BEGINNING TEACHING:
BEGINNING LEARNING
in   primary   education

BEGINNING TEACHING:
BEGINNING LEARNING
in primary education

Edited by
Janet Moyles

Open University Press
Buckingham • Philadelphia

Open University Press
Celtic Court
22 Ballmoor
Buckingham
MK18 1XW

email: enquiries@openup.co.uk
world wide web: http://www.openup.co.uk

and
325 Chestnut Street
Philadelphia, PA 19106, USA

First Published 1995
Reprinted 1996 (twice), 1997, 1998, 1999, 2000

Copyright © The Editor and Contributors 1995

A catalogue record of this book is available from the British Library

ISBN 0 335 19435 4 (pb)   0 335 19436 2 (hb)

Library of Congress Cataloging-in-Publication Data
Beginning teaching, beginning learning in primary education / edited
    by Janet Moyles.
        p.   cm.
    Includes bibliographical references and index.
    ISBN 0–335–19436–2 (hb) — ISBN 0–335–19435–4 (pb)
    1. First year teachers—Great Britain. 2. Student teachers—Great
Britain. 3. Elementary school teachers—Great Britain. I. Moyles,
Janet R.
    LB2844.1.N4B44   1995
    372.11—dc20   95–1199
                                                              CIP

Typeset by Graphicraft Limited, Hong Kong
Printed and bound in Great Britain by
Biddles Limited, www.biddles.co.uk

Contents

Notes on the editor and contributors

Martin Cortazzi lectures at the University of Leicester and specializes in primary education, linguistics and language teaching. His publications include two books *Primary Teaching: How it is* and *Narrative Analysis,* and articles on literacy, vocabulary learning, cross-cultural communication and learning English in China. He has recently given teacher training courses in Spain, Turkey, Lebanon, China and Taiwan.

Maurice Galton is a professor and Dean of the Faculty of Education and Continuing Studies at the University of Leicester. He has directed numerous research projects concerned with the observation of teaching and learning in the primary classroom (ORACLE 1975–83). His current work involves curriculum vision in small primary schools. He has numerous publications to his credit, the latest being *Crisis in the Primary Classroom.*

Barbara Garner is a part-time lecturer in primary education and also a classroom teacher. Having been an advisory teacher and a counsellor, she considers herself to be a generalist, though she has expertise in early years education and in primary maths. She has a wide range of interests and has published several papers on different aspects of primary education.

Linda Hargreaves took a degree in psychology at the University of Durham and went on to teach infants and juniors in Leicestershire. She subsequently gained an MA (Educ) and a Ph.D. at the University of Leicester and has contributed to observational research studies including the ORACLE project, the Science Teaching Action Research (STAR) project and a series of studies of curriculum provision in small schools.

Jane Hislam lectures in primary education at the University of Leicester, having been an advisory teacher for English. Her research and teaching interests are focused in the areas of children's literature, oral storytelling, gender issues and equal opportunities and she has lectured widely in her field. She has written several articles on aspects of story and two teachers' books on English.

Morag Hunter-Carsch lectures in primary education at the University of Leicester, having previously worked as a researcher. Her research and teaching interests are mainly in the area of reading and evaluating learning with particular reference to children with special educational needs. She has written and edited several books and articles on various aspects of literacy and its assessment.

Tina Jarvis is lecturer in primary science and technology at the University of Leicester. Her publications include *Children and Primary Science* and *Teaching Design and Technology*. Her research includes investigating English and Australian children's perceptions of technology and science, and the development of children's expertise in planning.

Neil Kitson lectures in primary education at the University of Leicester. He has worked for several years both as a teacher and as an advisory teacher for drama. He has published and broadcast widely on a variety of issues and is currently involved in developing materials in relation to competences for teachers.

Mark Lofthouse is senior lecturer in education and works from the Northampton base of the University of Leicester. Formerly a primary teacher, his current responsibilities include leadership of continuing professional development in Northamptonshire. His publications include many book chapters and articles and he is author of a history of The Church Colleges, one of several publications in the field of religious and denominational education.

Sylvia McNamara is a lecturer in education at the University of Leicester specializing in special educational needs and the social dimensions of the classroom. She teaches on a broad range of courses at various levels and has published widely both books and articles on issues associated with the social dimensions of schooling and group work issues.

Roger Merry is senior lecturer and head of the Primary PGCE course at the University of Leicester with research interests in cognitive psychology and special needs education. His previous publications range from book chapters and journal articles in these areas, to children's stories and activity books with characters like Sid Genius and Gertie Grimble.

Janet Moyles is Professor of Education at Anglia Polytechnic University and an early childhood education specialist, particularly in the areas of play and classroom management. Her books include *Just Playing?*, *Organizing for Learning*, *Play as a Learning Process* and *The Excellence of Play* (ed.). She has also written a variety of articles on different aspects of early and primary education. In 1994 she undertook an invited Fellowship at de Lissa Institute, Adelaide.

Wendy Suschitzky is a part-time tutor working within initial teacher education and particularly in relation to licensed teachers and their school-based mentors. Formerly an early years teacher, she has worked in community education and co-ordinated a project developing multi-cultural education and equal opportunities in children's learning and in HE.

David Turner worked as a primary teacher for several years before joining the Northamptonshire Inspection and Advisory Service undertaking a broad range of advisory work. He holds both an honours and masters degree specializing in educational management and lectures extensively on a broad range of topics including education and the law.

Martin Wenham is lecturer in primary education at the University of Leicester, specializing in several curriculum aspects but notably science, art and design, and technology. He is a practising artist and calligrapher and an ardent musician. He has written many papers on different aspects of primary education and has recently published *Understanding Primary Science*, a major work in this area.

Foreword

Professor Tim Brighouse

To be a primary teacher you need to be an optimist as well as a realist; you need to be generous without being sentimental. You must have intellectual curiosity and a keen eye for change in children; unless you notice changes in individual children on a daily basis, your 'eyesight' is not good enough. You will be energetic and a magpie for ideas. You can recognize teachers at a social event because they will see artefacts, everyday objects, even waste materials as sources of curriculum support. (If anyone asks me what is in my attic or my garage, I know this person is a primary teacher on the prowl for next term's explorations!)

As a primary teacher you will have the confidence to admit your weaknesses and you will be a risk taker. You will never stop learning yourself and you will take care to show this to the children whom you teach. You are indeed a privileged person. You work for children whose cognitive development is advancing at the greatest speed in human life and you see that infant through childhood and often into early adolescence.

The prize is that you, too, acquire the science and develop the art of being able to judge with uncanny accuracy the moments when a child – or group of children – has consolidated learning and is ready to be surprised into understanding or doing something they did not think they could do before. Such moments are beyond price – for you and for the children whom you believe can walk with genius. And, don't forget that you will communicate that belief by your tone of voice, your eyes and your every movement.

The isolated primary teacher is the lost professional, for teachers always profit from sharing ideas through planning together, from observing others doing the same job, through reading and discussion; in short, from extending knowledge of how children learn to read and how they develop their musical, mathematical, spatial and motor intelligences.

It will be your ambition to 'burn' about language, mathematical thinking and at least one of the arts so that you can communicate that infectious enthusiasm to the children. Scientific thinking – at least the observation and collection of evidence, the recording of results and the creation and testing of the hypothesis – will be your ally. If you have all that, you will be a 'good enough' teacher.

Paradoxically, it is always the lot of teachers to go home wondering if they are good enough. For there is always the thought that if only you had more knowledge, more skill or more resources, one of the pupils that day would have made the breakthrough in understanding which you had longed for. Those children and those moments haunt the primary teacher as much as the missed open goal irritates the footballer.

Yet it is the most companionable and intellectually satisfying of jobs, addictive in its rich variety of opportunities and human contacts.

As a primary teacher you will come to understand not merely the minds and personalities of the children you are teaching but also the theories of their learning and of their preferred styles of thinking. You will continue to learn beyond your initial education and training as you gradually become the confident expert practitioner.

This book is the product of a collective effort by the team of researchers, teachers and scholars at the University of Leicester's School of Education. Team work does not come easily in universities where individualism has full rein. Yet this volume illustrates the complementary talents of a remarkable team. Education at Leicester University has been a strength from the very beginning and particularly for the last fifty years. The present team of academics who have put together this book have forged for themselves an enviable reputation in the primary field. So, as the year 2000 approaches, to learn to be a teacher there is the best beginning for those who wish to shape the future of the next millennium.

You will have a head start in your career because you have been in good company, which is always a wise thing for a beginning teacher. Enjoy the book. Keep returning to different sections. Do not lose it. And still be reading it in ten years from now to remind yourself of some important point that suddenly comes into even bolder focus to illuminate your professional skills and life.

Acknowledgements

Many thanks and much appreciation should go to the many students, teachers and tutors who have contributed in various ways to the production of this book – not least those tutors who contributed chapters. Thanks should also be expressed to Cherry Fulloway and Linda Hargreaves for many of the photographs used in the book. Further acknowledgements are given in individual chapters.

Abbreviations and terminology used

We have tried to keep educational jargon to a minimum in the book but, inevitably, there are certain acronyms or phrases given specific meaning in education. The following represents a list of terminology which it would be useful for you to understand.

ATs   Attainment Targets within NC subjects
BEd/BA(Ed) Batchelor of Education/Batchelor of Arts (Education)
DES   Department of Education and Science, later to become the DfE
DfE   Department for Education, the government department which makes all central educational policy decisions
Early years or early childhood education
           Applied usually to the education of 3–7/8 year-olds
ERA   Education Reform Act
HMI   Her Majesty's Inspectorate (now OFSTED)
IAP   Individual Action Planning
In loco parentis
           adopting the role and responsibilities of a 'good parent'
IT   Information Technology
ITE   Initial Teacher Education (preferred by most people to ITT)
ITT   Initial Teacher Training
KS1 and KS2 The NC gives four age-related stages of education, with Key Stages 1 and 2 relating to primary children aged from 5–7 and 8–11 respectively
LEA   Local Education Authority
NC   National Curriculum

xiv *Abbreviations and terminology used*

NCC	National Curriculum Council (now subsumed within SCAA)
NQT	Newly qualified teacher
OFSTED	Office for Standards in Education
Parents	Anyone who has the legal guardianship of a child
PE	Physical Education
Pedagogy	The study of teaching and learning
PGCE	Post-graduate Certificate in Education
PoS	Programmes of Study in the NC
Pupils	Children in the context of school/ing
RE	Religious Education
RoA	Record(s) of Achievement
SATs	Standard Attainment Tasks
SCAA	Schools Curriculum and Assessment Authority
SEN	Special Educational Need(s)
TAs	Teacher Assessments
TP	Teaching Practice
Under 5s	Those children within the 0–5 age range (on educational courses, mostly applies to 3–5s)
Year groups	Those years which now constitute the years of schooling for primary childen from age 5 to 11, e.g. Year 1 = 5–6 year-olds, Year 2 = 6–7 year-olds, through to Year 6 = 10–11 year-olds. There is a designated Year R for reception children (those who are rising 5).

Photo 1   Beginning teaching: beginning learning?

Introduction

Janet Moyles

Cameo 1

A student teacher going into a junior school for his first placement was asked, 'Why on earth do you want to teach?'. He confidently replied 'Well, I really like being with children and helping them learn.' He was somewhat surprised at the teacher's response: 'Oh, if only that was what it is all about!'.

Cameo 2

From a new teacher's journal about work with a Year 4 class: 'The best moment this half-term was when all the children together performed a dance/drama about the water-cycle from beginning to end – five weeks work – and said they really enjoyed it! I felt a great sense of achievement because, in the first week's dance session, they didn't have a clue – and neither did I!'

Cameo 3

The student has spent nearly a week with a class of 5-year-olds on her first teaching experience. In planning the final day, the teacher has suggested that Julia might take the class for the Friday morning and 'try out' being a class teacher. Plans have been made and Julia goes through in her mind just how everything will go. The morning is spent on various activities and runs quite smoothly, if rather noisily. The teacher, who has just entered the classroom, reminds the student that the children will need some time to pack away the equipment. Julia uses what she believes to be the teacher's method of getting the children to put everything away, saying clearly 'Listen everybody . . . it's time to stop now. Put your things away and go and sit on the carpet.'

> Pandemonium reigns. The children appear to have gone berserk, rushing around the room, colliding with each other and dropping things on the floor. Even worse, the classroom looks like a herd of animals has passed through – and the teacher's standing there watching!

In the beginning . . .

Beginning teachers, whether students or those entering their first teaching posts, rightly have high ideals about the kind of teachers they want to be and the kind of classroom ethos they want to foster. Nearly always, as in the second cameo, they share a delight in actually being with children and participating in the fun and enjoyment of new learning. These are, however, only a very few aspects of the role of teacher, albeit arguably the best bits! As the teacher in the first cameo indicates, the requirements of the professional role extend well beyond 'just teaching' a class of children. There are many skills and attributes needed as will be evidenced through the chapters of this book.

The third cameo serves to emphasize that children and teaching can seemingly also be extremely unpredictable and that the balance of primary classroom life is sometimes poised on a ruler edge (if not quite a knife edge). The student did everything 'right' yet the outcome was disastrous for her confidence, at least in the short term. What this situation highlights is that it is not sufficient merely to emulate the actions and behaviours of another in order to learn to teach. How simple it would be if, as the government appears to believe, one could walk into a classroom armed with subject knowledge, the desire to teach and a belief that what one taught is what the children learn. The real world is far less predictable but infinitely more varied, exciting and challenging, as we shall discover.

Whereas we all might wish that someone could wave a magic wand and save us from Julia's encounter in the third cameo, these experiences are all part of learning to be a teacher. From the outset you need to be clear of one thing: *no-one can teach you how to teach* anymore than anyone can teach you how to learn. Both happen in tandem – or at least they should do – hence the title of this book *Beginning Teaching: Beginning Learning*. Learning to teach is all about what *you* bring that develops your professional personality in harmony with your own personality.

Every teacher is a mix of the personal and the professional and, whereas the professional may take a few knocks in the beginning stage like Julia, keeping the personal esteem intact is vital – 'I may be an awful teacher but that does not mean I am inevitably an awful person!' One common activity which teaching students often undertake is to identify what makes a 'good teacher' and to try to separate out those professional skills which may need to be developed and the personal skills already existing. Inevitably, this is not necessarily as clear cut as Figure 0.1 suggests but does show how

Photo 2　Beginner teachers must be prepared to be learners themselves

one group of students began to celebrate some of their many desirable competences, which ensured that they did not get overwhelmed or de-skilled from the perpetual onslaught of new learning.

In any profession, the learning curve is inevitably steep because there are always so many new issues to deal with simultaneously. Whatever apparently rigorous and difficult roles people have had in previous experiences, entrants to the teaching profession suddenly find themselves confronted with an overload of challenges. Because primary education concerns 3–11 year-old children – and often fairly large numbers of them at once – these challenges are nearly always immediate and unrelenting: the children just do not go away while we get our acts together! What needs to be acknowledged is that, with support and encouragement from others, the vast majority of people succeed as effective teachers and thoroughly enjoy their vocation. Any teacher education course, be it a four-year BEd or a

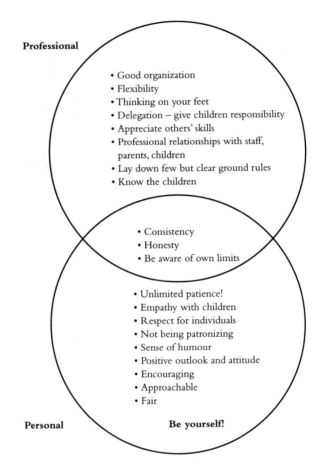

Professional

• Good organization
• Flexibility
• Thinking on your feet
• Delegation – give children responsibility
• Appreciate others' skills
• Professional relationships with staff,
  parents, children
• Lay down few but clear ground rules
• Know the children

• Consistency
• Honesty
• Be aware of own limits

• Unlimited patience!
• Empathy with children
• Respect for individuals
• Not being patronizing
• Sense of humour
• Positive outlook and attitude
• Encouraging
• Approachable
• Fair

Personal   Be yourself!

Figure 0.1   What makes a good teacher?

one-year PGCE, is only the *start* of a professional career; the beginning of learning about teaching.

Intentions of this book

This book addresses all those just entering teaching either as students or as newly qualified teachers. It will also be of interest to those whose job it is to help these individuals learn the craft of the teacher. The book has grown out of increasing concern on the part of one group of PGCE course tutors that the emphasis in teacher education is now so focused on *subject* curriculum that many of the underlying issues of primary practice are given insufficient prominence. By undertaking this venture, we hope to redress some of this balance and restore the concept of teacher *education* rather than the infinitely narrower notion of teacher *training* now so widely used in government circles and the media.

Firstly, a brief background to the current situation with regard to primary education is given together with an introduction to some of the concepts you will meet in reading the book as a whole. (On preceding pages there is a note of the abbreviations and special terminology used.) Secondly, the structure of the book is explained and information given regarding the chapters.

Primary education – how it is

In Britain, as in many other countries in the world, a deep economic recession in the 1980s led to relatively high levels of unemployment. On the understandable basis of attempting to give their children more than they themselves have experienced, being 'in work' became the ultimate goal of many parents for their children and, parallel to this, came the pressures of being 'well educated' in order ostensibly to achieve such employment. Rightly or wrongly education – or more properly *schooling* – became viewed, by politicians and the general public alike, as the panacea for many of society's problems. Huge accountability pressures were put upon teachers – teacher appraisal became a paramount issue at this time also (see Moyles 1988) – and it was inevitable that what was taught in the name of education also came under national scrutiny (DES 1988).

It was within this framework that the National Curriculum (NC) for England and Wales became a legislated requirement in 1989. Since then, the primary curriculum has been dominated by nine subjects: three core (English, maths, science) and six foundation (music, technology – later split into design technology and IT, history, geography, art and physical education, with RE as a compulsory addition). These subjects have to be taught by law to all children aged 5–16 years in state schools (5–11 in state primary schools), with maths and English (from 1995) being formally assessed in Key Stage 1 (KS1) at 7 years of age and Key Stage 2 (KS2) at age 11 years.

In addition, the NC aims to reflect the entitlement of all children to have access to a broad, balanced and relevant curriculum which accounts for differentiation, progression and continuity, in order that every child should achieve his/her full potential (DES 1989). In practice, this means that the subject curriculum has to be extended to include all the broader curriculum aspects such as health/sex education, equal opportunities, special needs, the European dimension, economic and industrial awareness, citizenship and personal/social education.

It needs to be remembered that a subject-dominated curriculum takes *knowledge,* and the handing *down* of that knowledge, as its basis. However, it is widely acknowledged that, for primary age children, the *processes* of their learning are far more important (see Kelly 1994). To teach primary aged children effectively, one must first recognize what they already bring to the learning situation, just as teacher education courses try to use the existing competences of students as the basis of professional development.

The subject dominance has impacted heavily upon teacher education: Circular 14/93 (DfE 1993) clearly spells out what initial teacher training (ITT) courses are expected to do. Essentially, a major part of course time is to be spent on subject curriculum (at least 150 hours devoted to each of the three core areas), irrespective of the age group of children to be taught – a bone of contention for all early childhood teachers (see Blenkin and Kelly 1994). In addition, there are specific periods of time (dependent on the overall length of the course) which students must spend in schools in direct contact with practising teachers and children. As well as the broader curriculum aspects listed above, the Circular also requires that other main priorities be addressed, namely:

- testing, assessment and recording techniques;
- continuity and progression;
- teaching methods;
- classroom organization;
- dealing with individual/special needs/giftedness;
- maintaining order and discipline.

On the wider professional front, new teachers also need to develop:

- effective relationships with professional colleagues (including support staff) and parents;
- a working knowledge of contractual, legal, administrative and pastoral responsibilities as teachers;
- a readiness to promote the spiritual, moral, social and cultural development of pupils;
- vision, imagination and critical awareness in educating their pupils.

It goes without saying that the combination of these demands is overwhelming to students, course providers and schools. Therefore, it is no surprise to find that many of these issues are now ineffectually covered on many teacher education courses despite continuing goodwill all round. Hence the need for a book of this type which explores just a few of these vitally important but neglected areas and a selection of related issues which we feel are important for beginner teachers.

The structure and content of the book

The book has three parts: one addresses the issues of teaching to learn, the second explores a variety of strategies needed by beginner teachers in learning to teach, whilst the third part deals with responsibilities, roles and relationships. Within each section there are several chapters, each of which carries its own questions, references and suggested further reading. Each chapter is written in a straightforward style and begins with one or more cameos of life in primary classrooms as it is experienced by beginner teachers offering an immediate point of reference with everyday encounters.

Firstly, in Part 1 Maurice Galton examines the background to how teachers manage large classes of primary age children and offers strategies for dealing effectively with the many demands this makes. Arguing for more responsibility for the children in their school activities, he exhorts you to consider carefully the variety of ways in which learning can be organized in the primary classroom, particularly emphasizing collaborative group work as a way forward in overcoming some of the problems of large class sizes. This is followed by my own chapter exploring aspects of the classroom as a learning context. Rather than dealing with the pragmatics of the classroom, the emphasis is on delving into teachers' beliefs and values, behavioural and home/school issues, children's independence and the processes of teaching and learning, to understand how structures and routine affect potential learning opportunities.

Part of any teacher's repertoire must include observing what is happening in the classroom context. In Chapter 3, Linda Hargreaves offers many examples of effective observational techniques which she has grounded firmly in a clear rationale for practice. She challenges you to think about the differences between looking and observing and emphasizes the importance of observation as part of teacher-based, formative assessment to help in the identification of a child's, and teacher's, needs.

Teacher education must start from the basis of acknowledging what beginner teachers bring to their own learning. Neil Kitson examines the background to the notion of teacher competences and explains what this means in the context of initial teacher education (ITE). The example given is of one of Leicester's PGCE course pieces of documentation through which students identify their strengths and needs and make individual action plans for future development.

In the much longer Part 2, 'Learning to Teach', the seven chapters focus on different aspects of dealing with children's learning and some of the processes and skills which underlie effective implementation of the whole curriculum. In Chapter 5, Roger Merry concentrates on how we can begin to understand children through identifying aspects of our own learning and reflecting on our approaches to tasks. He covers such aspects as perception, memory and learning strategies, reviews some general trends in how children develop and considers the curriculum in relation to purpose, relevance and attention to differentiation. Having emphasized how we each learn through our own experiences, I then take up some of these issues in Chapter 6, exploring how we can plan for children's learning within the context of their own interests and motivations while still complying with curriculum requirements.

Developing investigative skills, creativity and problem-solving strategies must have high priority for primary age children (as well as their teachers) for these provide the tools with which to approach the formal task of school learning. The next five chapters highlight these skills and processes. Firstly, in Chapter 7, using science, technology and maths situations, Tina

Jarvis illustrates some of the many concepts which provide a sound basis for learning and emphasizes the need to ensure that children are given sufficient opportunity to explore a variety of questions and solutions in a logical and systematic way. Martin Wenham, in Chapter 8, accentuates similar points but does so in the context of exploring children's approaches to aesthetic activities such as painting, sculpture, music, dance and poetry. He writes of the artist in us all, the links with scientific thinking and gives many examples of ways in which children's creative expression can be fostered by teachers.

Using a variety of examples, Jane Hislam's chapter explores ways of creating an effective classroom context for the development of children's imaginative powers through the structured framework of storytelling and oracy-based activities. Communication and co-operation are vital ingredients in primary education for teachers and children. Sylvia McNamara (Chapter 10) examines the many sound reasons for teaching children appropriate class social skills and shows how specific strategies, if well utilized by teachers, can circumvent discipline issues and give even very young children an overall responsibility for their own learning. Martin Cortazzi (Chapter 11), in writing of a 'hidden curriculum' of children's and teachers' perceptions of writing tasks, provides a wealth of information and ideas for encouraging children's writing across the primary curriculum. In using what children say about the writing process and its outcomes, difficult concepts are brought to life and issues of authorship and ownership are explored.

The third and final part has four chapters. The first of these focuses on the teacher's responsibility for keeping track of children's progress and achievement. Morag Hunter-Carsch outlines some of the theory and practices of recording, evaluating and assessing not only children's learning but monitoring the planning and implementation of the curriculum by the teacher. In Chapter 13, Wendy Suschitzky explores the many issues involved in working within equal opportunities guidelines. She emphasizes children's entitlement to a broad, balanced and relevant curriculum irrespective of sex, race, age or disability. This equally applies to teachers. Wendy is joined by Barbara Garner in the next chapter and together they explore the role of mentor teacher and the establishment of mutual respect and partnerships between beginner teachers and those who will support their professional development.

David Turner and Mark Lofthouse's final chapter shows clearly how the history of education and schooling continually informs and affects current practices particularly in relation to the teacher and the law. The writers emphasize the need for the primary teacher to adopt the role and responsibilities of a 'good parent', giving guidance on coping with professional responsibilities and how these are expressed in practice.

As will be obvious by now, the scope of the book is very broadly based, but by keeping the focus on the learning partnership between the beginner teacher and the children, we hope to have made it manageable and useful.

Primary teachers do need to have a good grasp of subject knowledge and how it can be translated into classroom practices and this is now covered in some detail in all ITE courses. But this is only part of a broader primary curriculum which subsumes many other factors as we have seen. Whatever the intensity and rigours of the primary curriculum, the children and their teachers both need to gain enjoyment and satisfaction from the educational process and a real desire to continue learning: school and learning should be fun for everyone. Beginner teachers are usually very welcomed by the children because they bring new ideas and different ways of doing things. As one 8-year-old child wrote in a letter to a student – the spelling faithfully reproduced: 'We are very greatful that you came to help us in your spare time and we're sorry that your liveing'!! Here's the hope that you will always be able to see the humorous side of school.

References and further reading

Blenkin, G. and Kelly, V. (1994) *The Early Years Curriculum and the National Curriculum.* London: Paul Chapman.

Department of Education and Science (1988) *The Education Reform Act.* London: HMSO.

Department of Education and Science (1989) *The Implementation of the National Curriculum in Primary Schools.* London: HMSO.

Department for Education (1993) *The Initial Training of Primary School Teachers: New Criteria for Courses*, Circular 14/93. London: DfE.

Kelly, V. (1994) A high quality curriculum for the early years – some conceptual issues. *Early Years*, 15 (1): 6–12.

Moyles, J. (1988) *Self-Evaluation: A Primary Teacher's Guide.* Windsor: NFER/Nelson.

Part I

TEACHING TO LEARN

1

Do you really want to cope with thirty lively children and become an effective primary teacher?

Maurice Galton

Cameo

Jenny read history at university, stayed on to do a PGCE and has now been teaching for five years in a suburban, 5–11, one form entry school. At the moment she has a mixed-age class of twenty-seven 7- and 8-year-old children. The room is arranged as shown in Figure 1.1.

There are five tables, one with seven, two with six and two with four children (each a mix of boys and girls). A typical lesson begins with Jenny talking to the whole class as they sit on the carpet in the quiet corner. She also brings the class back together at the end of the session. Operating as a whole class in this way generally takes up around 20 per cent of every day. For most of the remaining time the children work individually, completing mathematics worksheets, exercises in their English work books or occasionally working on art activities. At other times they will co-operate in groups on a science experiment or on a geography or history project. Typically, the children spend about 80 per cent of this remaining time working individually (64 per cent of the day). This means that about 16 per cent of the day involves collaborative activity of some kind.

Introduction

Today's primary classroom described above will, in most respects, still be very familiar to people whose primary education occurred some time ago, schools having changed little during the last twenty or more years. The question why children sit together but work individually has been a major issue in the ongoing debate about modern primary practice. Critics point to

Key
A   = Armchair
DU = Display unit
LC = Low cupboard
CA = Carpet area
S   = Sink
TD = Teacher's desk
TU = Tray units

Figure 1.1   Jenny's classroom layout
Note: Jenny's classroom is an amalgam of those listed in Alexander *et al.*
(1989: 249–50).

the fact, established in research studies in the UK and in the US, that sitting
together but working alone produces some of the lowest levels of concentration, whereas, during class teaching, children are on task for over 80 per
cent of the time. Moreover, increases in class teaching also produce better
performances on standardized tests of mathematics, reading and language.

In this chapter, we shall examine some of these varying views and make
suggestions about gaining effectiveness by making greater use of group
work, a neglected art in many primary classrooms (Galton 1981).

The debate about primary practice: new record, same old tune

Over the past few years, there has been what one commentator has described as 'a coordinated onslaught' upon primary practice 'by politicians

Photo 3   Group work in the primary classroom – or children seated in groups?

backed up by the tabloid press'. Simon (1993: 13) also quotes a government minister, Michael Fallon, announcing that 'the days of group project work are numbered' and that teachers should 'forget the fiction of child-centred learning and the pursuit of happiness'. Elsewhere, a review of recent research led the 'Three Wise Men' to claim that among primary teachers, 'there are persistent and damaging beliefs' that children 'should never be told things, only asked questions', and that 'teachers must never point out when a pupil is wrong' since 'proffer anything but unqualified praise and the child's confidence will be undermined forever' (Alexander *et al.* 1992: 104). Critics have generally assumed that individualization of teaching is associated with the use of 'discovery learning' methods where children are largely left 'to find things out for themselves' (Anthony 1982).

A central issue in the continuing debate about primary education has, therefore, been the perceived benefits or defects of these 'progressive' or 'child-centred' approaches. These first came to the ascendant in the 1930s and were strongly promoted by what we would now term 'lobbying groups' such as the Froebelian movement. However, as Simon (1993) again observes, the conditions which existed in most classrooms, particularly class sizes of around 50, prevented these ideas from gaining hold in most state schools.

Teaching styles in the primary classroom

The question of the effectiveness of 'child-centred' approaches began to concern researchers in the aftermath of the Second World War. During this time, the pioneering work of Dorothy Gardner attempted to show that children taught by less didactic methods produced as good, if not better, results than more traditional approaches based largely on whole class teaching.

By the mid-1960s little pockets of innovation had developed in various parts of the country promoted by chief education officers who were persuaded of the value of these new teaching approaches and campaigned actively for their wider use. These developments came to fruition when the evidence collected for the Newsom Report (1963) exposed the extent to which young adults from working-class backgrounds, although possessing suitable Intelligence Quotient (IQ) scores, nevertheless failed to gain entry into grammar schools at 11. The growing consensus within both major political parties that such problems could only be solved by ending selection at 11 and developing a comprehensive system of secondary schooling, coincided with the setting up of a committee to investigate primary education.

It has been argued by Jones (1987) that the committee's report (The Plowden Report 1967) and the structural changes associated with the abolition of streaming within the primary school, helped to create an impression that change in school was more radical than really it was. Over a quarter of a century later it is now agreed by most serious commentators that there has been no widespread adoption of the Plowden recommendations. Critics were particularly incensed by the report's claim that 'finding out had been *proved* to be better than being told' (my italics). These same critics, many of whom had no experience of state education other than at university, also strongly objected to developments, such as the integrated day, which attempted to link subjects by using topic or thematic approaches, although surveys of classroom organization and practice carried out at that time showed that only a limited amount of work was organized in this way. Later research (Mortimore *et al.* 1988) has confirmed this view.

Nevertheless, educational debates of this kind often prompt researchers into action. The results of one such research study (Bennett 1976) appeared to show that 'traditionalist' class teaching was a more effective means of ensuring pupil progress in the core skills of numeracy and literacy than more 'progressive' methods. Despite much subsequent controversy, Bennett's findings have been frequently replicated both in the UK and in the US. Where teaching effectiveness is defined solely in terms of pupil performance on standardized tests of mathematics and language, moderate positive correlations have been found between these measures and the extent to which children were taught as a whole class as opposed to being provided with individual assignments (Brophy and Good 1986; Mortimore *et al.* 1988; Alexander *et al.* 1992).

Classroom processes and pupil behaviour

Given this evidence accumulated over nearly two decades, the question why little systematic change has taken place in the ways schools organize teaching and learning, needs to be explored. There was little in Bennett's 1976 research which explained what it was that teachers who taught in this way did that enabled such progress to be achieved. The ORACLE (Observational Research and Classroom Learning Evaluation) studies carried out at the University of Leicester over the period 1975–83 (Galton 1987) attempted to answer such questions by directly observing teachers and children during lessons, in some cases over a three-year period. (Linda Hargreaves explores a range of such observational techniques in Chapter 3.)

The conclusions of these studies was that it was not in itself class teaching or individualized instruction which made the difference but the opportunity that the use of a particular method provided for a teacher to *engage in certain types of exchanges with children*. When addressing the whole class, for example, there was a greater probability that teachers would ask more challenging questions and that children would pay greater attention and concentrate more on their work. Consequently there would be fewer disruptions which distracted both teachers and other children from the tasks in hand. Another apparent advantage was that it enabled teachers to provide greater amounts of feedback to children about the quality of their work.

There were, of course, disadvantages in this whole class approach in that a sizeable number of children remained largely inactive during these exchanges, preferring to listen only when either the teacher addressed the whole class or questioned individuals or groups. However, *none of these kinds of exchanges between children and teachers is a unique attribute of class teaching*. It is possible to visualize a teacher, with children who are working on different individual assignments, engaging in the same kinds of exchanges or interactions. Indeed, in the ORACLE sample a small group of teachers who worked in this way did succeed in matching teachers who mainly used a whole class approach in their use of these interactions. These teachers worked at a very demanding pace engaging in conversations with individual children for nearly 90 per cent of the day compared to an average of 75 per cent in the rest of the sample. When the test results in the classes of these extremely active groups of teachers were analysed, it was found that they compared very favourably with those of the children who experienced greater amounts of whole class teaching.

Thus *it was not class teaching in itself which brought about success but what could be accomplished when teachers taught in this way*. The bulk of teachers, who preferred approaches based on individual assignments, were unable to match these class teachers in the use of certain types of interaction, such as asking challenging questions or providing feedback. In many classrooms where the teacher's preference was for individual assignments, there were more disruptions with the result that children spent considerably less time on task.

These lower levels of interaction did not arise because the teachers were any less capable when employing questioning techniques: rather their preference for setting individual assignments denied them opportunities to use these teaching skills largely, it would appear, because of the overdependence of children on the teacher as a source of information. Within this *dependency mode* teachers were obliged to spend most of their time ensuring that children were able to continue with their tasks. There were above average levels (compared to the rest of the sample) of exchanges where teachers either provided children with instructions about what to do next or provided information which was needed to complete a task. In such classes there were often queues of children waiting for the teacher, which decreased the time that children were able to devote to their task. In this environment teachers found it difficult to engage in extended challenging conversations of the kind likely to stimulate new ideas among their children. Studies of teachers in small primary schools (Galton and Patrick 1990) found that nearly 40 per cent of the teacher's exchanges with children during individualized instruction did not last longer than *5 seconds*. As a consequence, smaller portions of time were available for providing feedback in the presence of the child. Such teachers were often forced to correct work books without the child being present and to hand them back without an extended oral comment.

What happens in the typical primary classroom is, therefore, *a complete reversal of what critics alleged to be happening.* Whereas the public was encouraged to believe that, in the informal primary classroom (that is, classrooms where children sat in groups and were given individual assignments rather than taught as a whole class), children were never told anything but left to find things out for themselves, the opposite was taking place and, for the most part, children were being told what to do more frequently than under any other form of organization.

It would seem, therefore, that the weakness of individualized approaches to teaching and learning in the primary classroom does not lie in the method itself. Properly applied, teachers using such approaches can achieve comparable results to those preferring to teach children in larger groups. What prevents the method from being effective, under typical classroom conditions, is the dependency upon the teacher that many children exhibit right from the start of the infant school (Barrett 1986). As a result, the time available for teaching is often used inappropriately. To use individualized approaches successfully, teachers have to overcome what, in its extreme form, psychologists call 'learned helplessness'. Whole class teaching appears to work, in part, because it allows these dependent children to exercise this dependency undetected by the teacher.

Common sense would suggest that a balance needs to be struck between the different kinds of organizational strategies which teachers deploy in the classroom (see Janet Moyles and Sylvia McNamara's further discussions in Chapters 2 and 10 respectively). But the issue of *children's independence* and how to foster it assumes increasing importance once a third possibility for organizing children in the classroom, namely the use of grouping, is considered. Here the results of the ORACLE studies and other similar work, particularly that of Mortimore *et al.* (1988) at junior level and Tizard *et al.* (1988) in the early years, are particularly relevant. These two studies found similar patterns of organization to that described in ORACLE. The most striking of all findings concerned what Galton *et al.* (1980) termed the *'asymmetry of classroom interaction'*. Put simply this asymmetry referred to the observation that children, because they sat in groups but worked at individual assignments, did not interact with the teacher or a peer for nearly 80 per cent of the time in class. In contrast, the teacher engaged in one-to-one interactions with particular children, in turn, for the majority of the school day. This pattern was a consequence of the fact that there were on average 30 children for each class teacher. In the course of a 25-hour week, with 80 per cent of the time devoted to individual work, a child might receive, on average, 40 minutes of a teacher's attention, that is only eight minutes per day!

One obvious way of compensating for this isolation is for the children, when the teacher was elsewhere, to support each other in their work by co-operating in groups. Such activities, at least in theory, allow children to develop skills of oracy and debate as well as social skills of tolerance and courtesy when listening to another person's point of view without inter-ruption. Conversations of this kind take on a greater importance when set against the fact that, during whole class teaching, the majority of children do not participate in the exchanges but listen to the teacher talking for nearly 75 per cent of the time. It is precisely because most teachers recog-nize the advantages and disadvantages of whole class teaching and the need to provide opportunities for children to engage in extended conversation, that they usually reply, when asked about their preferred teaching strate-gies, 'I use mixed methods'. What is at issue, however, is the balance struck between these different approaches.

Has the National Curriculum made a difference?

The NC was intended to raise standards, not only by providing greater coherence and continuity in what was taught, but also in the manner in which this content was transmitted. However, the largest examination of the impact of the NC, the Primary Assessment Curriculum and Experience (PACE) project (Pollard *et al.* 1993; Sammons *et al.* 1994) has provided evidence in interim reports that little has changed within the primary class-room. For example, percentages of time on task were of the same order as those in the earlier observational studies of the 1980s. Similarly, collabora-tive group work in junior classrooms continued to be a 'neglected art'. Although at KS1, in comparison to the only other observation study avail-able (Tizard *et al.* 1988) there was more pupil-teacher interaction in whole class settings, the Tizard study was unusual in that it deliberately chose classes where there were high proportions of children whose first language was not English. Such children clearly need higher proportions of indi-vidual attention.

At first, when this evidence suggested that the 'logic' of the NC was not producing the desired changes in practice, the view was taken by officials that this was a matter of lack of confidence: as familiarity with the programmes of study and the assessment targets increased, teachers would begin to re-evaluate their pedagogy. When, however, the evidence continued to show that the new subject content was still being 'bolted on' to existing practice, the focus of attention shifted. Failure to bring about changes in practice was now attributed to another of the supposed characteristics of child-centred teaching, namely the use of integrated subject teaching. This view was persistently paraded despite the careful analysis of research studies showing that the integrated day, for the most part, existed in theory rather than practice (Simon 1981; Alexander 1992). Scapegoats for this supposed state of affairs were also readily available. It was the LEA's insistence in maintaining these undesirable features as part of 'good primary practice' along with the reactionary views of those responsible for ITT who were blamed for this reluctance by teachers to modify their teaching. Government ministers were reinforced by the evaluation report of the Leeds Primary Needs Project, the attempt to improve the quality of provision in the city's inner city schools at the cost of some £13 million (Alexander 1991). This report led to the setting up of an enquiry, the so-called 'Three Wise Men's Report' (Alexander *et al.* 1992). These 'wise men' doubted the effectiveness of the existing elementary tradition of a single class, generalist primary teacher and recommended instead the use of more class teaching and more specialist teachers.

Teaching children to think

The emphasis in the 'Three Wise Men's' report on classroom organization, planning and assessment derives from a secondary school model where pedagogy and the style of teaching and learning is mainly determined by the subject matter. Decision making is largely to do with strategic questions and has little to say about teaching at a tactical level which is the main concern of a pedagogy based upon *how children learn to think* (see Roger Merry's discussion in Chapter 5). Although the nature of the learning will have some bearing on strategic decisions, the latter will be strongly influenced by contextual variables. Science may be taught in groups because there is insufficient apparatus to go round the whole class. Such decisions are primarily *managerial* ones.

Tactics, on the other hand, are concerned with the appropriateness of certain classroom transactions for effectively transmitting a particular form of knowledge. Although tactics are related to strategy they are not necessarily driven by it. For example, under present classroom conditions it appears easier to facilitate exchanges involving what are termed 'higher order questions' in whole class settings. But if we could change the conditions, as some teachers did in the ORACLE study, then similar high levels of questioning can take place during one-to-one interactions.

Researchers interested in these tactical issues do not dispute that improving the management functions of teaching can lead to an increase in learning outcomes. They do believe, however, that standards will only rise when the *study of pedagogy* – the use of appropriate teaching tactics to facilitate the learning processes involved in any task demand – becomes a central element of a teacher's professional development. (The chapters in Part 2 forcibly emphasize these points.) This requires the teacher to know something about teaching and about learning processes and the relationship between the two. This is why pedagogy has been defined as the 'science of the art of teaching' (Gage 1985). The need for teachers to become reflective and evaluative about their practice is the focus of Neil Kitson's work in Chapter 4.

In seeking to develop an effective pedagogy, however, we need to reject the view that effectiveness can be described solely by the application of the teacher's 'common-sense appraisal' of what is and is not effective. This is because a teacher's perception of what goes on in the classroom is selective and generally attributes causality to factors which lie outside their personal control (for example, socio-economic background as discussed in Chapter 2). Failures of children to learn are not blamed on the way the topic was taught but to external factors to do with the children's home background or their limited powers of concentration. Interestingly, as Cortazzi (1991) has demonstrated, teachers also rarely claim credit for any outstanding pupil achievement. Because, therefore, the teachers' analysis of classroom problems places less emphasis on possible weaknesses in their own behaviour, the teaching solutions chosen will tend to suit the teacher but may not be best suited for the children's needs. What is required, therefore, are other sources of ideas about teaching and learning that can be used to validate the teacher's own analysis. Among such sources would be theories of *how children learn to think* (Wood 1988).

How, given that there exists no clear-cut view about children's development, is it possible for teachers to use theory, in conjunction with their own common-sense experience, to select the most appropriate teaching methods? One possible way forward is to introduce a third element into this verification procedure using empirical data collected from process-product classroom observation studies such as ORACLE. The evidence from these studies suggests that the use of direct instruction, not to be confused with direct teaching, is most appropriate for teaching children to solve relatively simple problems involving procedural routines, content knowledge and factual information. The teacher's role in this kind of problem solving is very similar to the computer programmer who provides the machine with the procedures necessary to work out a solution. As well as the actual calculation, this also involves routines for accessing, storing and retrieving information and rules for making decisions (for example, how to proceed if a result is higher or lower than a given value). The efficiency of the computer depends on this speed of processing and its capacity to store large amounts of information in chunks. The effectiveness is also increased by the use of 'sub routines': regularly used procedures which can be auto-matically called up when needed rather than starting from scratch each time.

When this information processing model of 'man as computer' (Meadows 1993) is applied to learning by direct instruction, there are strong parallels. The children are given new information; they are shown how to remember it and are taught how to use it in various procedures to solve problems. The children then practise these procedures until they can use them auto-matically. However, just as with the simple computer model, where if the nature of the problem solving changes appreciably the computer has to be re-programmed, so too when we move from teaching how to multiply whole numbers to multiplying fractions or decimals, we have to begin the process of direct instruction again. Once we move to generalities, for ex-ample, understanding the principles of multiplication irrespective of the particular application, direct instruction appears to be less effective. This form of thinking or concept development involves the acquisition of new ideas (or the invention of them) and an ability to make appropriate use of them. In the process we may have to identify the nature of a problem, analyse its components, determine whether we have sufficient knowledge to solve it and be able to monitor whether our efforts are likely to be productive. This ability to regulate our thinking processes, or to 'control the domain of cognition' (Meadows 1993: 78) lies at the heart of what has been called by Brown and Palincsar (1986) *'learning as theory change'*. It is necessary for all ages of primary children.

The 'man as a computer' model is not very helpful for understanding these 'metacognitive' processes but the ideas of the Russian psychologist, Vygotsky, based upon co-operative learning are (see Wood 1988: 24). Here the more competent help the less competent move to a position where they can become 'self-regulating' in their thinking. To assist the less competent learner, the more competent must provide a 'scaffolding' or framework by means of which these metacognitive processes can be internalized. Once this state is achieved children can become independent thinkers. Part of the scaffolding for discussion during collaborative learning involves systemati-cally considering all cases in support of the argument, then all counter examples. Cases which are neither for or against are then isolated and used to suggest possible alternative ways of presenting the original proposition (Brown and Palincsar 1986: 39). Groups are taught to apply this strategy until the process becomes automatic. These procedures, therefore, along with more fundamental skills such as learning to listen carefully, commu-nicate one's views and handle conflict within the group, need to be taught initially through direct instruction – some strategies are provided in Chap-ter 10.

Decisions about classroom organization should then follow from this analysis. In direct instruction class teaching will be most effective because it maximizes teacher contact: when teaching procedures or skills such as listening the whole class can be involved. When new information is being offered, including demonstrations of relatively simple problem solving using this information, ability groups are likely to be preferred. Once, however, thinking processes involve metacognition (such as generating ideas for story writing, hypothesis generation, evaluating historical evidence) mixed ability groups are required. This suggests that the current practice of having two different subject areas in operation, but with one requiring direct instruction and the other co-operative learning in groups, should be the preferred strategy.

Do as you think but behave as I say

Even with these strategies in place there remains a question of motivating children to participate enthusiastically in these activities. Even when children have the necessary prior knowledge, some appear reluctant to engage in more demanding cognitive activities, preferring, instead, to feign dependency. Children who feel confident enough in their learning – with high self-image and self-esteem (both academic and social) and little fear of failure – will be more willing to initiate exchanges with teachers in which they are open about the difficulties encountered and the solutions used in attempting to solve a problem.

Elsewhere, I have argued (Galton 1989) that much of the current dependency is created by the discontinuity which exists between the management of learning and the management of behaviour in the primary classroom. *Learning is managed so that children are expected to do as they think while in matters of behaviour teachers require the children to do as they say.* This invests more complex learning tasks with a degree of ambiguity, in that children are never certain of what teachers require of them in a particular situation and whether the teacher's utterance is concerned primarily with learning or with control. Consequently junior age children 'hedge their bets' and use various avoidance strategies to ensure the teacher initially interacts with another member of the class. By watching and listening carefully to this initial exchange the rest of the class are able to discern the teacher's intentions.

More than any other part of their practice, teachers, once they have acquired an effective means of classroom control, tend to stick with it for the remainder of their teaching lives. The approach they favour will largely depend on their experience during initial training and the practice favoured by their mentors (the mentoring process is discussed by Wendy Suschitzky and Barbara Garner in Chapter 14). There is, therefore, a case for things remaining as they are and leaving teachers to continue to do what they already do while helping them become more effective classroom lecturers and disciplinarians. However, research suggests that such an approach will not create a classroom climate which encourages creativity and imagination and persuades children of the value of solving difficult problems co-operatively (see Chapters 7, 8 and 9 respectively). These are skills which industrialists tell us will be required of workers in the twenty-first century. It would seem, therefore, that despite the calls of government ministers and the media for a return to more traditional teaching approaches, there is little option but to continue the search for ways of successfully implementing these necessary changes in pedagogy.

Conclusion

For the beginning teacher the future is one of many exciting challenges. The issue of pupil dependency has been with us now for a long time and it is hardly to be expected that you should immediately solve all the outstanding problems of primary education! You would be wise to concentrate on first mastering the basic skills of direct instruction involving demonstration, questioning, discussions, tutoring and seat work which 'make the difference between superb, average and atrocious classroom teaching' (Gage 1985). It takes time to develop the kinds of relationship which encourage children to become independent thinkers. Jenny, our teacher at the beginning of the chapter, like other teachers in Nias's (1988) study, feels that only after five years is she able to feel 'relaxed, easy, not frightened any more in the classroom' and is 'ready to pass on more and more of the responsibility for the learning to the pupils' (Nias 1988: 133). All of us have good days and bad days. As the good days begin to outnumber the bad days, I hope those who read this book will be confirmed in the view that coping with 30 lively young children is one of the most rewarding and intellectually challenging careers available.

Things to do when observing your teacher/mentor

1 Compare the classroom arrangement in Figure 1.1 with a classroom you know. Ask the teacher/mentor to explain why things are as they are.
2 Observe children answering questions during class discussion. Can you detect avoidance strategies? How does the teacher cope with them?
3 Follow the teacher's movements when children are working on individual assignments. How long do the exchanges between the teacher and children last? What do children do when the teacher is engaged elsewhere in the classroom?
4 Discuss with the teacher the preferred means of controlling children's behaviour. What effect does the teacher's approach have upon the children's engagement and motivation?

When you have collected this information re-read the chapter to see how far you agree or disagree with the views expressed.

References and further reading

Alexander, R. (1991) *Primary Education in Leeds*. Twelfth and Final Report from the Primary Needs Independent Evaluation Project: University of Leeds.

Alexander, R. (1992) *Policy and Practice in Primary Education.* London: Routledge.
Alexander, R., Rose, J. and Woodhead, C. (1992) *Curriculum Organisation and Classroom Practice in Primary Schools.* London: Department of Education and Science.
Alexander, R., Willcocks, J. and Kinder, K. (1989) *Changing Primary Practice.* London: Falmer Press.
Anthony, W.S. (1982) Research on progressive teaching. *British Journal of Educational Psychology,* 52: 381–5.
Barrett, G. (1986) *Starting School: An Evaluation of the Experience.* Final Report to the AMMA, CARE, University of East Anglia.
Bennett, S.N. (1976) *Teaching Styles and Pupil Progress.* London: Open Books.
Brophy, J.E. and Good, T.L. (1986) Teacher behaviour and student achievement, in M.C. Wittrock (ed.) *Handbook of Research on Teaching,* 3rd edn. New York: Macmillan.
Brown, A. and Palincsar, A. (1986) *Guided Co-operative Learning and Individual Knowledge Acquisition,* technical report 372. Cambridge, Mass.: Bolt, Beranak and Newham Inc.
Cortazzi, M. (1991) *Primary Teaching. How it is: A Narrative Account.* London: David Fulton Publishers.
Cowie, H., Smith, P., Boulton, M. and Laver, R. (1994) *Co-operation in the Multiethnic Classroom.* London: David Fulton Publishers.
Gage, N.L. (1985) *Hard Gains in the Soft Sciences: The Case of Pedagogy,* A CEDR Monograph. Indiana: Phi Delta Kappa.
Galton, M. (1981) Teaching groups in the junior school: a neglected art. *Schools Organisation,* 1 (2): 175–81.
Galton, M. (1987) An ORACLE chronicle: a decade of classroom research. *Teaching and Teacher Education,* 3 (4): 299–314.
Galton, M. (1989) *Teaching in the Primary School.* London: David Fulton Publishers.
Galton, M. and Patrick, H. (1990) *Curriculum Provision in the Small Primary School.* London: Routledge.
Galton, M., Simon, B. and Croll, P. (1980) *Inside the Primary Classroom.* London: Routledge and Kegan Paul.
Jones, D. (1987) Planning for progressivism: the changing primary school in the Leicestershire authority during the Mason era 1947–71, in R. Lowe (ed.) *The Changing Primary School.* London: Falmer Press.
Jones, D. (1988) *Stewart Mason: The Art of Education.* London: Lawrence and Wishart.
Meadows, S. (1993) *The Child as Thinker: The Development and Acquisition of Cognition in Childhood.* London: Routledge.
Mortimore, P., Sammons, P., Stoll, L.D. and Ecob, R. (1988) *School Matters: The Junior Years.* Wells: Open Books.
Ministry of Education (1963) *Half Our Future: A Report of the Central Advisory Council for Education (England),* The Newsom Report. London: HMSO.
Nias, J. (1988) Informal education in action: teachers' accounts, in A. Blyth (ed.) *Informal Primary Education Today.* London: Falmer Press.
Plowden Report (1967) *Children and their Primary Schools,* report of the Central Advisory Council for Education in England. London: HMSO.
Pollard, A. with Osborn, M., Abbott, D., Broadfoot, P. and Croll, P. (1993) Balancing priorities: children and the curriculum in the nineties, in R. Campbell (ed.) *Breadth and Balance in the Primary Curriculum.* London: Falmer Press.
Sammons, P., Lewis, A., MacLure, M., Riley, J., Bennett, N. and Pollard, A. (1994) Teaching and learning processes, in A. Pollard (ed.) *Look Before You Leap. Research Evidence for the Curriculum at Key Stage 2.* London: Tufnell Press.

Simon, B. (1981) The Primary School Revolution, Myth or Reality? In M. Galton, B. Simon, and J. Willcocks (eds) *Research and Practice in the Primary Classroom*. London: Routledge and Kegan Paul.

Simon, B. (1993) Primary Education. *Education Today and Tomorrow*, 44 (3): 13–14.

Tizard, B., Blatchford, D., Burke, J., Farquhar, C. and Plewis, I. (1988) *Young Children at School in the Inner City*. Hove: Lawrence Erlbaum.

Wood, D. (1988) *How Children Think and Learn*. Oxford: Basil Blackwell.

2

A place for everything?
The classroom as a teaching and learning context

Janet Moyles

Cameo 1

Billy, aged 4 years, watches the new teacher closely in the nursery classroom, scrutinizing her face with a puzzled expression at every opportunity. He does this for several days, saying nothing, and the teacher bides her time feeling that Billy is simply getting used to her being with that class. Eventually, she asks Billy why he seems so puzzled. 'What you got that blue-stuff on your eyes for?' Billy asks gruffly (meaning the teacher's eye shadow). Instead of rushing in with an answer the teacher reflects for a moment and then asks of the boy 'Why do you think it's there?'. Quick as a flash Billy retorts – 'Is it 'cos your 'tending to be a witch?'.

Cameo 2

The beginner teacher takes great trouble to set up a new 'travel agents' stimulus area in the classroom. It has an appropriate sign, brochures, pens and paper, telephone, maps of the world, travel posters for Disneyworld, a computer, a cash-till and a furniture arrangement which, as far as possible, reflects a real travel agency. Next morning, when the class of 8-year-olds arrive, there is great delight in the area and everyone wants to be the first to play. There is much jostling, pushing, arguing and, eventually, a few tears as the travel agents ends up in a demolished heap. The young teacher is devastated by the quick demise of her hard work and vows never to set up such an area again.

Cameo 3

It is customary at the end of the day, for the Year 1 children in Mrs Trent's class to sit on the carpet for quiet reflection and a story. The children mostly listen quietly and attentively to each other and to the teacher. However, there are always one or two children who constantly tug at the fraying edges of the carpet and set other children off pulling at the loose threads. Mrs Trent asks them in a kindly but firm manner, several times, to 'Please stop making the carpet worse' but every day her story is interrupted, and eventually stopped, in order to remove the offending children.

Introduction

The cameos raise very different issues about the classroom as a context for teaching and learning. On the one hand, a primary teacher needs to be a very organized and aware person, with a clear rationale for managing such things as a broad curriculum, teaching and learning resources, mounds of paperwork whilst, on the other hand, being able to give maximum time and effort to managing children and their learning. Young children, like Billy, are no less intelligent or less thinking than adults; they just operate at a different level of understanding and constantly work and play to understand the contexts in which they find themselves and the experiences presented.

No doubt you are questioning why, in the second cameo, despite all this teacher's care and effort, did she apparently not succeed? What more did she need to understand about the children and the learning context in order to achieve her intentions? Similarly, in the third cameo, why does this experienced teacher fail to pay attention to something relatively small which continually undermines her authority during story time and, worse still, causes interference to children's concentration, enjoyment of the occasion and potential learning? The answer to these and other questions lies in understanding some crucial factors (some of which have been explored by Maurice Galton in Chapter 1) which inextricably interrelate in the primary classroom and significantly affect its organization and management, namely:

- teachers – their beliefs and values and how these underpin all other elements of classroom organization and management;
- children – their family backgrounds, age phases and individual learning and behavioural needs which must be addressed;
- the learning context – the classroom and its resources (including people).

In this chapter, albeit briefly, we will examine these three issues and what they mean to the beginner teacher, using examples from classroom experiences and questions to focus attention on the issues.

Beliefs that matter

All of us bring to teaching memories of our own lives in school, perceptions about what it is to 'teach' and beliefs about how classroom systems

B elieve in what you do
ase what you do on children's interests and needs

A pproachable personality is vital
lways try to think positively and react thoughtfully

S ense of humour is essential – second sight is useful!
tructured approach to planning and management

I n touch with differing abilities and interests
ntegrate all children into class whatever race, sex or disability

C ontrol and respect must be <u>earned:</u> children treated equitably
ommunication skills must be excellent

T otally firm, fair and flexible
reat everyone with respect

E xplain things clearly and explicitly
xpect to be listened to and listen in return

A ware of everything and open to new ideas
nalytical and self-reflective

C onfident, calm, caring, collected and child-orientated
reative and imaginative

H appy classroom and happy, secure children
ome background is acknowledged and understood

I nfinitely patient and consistent
maginative and enthusiastic, inspiring and in-touch

N egotiate learning intentions and outcomes
eed for planning, observation and evaluation recognized

G eneral knowledge and common sense is used in teaching
ET ORGANIZED!

Figure 2.1 Basic teaching

should be. As part of coursework, some PGCE students explored the notion of 'Basic Teaching' and their thoughts are shown in Figure 2.1.

The very first statement, 'Believe in what you do', is simple but profound. Within us all lurks the 'ghost of pupil past' which influences both negatively and positively what we believe about children, teachers and education. You will, no doubt, have heard people say things like: 'Children today are not as well behaved as they used to be'; 'Education's all about getting a job'; or even 'Teachers have a cushy life with all those long holidays!'. These beliefs about children, teachers and education may or may not reflect how *you* feel about these things but certainly echo others'

Photo 4   Teach children the safety rules – and then trust them!

perceptions. Holding such views would make a vast difference to the way each of these people might themselves teach children, organize the curriculum, or manage the classroom. Hence, one can begin to understand why there are so many different views about education prevailing in our society. An added difficulty within teaching is that whilst the schooling system operates for all, ostensibly on the basis of equality of opportunity, each individual within the system – child and teacher – is different and has differing levels of expectation, capability, understanding and need.

Not only as a beginner teacher must you engage with what other people express about their beliefs and views regarding these educational issues, but you must determine what YOU believe. Without this personal construct – of children, the teacher's role and the learning context – it is an uphill struggle to establish yourself as a competent and confident class teacher.

People aged 3–11 years

When they enter school somewhere between the age of 3 to 5 years, children already bring with them a rich gamut of experiences. Parents and other family members are their first 'educators' (DES 1990) and teachers cannot ignore this. From the time they enter school, children are also developing greater and greater levels of independence in their actions and thinking – the very move from home to school represents the main beginning of independence from the family. Having made that break, how children react to being in a classroom framework with a large number of (relatively unknown) other children and adults and how this affects their behaviour and self-concept warrants investigation.

Family background

Whatever children bring with them, an effective teacher will ensure that early experiences are endorsed within the classroom structures. For example, children from different ethnic backgrounds will have their cultures represented within home corner materials, and 'the family' will reflect a range of types of structures to be found in modern society. The effective teacher will also want to *extend* children's experiences and offer them a range of broader options. One example might be the child who arrives with very stereotypical gender views (like the 3-year-old boy who told me it was women's work to pick up the jigsaw pieces from the floor!) or those who have not yet learned to cope with children different from themselves (see Chapter 13). Remember, we cannot change anything so fundamental as the child's background. What has to 'change' is the way different children are dealt with in school on the basis of accepting their background as a starting point for managing learning and ensuring continuity and coherence.

Continued contact with parents is a specific feature of primary education and most parents want to work with you in achieving the best for their children (see Hughes *et al.* 1994). In primary classrooms, teachers are 'in loco parentis' (as David Turner and Mark Lofthouse explain in Chapter 15), replacing the parent in dealing as diligently as you can with the children's needs during the school day.

Managing learning with different age groups

Most primary ITE courses will specialize within either the early years phase 3/5–8 year-olds, or for junior/middle years phase of 7–11/12 year-olds. Courses will normally make some differentiation between these phases but will emphasize the notions of continuity and progression across primary education. Just because a child is 7 years old does not mean, for example, that they no longer need access to concrete aids for number work or should cease to have experiences with constructional toys. Throughout the primary years children are developing a whole range of skills and constructing knowledge and understanding through their interactions and, as they increasingly gain ability to work from more abstract concepts, their teaching and learning needs and the organization of these will gradually change. For example, older children may be expected to work more collaboratively and undertake more complex problem-solving tasks which will require a very different classroom organization and teaching style.

For younger children, it is not a question of 'watering down' the activities which would be given to junior children: far from it! Rather it is necessary to understand the distinct emphases required in focusing upon young children, in developing their learning effectively and in examining the particular classroom strategies required by the teacher. Figure 2.2 represents an attempt to explain to PGCE students the differing emphases between teaching early years and older children.

The main headings within the diagram in Figure 2.2 do not necessarily change for older children but the focus becomes increasingly more dominated by curriculum, in particular a growing knowledge base in relation to subjects (see Chapter 6). Teachers of younger children equally require a sound knowledge of subject curriculum for it is probably a truism to say that the younger the child, the securer your own knowledge of different curriculum aspects needs to be. Whereas one explanation may be sufficient for an older primary child, the same concept may need explaining in many diverse ways to find an explanation which 'fits' the younger child's more limited experiences. This means creating classroom structures which allow this sustained language contact with children (Bennett 1992).

A sound understanding of child development and the process of learning is vital for all primary teachers if they are to organize and manage the classroom appropriately for different age groups. Regrettably, this is one aspect which has received decreasing emphasis on primary ITT courses over the last few years (Blenkin and Yue 1994). Beginner teachers must be prepared to ask appropriate searching questions related to children's development during curriculum sessions and to enhance their own understanding through reading and observations of children of across the age phases.

Children's independence

Children across the primary school years are developing independence in a variety of ways, particularly in thinking, confidence/self-esteem and development.

Thinking

Like Billy in the first cameo, many children work out explanations for themselves about phenomena (Tina Jarvis explains this more fully in Chapter 7). He is not being rude or cheeky, trying to be funny or being 'cute', he is simply making a guess based on prior experience (in this case an All Saints' Day celebration). This trial and error way of working is very typical of primary age children and should be fostered for we all learn a great deal by our mistakes and our guesses. The management of learning situations must allow children to raise serious, sensible questions which receive equally serious answers. The type of 'What colour is it?', 'What shape is it?' questions, so frequently asked, are actually confusing to young children who

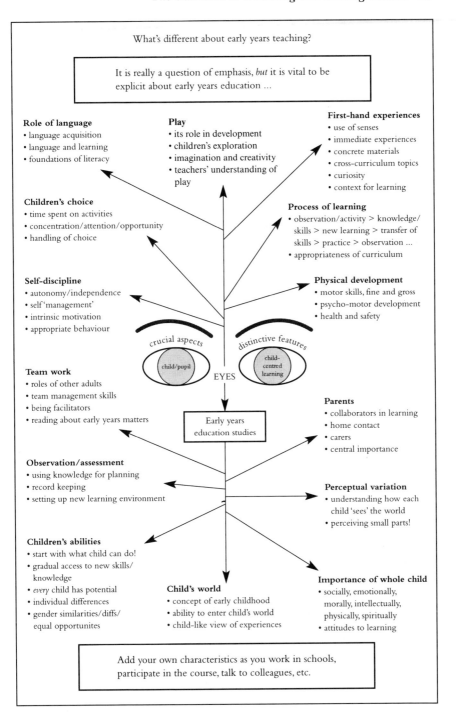

Figure 2.2

are well aware that the adult knows the answers already and, therefore, see no point in responding. Children often think it must be some kind of 'catch' question which leads to some failing to respond through uncertainty or embarrassment which, in turn, may lead the teacher to believe that the child has poor language skills. The classroom structures need to allow opportunities for exploring open-ended questions, more appropriate in developing higher-order thinking skills to challenge understanding and ensure the teacher learns about the children's learning.

Confidence

The children in the second scenario were so keen and confident in the classroom context that they temporarily 'forgot' the conventions of behaviour which they had been taught. They would need to be told that their *behaviour* was inappropriate on this occasion, rather than being 'blamed' for what had happened to the travel agency. Being blamed leads to children eventually deciding that they are 'no good' or making the 'I'm useless' type of comment, a form of 'labelling' so destructive of self-worth. The problem with labels is that people so often live up to the image the label suggests, so that being 'naughty' or 'good' or 'difficult' leads to exactly that kind of behaviour being exhibited. In turn, being 'difficult' gains some children the level of attention they demand (inevitably meaning that other children get less) and generates a self-fulfilling prophecy on the part of teacher and child with the child becoming more difficult and the teaching continually reaffirming the label. As a consequence, classroom management is made more problematic in that much time and energy is taken up in dealing with the difficult children rather than ensuring teacher time is more equitably distributed (see Campbell (1992) for discussion on teacher time). Giving children the responsibility for making decisions about classroom rules and routines, ensures that they take ownership and responsibility for their own actions as well as democratic decisions about other people's behaviour.

Development

Children of 3–8 years are gradually developing physical competence which allows greater independence of movement and action. It is positively cruel to keep children in this age phase sitting still for long periods of time! (After 8 years, children tend to refine and hone existing skills through general maturity rather than making any great leaps in development, see Davenport 1994.) Although the children in the third scenario appear to be 'naughty', children naturally manipulate things around them and explore increasing control over their fine motor skills. Ironically, it may well be that fraying the carpet edge was actually helping one child to concentrate! It could equally be that one of the 'frayers' is still socially quite immature and finds sitting within a confined space in close proximity to others quite distressing. Perhaps one or both of the children have not yet acquired age-appropriate levels of emotional stability, in which case fraying the carpet may be a symptom of underlying anxiety about, for example, whether the parent or carer will turn up at the end of the day. The message is: *understand the children as individual people* and organize and manage the classroom with this knowledge in mind. Think of them as people with all the emotions and needs which you yourself have – though at a different phase in life. Make one-to-one as well as collective relationships with them. Dealing with individual needs is not simply a matter of considering a child's learning needs but of understanding 'where they are' physically, socially and emotionally as well. For the children who cannot physically sit still for any extended period, it may be more appropriate that they draw a picture during story time or are asked to make pictorial or written notes during periods of teacher exposition to the whole class. This kind of thinking is at the very heart of child-centred education, the provision of a differentiated curriculum and effective classroom management.

Organizing and managing the learning environment

The classroom represents 'home' for five or more hours of each weekday during term times to children and teachers alike. Its prime function is to 'house' the teacher and the learners in a kind of 'workshop' (or playshop!) context which supports these crucial interactions between them. The teacher must translate knowledge of children and pedagogy into classroom organization and management structures to everyone's benefit, no mean feat given that few people will have been totally responsible for 30+ other people before! The vital elements which must be considered are:

- the physical context;
- structures (including routines) and resource management;
- rights, responsibilities and rules;
- behaviour;
- communication.

Each of these will be explored briefly. (For fuller information see Moyles 1992 and 1994.) While you read, try to think about classrooms within your recent experience so as to give substance to the discussion.

Physical context

The classroom or class base is part of a larger school building which was built in a particular time in history under the philosophies of education which existed at the time. Very early state elementary schools, for example, had large halls where vast numbers of children were taught en masse to read, write and do basic number activities. Schools built in the 1920s to 1930s show a growing emphasis on outdoor activities for children, being characterized by having open-air quadrangles (often containing gardens and outdoor play areas) around which long draughty corridors spawn individual

Photo 5   Display is part of creating a stimulating environment

classrooms, with up to 50 children in each! Designs of schools built in the 1960s and 1970s reflect a belief in the interactive and collaborative nature of children's learning and are often open-plan, where two or more classrooms are merged together and teachers are intended to function as a team. Whatever the building, teachers must operate current ideologies and practices making the most of whatever they have so as to offer the best possible experiences to the children.

Take a moment to turn to the classroom plan in Figure 3.3 (Chapter 3). It reflects a very typical kind of layout for an infant classroom and contains direct 'clues' as to the activities of the children and, therefore, the practices of the teacher. Many areas of curriculum, including subjects, are represented within the layout, for example language and social skills (the home corner café), literacy (the book corner), design technology (constructional toys and 3-D models), art (painting table), science (water play) and sorting and puzzles (mathematics). It is likely that children will be given some choice of the activities they undertake, albeit choosing from those activities provided by the teacher in specific areas of the room.

Contrast this with Jenny's classroom (Figure 1.1, Chapter 1) where group work tables are undesignated in terms of activity, suggesting that this teacher may well direct children's activities quite specifically and may operate at an expositional or instructional level from the position of the teacher's desk. The provision of a carpet area suggests that there may be occasions when children work at floor level or perhaps have quiet reading opportunities or gather together in a large social group for story or discussion.

What a lot there is to be gleaned by interpreting different classroom layouts! What this exposes, however, is that the teacher's ideology super-imposes on any physical classroom space a way of working for that teacher and the children. Such aspects are worth noting on your next visit to a classroom.

Equally, there is much to learn from the way in which teachers organize the seating arrangements (see Chapter 1). People whose ideology lies in a child-centred type of education can be quite horrified at the sight of rows of desks and chairs which tends to signify whole class teaching. However, the organization of the desks or tables needs to be contingent upon the type of activities which are taking place – the 'fitness for purpose' notion (see Alexander *et al.* 1992). Collaborative group work requires tables to be organized in such a way that co-operation and interaction between children can take place, for example, that they can all see each other's faces and share resources. Such arrangements, however, can positively hinder children attempting to undertake concentrated, individual work or hinder the teacher in trying to give a demonstration to a whole class.

Carpet areas are excellent for bringing a cosy 'togetherness' to shared events in the classroom, be it story (as in the third cameo), children telling their 'news' to others, discussion or singing together. They may not be so useful for older children (physically large 11-year-olds can find sitting on a carpet cross-legged rather demeaning) or for a teacher's detailed exposition on a special topic. It may be far more useful if the carpet area is detailed as a stimulus area (see Moyles 1989) so that children can follow up such a teacher-directed session with a more first-hand, direct experience, as might be the case with the travel agency (once the ground rules are established!).

When entering a classroom in which you are going to work for the first time, it is advisable to make a plan as this both helps to fix the area in your mind and also offers the opportunity of re-checking outside school when you are thinking through future learning activities. It is also useful for obser-vation purposes as suggested by Linda Hargreaves in the next chapter.

Structures and routines

By structures is meant the way the classroom operates so that children are clear what they are doing and do not need to expend time and energy in constantly finding out where things are and what they must do. Routines represent the order in which things happen and are usually related to the daily and weekly timetable for the class.

Timetables are usually determined by the school, at least in outline, with several sessions being 'fixed times', for example, hall periods or assemblies.

Teachers have the task of deciding on the best use of time within what is left either individually or in year groups. Making good use of children's and teacher's time is vital as there is always so much to fit in with the subject and broader curriculum implementation. If observation reveals that children are spending much of their time waiting for teacher attention, this may be because the daily structures and routines are inappropriate. Perhaps children are too dependent upon the teacher for resources or tasks (see Chapter 1), or are given insufficient guidance on what to do when they are 'stuck'. A class discussion generating a set of ideas of what to do when you need help, such as ask another child, look in a book, do another task until the teacher can see you, can quickly alleviate this problem even with young children.

Routines are helpful though you must guard against them becoming 'routinous' and, therefore, boring. A little deviation from routine helps to keep children and teacher alert and interested, for example try having the story after morning playtime instead of the end of the morning or afternoon ensuring it can be used as the basis for the next session (Jane Hislam gives some suggestions in Chapter 9).

Such routines as those involved in children entering and leaving the classroom or in tidying up need attention. Does it happen smoothly or do the children fidget and tussle with each other? Often, as in the carpet cameo above, children and teachers simply get overly familiar with a situation and what should be dealt with quickly then becomes a constant thorn in everyone's side! Routines are useful but familiarity can breed contempt! (The caretaker might be asked to repair that carpet.)

Demanding levels of responsibility from the children appropriate to their age by, for example, ensuring that they are responsible for the access/ retrieval and upkeep/maintenance of resources (we need *all* the pieces in a jigsaw!), ensures that they are not dependent upon the teacher for every item of equipment. (Maurice Galton raises the issue of teacher dependency in the previous chapter.) This also means that materials should be located and labelled appropriately; older children can do this in negotiation with the teacher and even the youngest children can do the labelling though location may be the teacher's decision. Train and trust the children! Expect them to behave appropriately in all matters and most of them will. A quality classroom is likely to be one where there is a place for everything and everything is mainly in its place! You should not use precious time at the end of each day in sorting out the classroom when there is marking, preparation, display, records and a wealth of other tasks upon which your time is more profitably spent.

Rights, responsibilities and rules

Children and teachers have the right to the best possible classroom experiences – and that also means behaving appropriately towards each other. Issues should be discussed, the responsibilities of each party determined and ground rules established. Both should feel able to raise issues which mean they cannot work effectively in the classroom, for example both teachers and children are affected by noise – constant shouting or nagging will usually make this situation worse, whereas discussion about alleviating the situation can result in a quiet working atmosphere being maintained by the children. As a general rule, children should be given responsibility for going to the toilet without asking though this may be dependent upon the school layout. A sensible rule which children will readily accept is 'one at a time'. Whatever the rule, it should be established quickly, with firmness and consistency: this applies equally to any rules made. When asked about their 'best' teachers, a majority of junior age pupils chose fairness and consistency as the chief qualities (see Cullingford 1991). If, for any reason, changes to the rules are required, these should be communicated, re-negotiated, written up and read out for all to see and hear and firmly put into place as efficiently as possible (see Calderhead 1984).

Behaviour

It would be trite to suggest that if you get the classroom organization and management sorted out there will be no behaviour problems. You have, however, only to think about the number of times there is a fuss and disagreement over quite minor incidents – a child tripping over another, arguments over resources – to realize that many behavioural issues are at least related to classroom structures. Bored children also misbehave so achieving work at an appropriate standard relieves some problems. Most primary children enjoy school, appreciate the relationship they have with teachers and want to be part of the stimulating activities. Many behavioural problems are contained within acceptable boundaries once teacher and child have 'got the measure of each other' and a working relationship agreed. This happens when the teacher makes time to work with individuals, knows their names and responds to their needs. Treating children as people and giving them appropriate respect means that many children will respond with appropriate levels of responsibility and care for others.

Communication

At explaining to children what to do and how to do it, primary teachers usually excel. Communication, however, often breaks down because teachers fail to tell children *why* they are undertaking certain activity and what they are expected to *know* and *do* as a result. So much is taken for granted in the primary classroom and yet, as many cameos in this book show, children often have a very different level of understanding to adults and need explicit guidance (see Edwards and Mercer 1987).

There will be many different levels at which you communicate with children requiring different *classroom groupings*. Talking to them as a whole class to establish the groundwork for something to which all children will contribute or demonstrating a new technique are examples. Grouping by ability for some activities will mean that you can work to stretch the abler children or give closer attention to a group requiring additional help. Grouping by task will be helpful where resources are perhaps limited and only a few children at a time can have access to, for example, science equipment. With younger children, groupings are commonly by friendship and there may also be occasion where sex groupings might be used, particularly where the teacher is attempting to encourage boys to use the home-corner provision or girls to become more adventurous with the constructional materials.

Communication with other adults is also an important skill. As a student on a teacher education course, there will be many occasions on which you will work with others as part of learning about classroom practice. In fact, students sometimes feel like 'piggy-in-the-middle' when they receive regular, if sometimes conflicting advice, from a range of tutors and class teachers! Regular communication with a more experienced teacher such as a mentor, can ensure that adversity is kept in perspective and the classroom runs as smoothly as possible – time needs to be set aside for mentoring as Wendy Suschitzky stresses in Chapter 14. These types of communication happen with less frequency as one becomes a teacher with full responsibility for the class – in fact it can be quite an isolated job in a typical closed classroom situation. You may well have help from nursery nurses (if you work within the early years) and ancillaries, parents, further education students, sixth formers, and professionals whose advice is sought about particular children. You must help them to help you and the children. Be clear before they arrive what their role is and what support is needed. Unless it is vital to the activity that they sit and listen to the story, for example, request their help in preparing the next batch of materials, repairing books, labelling materials or working with individuals.

One level of communication which is often forgotten is that of communicating with yourself – reflecting on your experiences and needs. What did YOU do today? How did you feel about it? What skills have you used and what needs do you have for tomorrow or next week? (Claxton 1990). Take time out to reflect upon your beliefs about teaching and learning and talk to others about your successes and occasional disasters!

Conclusion

When considering classroom organization and management issues it is inappropriate to focus wholly upon the pragmatics of organizing a physical space, for each one carries its own unique constraints. It is far more vital to get at the roots of why different teachers' practices are as they are. The crucial aspects involved are what teachers believe – about themselves, the children, the purposes of education and schooling, curriculum processes and the ethos of the particular school. Having a clear rationale for organizing and managing a classroom in a particular way needs to be explored by beginner teachers based on their own beliefs and developing ideology. Constant reflection on how it all works is crucial to continuing success and evolution of effective practice.

To put all this in perspective, let us return to the second cameo. This teacher felt that her course had taught her that children would learn much about the work of travel agents (as well as some geographical knowledge, multi-cultural understanding and opportunity to use number skills) from having this first-hand experience presented to them in the classroom. However, this element was still not really part of her own value system or within her understanding of children's responses to such experiences. She had been taught on her ITE course, but had not yet absorbed it into her own value systems, that most children need exploration of new materials and contexts before being expected to deal in any depth with the concepts presented (see Chapter 6). The student could have:

- given children the responsibility for setting up the travel agency in the classroom, so that at each stage they were exploring the materials and the context;
- asked the children to present rules for use of the travel agency and to decide what was and was not acceptable behaviour;
- made her own rules as to how the travel agency should be used and put up an appropriate sign;
- allowed children to use the travel agency only when she was available to supervise their activities.

If your instinct is towards the first and second options, it is likely that you are a 'child-centred' person who puts thoughts about the children's learning experiences first. If you chose the final two options, these, on the whole, reflect a more 'teacher-centred' reaction. Which one would you have chosen? Why? How would this have affected your classroom organization and management?

References and further reading

Alexander, R., Rose, J. and Woodhead, C. (1992) *Curriculum Organisation and Classroom Practice in Primary Schools*. London: DES.

Bennett, N. (1992) *Managing Learning in the Primary Classroom*. Stoke-on-Trent: ASPE/Trentham Books.

Blenkin, G. and Yue, N. (1994) Profiling early years practitioners: some first impressions from a national survey. *Early Years*, 15 (1): 13–22.

Calderhead, J. (1984) *Teachers' Classroom Decision Making*. London: Holt, Rinehart and Winston.

Campbell, J. (1992) *Managing Teachers Time in Primary Schools: Concepts, Evidence and Policy Issues*. Stoke-on-Trent: ASPE/Trentham Books.

Claxton, G. (1990) *Teaching to Learn*. Oxford: Blackwell.

Cullingford, C. (1991) *The Inner World of the School: Children's Ideas about Schools.* London: Cassells.

Davenport, G. (1994) *An Introduction to Child Development*, 2nd edn. London: Collins.

Department of Education and Science (1990) *Starting with Quality* (The Rumbold Report). London: HMSO.

Edwards, D. and Mercer, N. (1987) *Common Knowledge: The Development of Understanding in the Classroom.* London: Methuen.

Hughes, M., Wikeley, F. and Nash, T. (1994) *Parents and Their Children's Schools.* Oxford: Blackwell.

Kyriacou, C. (1990) *Essential Teaching Skills.* Oxford: Basil Blackwell.

Merrett, F. and Wheldall, K. (1990) *Positive Teaching in the Primary School.* London: Paul Chapman.

Moyles, J.R. (1989) *Just Playing? The Role and Status of Play in Early Childhood Education.* Milton Keynes: Open University Press.

Moyles, J.R. (1992) *Organizing for Learning in the Primary Classroom: A Balanced Approach to Classroom Management.* Milton Keynes: Open University Press.

Moyles, J.R. (1994) *Classroom Organisation.* Bright Ideas for Early Years Series. Leamington Spa: Scholastic Publications.

Waterhouse, P. (1990) *Classroom Management.* Stafford: Network Educational Press.

3

Seeing clearly
Observation in the primary classroom

Linda Hargreaves

Cameo 1

A Year 2 teacher was concerned about the noise level in her class and decided to carry out some observations to find out what was really happening. She decided to focus on the most and least talkative children in the class, Paul and Maria respectively. Here are her impressions of these two children.

Paul seemed to talk all the time – to the teacher or to his friends. He blurted out his ideas and wouldn't listen to others. If he couldn't get the teacher's attention, he told those nearest to him. If he wanted help, he wanted it immediately.

Maria, on the other hand, seemed very quiet. She would hardly talk at all. She did not take part in class discussions, even when asked directly for her opinion. She rarely came to talk to the teacher on a one-to-one basis either to share information or to ask for help.

The teacher used the simple observation technique of glancing at each child every 20 minutes or so and noting down the behaviour observed on a page divided into two columns (see Figure 3.1).

The observations did not match the teacher's impressions. Before making the observations she would have underestimated Maria's confidence to help other children and Paul's ability to concentrate.

Cameo 2

A Year 5 class was working in groups on a co-operative task to make a paper bridge to span a certain length and to carry a specified minimum weight. The class teacher regularly used structured observation of the children during practical sessions as a way of assessing their skills and understanding. The children were quite used

Time	Target Child 1 Maria	Target Child 2 Paul
9.30	doing maths — working alone	out of place — getting a pencil
9.52	talking to R. and pointing at R's book	writing quietly
10.10	standing behind R and H; talking and pointing to books	writing quietly
10.25	reading alone	out of place — bringing work to be marked

Figure 3.1 Observations of two children at approximately 20 minute intervals

to being self-sufficient at these times. That day the teacher was using a photocopied sheet (see Figure 3.2) which had a grid for structured observations in the top half and space underneath to write down exactly what the children said or did, as evidence of their skills.

The teacher observed them as they tested their bridges. She had already put ticks on the grid whenever one of the girls in the group said something which involved planning skills, measuring and evaluating either their methods or approach. So far the grid record showed that Dawn and Julie had done most of the planning and Julie had talked about, and actually done, the measuring. By this stage in the session, Group 3 had put their 1kg, 500g and 200g weights, rather precariously, on the bridge, and had only 10g and 5g weights left in their box. Some of these were made of blue plastic and the others were made of metal. The teacher waited to see what they would do and then heard Yvette's suggestion and Dawn's agreement which indicated some lack of understanding about the meaning of '10g'. She quickly wrote down what the children had said on the observation sheet.

Y: Let's put the blue ones in first then it'll be more weights.
D: Yeah, good idea! (laughs)

When they had finished the teacher asked why they had used all the blue 10g weights before they used the metal ones. The reply was 'They're lighter 'cos they're plastic so you need more.'

The children's reports on the task simply showed the total weight which the bridge would support before it crumpled. If the teacher had

Date ..20..9........ Curriculum area(s) .sci./tech.....
Topic..forces............Task...bridge task..........

Group 3	planning	measuring mass	measuring length	evaluation/reflection
Dawn	✓✓✓		✓(talks)	
Julie	✓✓✓	✓?	✓✓✓	✓
Yvette	✓	*?check		

Examples/notes:

D: — now it'll need loads of these
      little ones

J : count them into 10s so it'll be
      100g. in each pile

Y : Let's put the blue ones on first so
      it'll be more weights

D: Yeah · good idea (laughs)

Figure 3.2 Group work observation grid: observing science and technology activities

not observed the children, she would not have known about their fundamental misunderstanding of standard units.

Cameo 3

The staff of a nursery unit routinely used observation of the children's choices of activity in their record-keeping system by plotting the child's movements on a plan of the nursery. Generally, this was done for each child once a term unless the plan showed that a child was choosing a very limited range of activities, or was flitting from one activity to another without really settling down. An example of a plan is shown in Figure 3.3. Sometimes they noted the time the child arrived at an activity and the time s/he left it, but usually they just recorded the order of the activities and added a plus (+) sign for each ten minutes that the child stayed at one activity.

The child's choices, plotted on the plan as in Figure 3.3, usually sufficed as a clear, graphic record. The staff used the tracks as a basis for discussion about the children's progress in the nursery and recently the tracks had shown that boys were rarely choosing the book area and that four children seemed regularly to avoid the puzzles and activities, needing fine motor co-ordination.

Introduction

These examples show some of the ways in which teachers have used class-room observation to find out about children's behaviour and learning. Observation is a term which includes *listening* to children as well as *watching* them because listening (*without* joining in) offers teachers unrivalled access to investigating and understanding children's concepts, learning and behaviour. In addition, once qualified, teachers get relatively little chance to observe each other and so it is vital to take every opportunity to observe closely the way other teachers' work and exactly what the children do in different learning situations. Using the cameos as real-life examples, this chapter will cover:

• looking and observing;
• the uses of observation;
• ways to record children's activities;
• observing teachers.

Looking and observing: what is the difference?

On visiting a school, people quickly begin to form impressions. Certain salient signals attract their attention:

• rapid arpeggios on a clarinet;
• children's laughter;
• the smell of fresh baking;

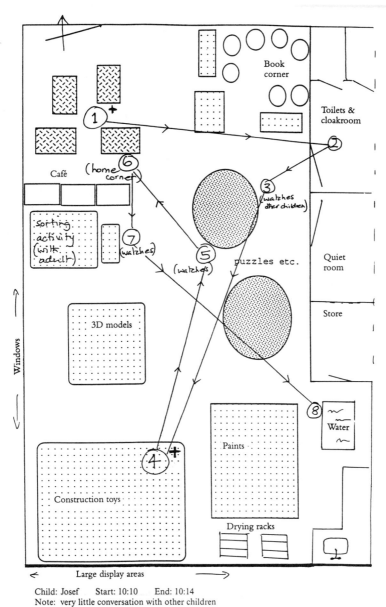

Book
corner

Toilets &
cloakroom

Café

(home
corner)

Sorting
activity
(with
adult)

(watches
other children)

(watches)

(watches)

puzzles etc.

Quiet
room

Store

3D models

Windows

Water

Paints

Construction toys

Large display areas

Drying racks

Child: Josef   Start: 10:10   End: 10:14
Note: very little conversation with other children

Figure 3.3   Using a classroom plan to track a child's choices of activity

Photo 6   Observing for learning in the outdoor environment

- cans and crisp packets all over the field;
- a calligraphy display;
- a teacher's raised voice;
- a cabinet of sports trophies;
- a whiff of cigarette smoke.

Such impressions are likely to give a false picture. The visitors will attend selectively to the signals which reinforce the rumours they have heard, for example that the school 'is good for music'; 'has a happy atmosphere'; 'keeps the children in order' or 'is untidy and run-down'. They will screen out the signals that do not fit.

On meeting a new class of children, the same thing can happen as teachers form impressions of the children: he is *always* talking; she *never* listens; those two *won't* try; this one *can't* concentrate. It may be that the negative impressions are formulated quickly because the teacher feels that something must be done about these things. Sometimes, unfortunately these impressions persist and can influence the teacher's expectations of a child and judgements of the child's work. This could have a significant and long-term effect on a child's progress in school. Planned observation is a vital check on this process, as shown in the first cameo.

Observing in classrooms

Unlike impressions, observations:

- are made for a *purpose*, for example to assess a child's skills or to see how a certain resource is used;
- have a *specific focus*, for example to record the level of a child's motor skills or oral skills or how children interact in a group;
- are made at set times including times when the child is *not* interacting with the teacher, as well as times when he or she *is*.

In addition and very importantly, observations are written down so that they can be interpreted, analysed and reflected on, away from the bustle and quick decision-making atmosphere of the classroom. In other words, when observing, as opposed to mere looking, the teacher decides in advance:

- what to look for;
- who to look at;
- where and when to look.

Uses of observation

Observation gives information about what actually happens in the classroom so that teachers can base their judgements and their planning on the *process* as well as the *products* of classroom activities. It can be used:

- to provide before and after evidence to show what *progress* a child has made as a result of some teaching or simply over a certain time period;
- to *compare* the effects on children's behaviour of different teaching approaches, different ways of grouping children or of managing the class;
- as *feedback* for the teacher in the evaluation of classroom activities, for example if an activity was set up with the aim of getting the children to practise formulating questions, or explore colours by mixing paints, an observational record would help the teacher to find out whether it *actually did* encourage question formation or experiments in paint mixing.

Several recent educational innovations have meant that observation is becoming a routine matter for many teachers. In 1980, the Open University/ Schools Council project on school-focused curriculum evaluation work, *Curriculum in Action*, introduced classroom observation to teachers as a useful information-gathering tool. Since then, the NC and standard attainment tasks (SATs) have demanded observational assessment of 7-year-olds, whilst the introduction of teacher appraisal has increased teachers' usage of observation. It is now accepted as a principal tool for finding out about teaching and learning in:

- the evaluation of learning activities;
- the monitoring of children's behaviour;
- the identification of effective teaching techniques;
- teacher education;
- school inspections.

The ultimate aim of classroom observation is to improve the children's opportunities to learn and to ensure that they get the best out of those opportunities. Firstly, by observing one child the teacher can find out about that child's way of working or 'learning style'. Secondly, by observing a group of children working together, the teacher can identify the cognitive skills and social skills used by the children through their interactions with other group members. Thirdly, by being observed by a colleague, or by taping part of a lesson and listening critically to it, teachers can learn about their own habitual teaching style and aim to develop a range of styles suited to different teaching and learning objectives.

Classroom observation is especially valuable for beginning teachers because, in most cases, they have i) more to learn about children than their more experienced counterparts, and ii) a classroom partner to help them make the observations. Moyles (1989) provides a very useful summary of ways to observe early years children, which are equally applicable at any stage of schooling.

What kinds of observations and recordings do teachers make?

The many different methods of making and recording classroom observations include long-hand continuous accounts of classroom events, the use of video and ticking categories on a checklist. The various methods are based originally on two different research traditions:

1 *Participant* observation is derived from anthropological and sociological research where it involved taking copious open-ended, long-hand field notes over a long enough period of time for the observer to become accepted as a participant in the observed group. Class teachers already are participants and can make notes about teaching and learning situations with some confidence that they understand them, although any newcomers to a particular class should take care to check their interpretations of any observations made with the teacher or children concerned.

2 *Systematic* observation, used in psychological studies, requires observers to record systematically on grids or checklists which have been set up – or pre-coded – before the observations begin (Morag Hunter-Carsch describes some of these in Chapter 12). Systematic observers are concerned with how much or how often specific behaviours occur in certain settings and, perhaps, at certain times or phases of an activity or lesson. By pre-specifying the range of behaviours to be recorded in this way, the researchers try to minimize the level of inferential judgement about what is happening and so obviate the need for extended immersion in the

culture of each classroom observed. Good examples of primary-phase research based on systematic observation include the ORACLE project, described by Maurice Galton in Chapter 1. Croll (1986) offers a definitive text on systematic observation.

Open-ended or structured observation?

If the aim is to find out what the children say or do in certain situations, long-hand notes will be most useful. For example, if the teacher wants to know exactly how two children set about the kind of co-operative task described by Sylvia McNamara in Chapter 10, the teacher might take notes about what the children do in the opening phase of work on the problem. If, however, teachers already know what types of behaviour they are looking for, then the use of a checklist will be the most efficient observation method. Having set a problem to solve, the teacher might want to observe the children's spontaneous or existing levels of use of 'entry' and 'attack' procedures, before planning teaching on problem solving. The teacher would then use a checklist or grid like that in Figure 3.2, but list 'entry' procedures such as:

- explores the problem;
- makes guesses;
- defines terms and relationships;
- organizes the information;

and so on (see Burton 1984). Both traditions have something to offer classroom teachers and the examples which follow draw on both techniques.

Using open-ended observation

Long-hand notes are particularly useful for individual child studies, provided that a factual account without value laden terms is kept and this needs practice. For example, 'S. wanders lazily to get book from drawers and strolls back to seat – flicks idly through pages to new page and gazes at blank page' presents a particularly negative view of what S. actually did through the choice of words such as *lazily, strolls, idly* and *gazes*. What S. actually did was: walk slowly to drawers and get book out; walk back, looking around; turn pages to find place and look at blank page.

Open-ended observations are ideal for individual child studies and can be kept to a simple format so that observations over a similar period of time can be made of other children, or if the same child in a variety of situations, such as during a craft activity, when reading alone, when playing and when working in a team.

The *Individual Record Sheet* (Figure 3.4) combines a simple, structured format with spaces for long-hand notes to be taken. This type of record is particularly useful to provide evidence which might support or refute a teacher's initial impressions of a child. A child's behaviour in a variety of different settings such as working alone, working in a group, playing in the

Child's Name: ......Simon....(S)..............................

Activity: ...Science : circuit with batteries and buzzers...

Sitting/working with: ....Katie....(K).....................

Each row is for 30 or 60 seconds' observation. This could be organized as a five minute block, 1 minute every 5 minutes, 2 x 5-minute periods or 10 observations spread over a session, day or half-day.

Time	What is target child *actually* doing?	Child interacts with:	Resources/ equipment being USED
9.30	Simon attaches wires by holding in place. Presses buzzer. "mine's working!"	katie	battery wires buzzer unit
9.31	continues to press buzzer demonstrates to 3 children	3 children and Katie	"
9.32	watches other children doing theirs. Tries buzzer again no buzz. Partner tries t	Katie	"
	attach wires —says 'We have to 'tach them'. S. 'Do we?' Try t manipulate croc. clips	"	and crocodile clips
9.34	Katie tries t attach clips but they come off the terminals K: "It's not going to work"	"	"
	Simon works buzzer again by holding wires on. Katie says 'Clip the black one on'	katie	
9.35	Tries t clip π to battery. It falls off " Ha! ha! ha! " both Boy(R)comes over to watch.	katie R.	"
9.36	S. 'Ugh it's hard'. K. 'should we ask Mrs. P.?' (S. ignores) Boy (R) watches. "Is it hot?" — S is holding wire on battery.	R	"
	S 'No it's cold' Carries on buzzing. Puts buzzer to face (to test for hot?) K. "we've got to clip them on" How do we clip them on?		"

NOTES: Simon seems to see getting buzz as aim — He is not interested in making a circuit.
N.B. clips difficult for children to use. Too stiff?.

Figure 3.4   Individual observation sheet

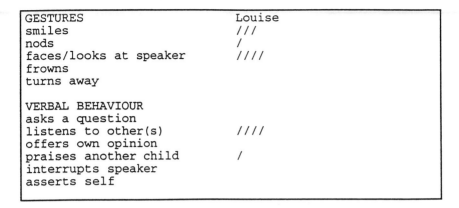

```
GESTURES                  Louise
smiles                    ///
nods                      /
faces/looks at speaker    ////
frowns
turns away

VERBAL BEHAVIOUR
asks a question
listens to other(s)       ////
offers own opinion
praises another child     /
interrupts speaker
asserts self
```

Figure 3.5 Individual checklist showing social skills

playground or taking part in an expressive activity such as dance or musical composition (such as those described by Martin Wenham in Chapter 8) could be recorded to furnish a rounded picture of the child's work and social styles.

Using structured observation

Cameo 2 uses a format for a structured observation system, based on a checklist or grid, where a grid is simply a checklist to be used when observing a small number of children at the same time. There are many areas where the teacher knows in advance what skills or behaviours s/he is looking for. These might be cognitive skills or the problem-solving example above, or social skills. If several teachers are going to observe the same aspects of children's behaviour, a checklist, with shared definitions and examples of what the behaviour will be, is most valuable. Checklists are also quick to use because there is no need to write notes and because a time pattern such as observing events during every third, fifth or tenth minute, or recording what is happening every 30 seconds can be imposed.

In Figure 3.5, the teacher has noted each time Louise showed any of the actions on the checklist during the time that Louise was being observed. This is called a category system and it shows the relative frequencies of Louise's various social actions.

In Figure 3.6, the teacher has observed four children and simply noted each action once. This shows the minimum number of times each action occurred but it shows which children did or did not use these actions. The pattern of ticks shows different social styles for the children. It suggests that Louise participated positively non-verbally but did not speak and that Jack was more self-assertive than the others. Mark did not listen to the others and Clare was more supportive of the others, in this situation.

	Clare	Jack	Mark	Louise
GESTURES				
smiles	/	/		/
nods in agreement	/			/
faces speaker	/	/		
frowns			/	
turns away			/	
VERBAL BEHAVIOUR				
asks a question	/			
listens to other(s)	/	/		
offers own opinion		/	/	
praises another child	/			
interrupts speaker		/		
asserts self		/		

Figure 3.6   Group observation grid of social skills used

	(skill 1)	(skill 2)	(skill 3)	(skill 4)
(child 1)				
(child 2)				
(child 3)				
(child 4)				

Activity/topic ....

Resources in use: ....

Notes:

Figure 3.7   A group work observation grid

The Group work Observation Grid (Figure 3.7) can readily be copied and the column headings can, of course, be changed to suit the focus of the observations.

Alternative methods of observation

Video and audio recording

Video and audio recordings are especially useful for emphasizing detail, for example to record children's work in physical education, dance and musical composition or children's actual words in an oral task. They can be used to assess individual or group progress if repeated after one or two months, as well as for class evaluation of a composition or performance in the making. For example, a series of short video recordings of a sample of children made, say, twice a term of children's gymnastic skills, throwing and catching skills can show marked developments which, because they are gradual, might not be fully recognized on a day-to-day basis. In music, children's appraisal skills can be developed as they listen critically to their own singing or playing: in effect they are observing themselves. *But* when using video or audio recording do remember:

1 the children will need time to get used to being filmed or taped – they cannot be expected to be perfectly natural so do not expect them to be for the first few times;
2 the teacher needs to get used to using a camera or recorder (remembering to switch it on – or to ask a child to switch it on – at the right moment is crucial!);
3 viewing or listening to the recording and making notes about it takes at least as much time as the recording actually took to make;
4 background noise can mask the desired sounds;
5 videos need to have the target child quite close up but then context can be lost.

Maps and plans

A map type observation was used in cameo 3 at the beginning of the chapter. This kind of record is ideal when children are likely to be moving about over a large area, as in PE, drama, or play activities, or when getting resources. It can also be used to plot how a teacher's attention is distributed across a class. In a classroom where the children usually sit down at tables a 'map' of the classroom with circles or 'blobs' to represent each seat as in Figure 3.8 can be used to record various aspects of classroom action and interaction as suggested by Hopkins (1993). 'Blob' plans can be used to record behaviour in a variety of settings such as the following.

1 To record observations of children's choices and movements in a setting such as a playground, nursery or reception unit or a practical workshop in which the children are free to move around (cameo 3). The results

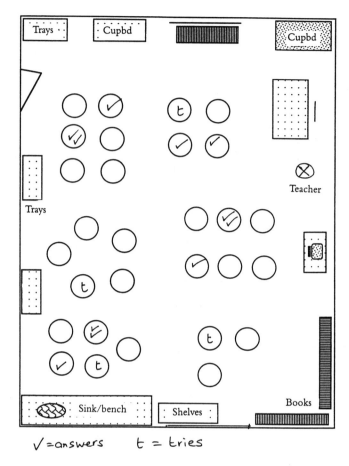

√ =answers   t = tries

Figure 3.8 Using a 'blob' plan to record participation in a teacher-led discussion

would be useful for keeping a record of children's behaviour or preferences. The following questions can be answered in terms of the plan:
• which activity did the child stay with for the longest period?
• did the child return to the same activity several times?
• does the child avoid certain types of activity?
2 To make several plots of how many children are in each area during an activity session to study the relative popularity of the activities.
3 To mark out the *teacher's* movements as he or she moves from group to group. One could plot:
• the teacher's movements about the class when children are working individually and requesting help;
• how long s/he stays at one table;
• which tables get the longest and shortest visits;
• whether every table gets a visit in the time allowed.

4 A classroom plan can be used to record observations of which children
answer questions in a class discussion. In Figure 3.7 each blob represents
a child. By marking a tick in the blob when a child answers a question,
the distribution of the teacher's attention can be studied, through questions such as:
- which children participate most in a whole class discussion or question
  and answer session?
- is it always the same children who volunteer answers?
- do some volunteer but are not asked?
- what are those who are not taking part actually doing?
- are boys asked more often than girls?
- do boys offer answers more than girls?
- what is the difference between the participation rates of higher and
  lower achieving children, or those who speak a different language at
  home?

After some practice with the 'blob' plan, a code to show whether the child
is a boy or girl (b/g); whether they volunteered or were named (v/n);
whether they offered but weren't asked (t = tries) or got the chance to give
a long response (s = stars), could be made. Use + or – if the child receives
praise or admonition. The code can be extended according to what you
want to observe.

Observing teachers

In this last part of the chapter, several ideas for observing other teachers
are presented. These will be very useful from the earliest school visits to
observe other teachers' classroom styles, but later they could be used to
analyse and evaluate your own teaching for the purposes of identifying
competences as indicated by Neil Kitson in Chapter 4. A tape recorder, a
colleague, or a mentor could record the teaching session.

The most well-known and widely used method for the observation of
teacher talk is Flanders's Interaction Analysis Categories (Flanders 1970).
Although inappropriate in a typical primary classroom, FIAC combines
what can be described as 'managerial' and 'information-giving' talk by the
teacher. These two functions of teacher talk are described below.

Two types of teacher talk

Beginning teachers soon discover that a normal conversational style can be
relatively ineffective in gaining the attention of a class of children. Experienced teachers, on the other hand, can talk to the children in an apparently natural way and still command their attention and co-operation. They
make it look easy and *because it looks so easy*, it is easy to overlook *exactly*
what the teacher is saying and doing. It is very useful, therefore, to observe
closely what teachers say and how they say it.

The first type to observe, is *managerial talk*, when teachers are managing the children through a change-over of some kind and are, for example:

- gaining the children's attention;
- starting off the activities;
- changing children from one activity to another;
- clearing up and ending an activity session;
- sending children to play, or to another room.

The second is *teaching talk*, when teachers are maintaining the children's attention and actually teaching and are, for example:

- introducing a topic;
- asking children questions;
- answering children's questions (without being side-tracked);
- giving information or instructions;
- inviting children to make suggestions;
- dealing with interruptions or attention-seekers;
- summing up a session.

Just one session spent observing (*not* just watching) an experienced effective teacher do these things will be invaluable. It will be even more useful to talk over the observations with the teacher after the session.

Using the teacher observation sheets

The teacher observation sheet (Figure 3.9) can be used to record both managerial and teaching talk but will be most useful for the former.

Column 1 – Time: There is no need to record this for every utterance – just note the beginning and end of each episode.

Column 2 – Teacher's location: Note where the teacher stands or sits: at the front, side or back of the class; at one of the children's tables; at the teacher's table/desk.

Column 3 – Teacher's actual words: Try to write down exactly what the teacher said, noting particularly how she or he i) begins a question or a statement; ii) responds to a child's suggestion.

Column 4 – Teacher's audience: Note down who is expected to listen to the teacher – the whole class, one group, one child, one child or group addressed but so that the class can hear.

Column 5 – Non-verbal behaviour: These aspects of teacher talk are so easily overlooked that it is worthwhile to observe them on their own, without noting the words. Note the teacher's:

- position – standing (how?) or sitting and which way s/he is facing relative to the children;
- arm and hand positions;
- eyes – exactly how are they used for communication, are they scanning the room, focused on one group, sweeping and stopping, inviting interaction – or not?;
- mouth/facial expression – smiling, dead-pan, expectant, frowning;
- style of speech – pace, pauses, tone.

ACTIVITY/TOPIC AREA...

Phase of session (underline): beginning   middle   end

Time	Locat-ion	Teacher's words	Non-verbal behaviour	Aud-ience

Notes about session: (any special features?)

Figure 3.9 Teacher observation sheet

Three phases of observation will be useful; one for the introduction or first five to ten minutes of the session, one for any change-over or check-up time in the middle and one to record from the *very first signs* that the session is ending to when it is over.

Reflecting on the observations

After making these observations identify how the teacher manages to:

- get the children's attention – through actions, words, or movement;
- keep the children's attention – a change of tone of voice, questioning, simple direct phrases, and so on, and how did the teacher encourage, speed up or calm down the children's behaviour;
- end the session – general announcement, quiet instruction to individuals, proffering a five-minute warning. How did the teacher organize and control the children leaving the room?

Observing teaching talk

At a later stage, try to observe a teacher working with a whole class, *and* with a group so that you observe an expert demonstrating these *actual processes of teaching*. Sometimes teachers themselves do not recognize what they are doing as a skilled performance, so the beginning teacher may need to ask to observe an experienced teacher working with a group or individual children.

At first, it can be difficult to disentangle the different constituents of the teacher's talk. Wragg (1994) suggests a good way to start is by simply writing down verbatim two or three of the teacher's questions and the responses given to them by the children. Discussion with the teacher after the session can include the nature of the questions, why they were asked and, if applicable, why they were directed at certain children.

After some practice at identifying different types of talk, a checklist of the different types like that shown in Figure 3.10 might be used to look at how they are used in a teaching session. The checklist could be used for, say, two three- or five-minute sections of teaching. Note the opportunity to use a 'don't know' category so that rather than panicking that the 'right' category cannot be found, the teacher's utterance can be placed somewhere and the observation can continue.

Points to consider: hints and stumbling blocks

As cameo 1 showed, it is possible to teach and observe at the same time but the beginner teacher should not expect to be able to do this immediately. Observing should become part of your teaching so that you are consciously *making* observations – even if that means noting the observations down as soon as you can after the events – and not relying on general impressions. These observations are an important part of teacher-based, formative assessment to help in the identification of a child's, and teacher's, needs. When first starting to use classroom observation, be aware of the following points.

1 Observation is selective. Like a magnifying glass, it will help the teacher to see one area of classroom life more clearly, but it cannot cover other areas at the same time. Other aspects have to be reserved for another observation session.

Type of teacher talk date ...... topic .... times: start ...... ends	1 number of uses in 3 min	2 number of uses in 3 min
QUESTIONS asking for a recap. of previous work asking closed questions (facts, recall) asking open questions (ideas, suggestions), other question (make note)	/ /// /	
TEACHER RESPONSES listening to a pupil (for 10 seconds minimum) positive feedback (more than just 'good') negative feedback other response (make note)	/ /(+++)// /	
STATEMENTS giving information (telling facts) giving instructions (how to do something), other statement (make note)	///	
ROUTINE TALK keeping control small talk, jokes, chat other	/ //	
Help! don't know what type of teacher talk	//	

Figure 3.10 A tally of types of teacher talk

2 Observation requires practice. It can be frustrating and difficult to concentrate on one aspect of the classroom for even a short period when normally the teacher tries to be very vigilant and repeatedly scans the whole room to pre-empt problems arising.

3 In the early stages of using any timed observations and/or a checklist, the time between observations often seems too short to find the appropriate place on the checklist or grid. This feeling of being rushed soon disappears as the observer learns the way around the checklist with practice.

4 For teachers, observation is particularly frustrating because of the urge to intervene and teach, especially if the children are missing the point of the activity. Self-discipline is vital here, because by not intervening, the

teacher-observer can see how the children deal with the problem. By intervening, s/he would i) prevent the children from sorting it out for themselves; and ii) miss the expression of any further misunderstandings.

5 The children need time to get used to being observed and have to practise being self-sufficient when their teacher is observing. Teachers who observe regularly: usually tell the children that they are observing the children soon get used to it and do appreciate some feedback from the observations.

Final comment

If, after reading this chapter, you feel that classroom observation sounds too onerous, please remember that even a few minutes of focused observation of a child or another teacher is very worthwhile. It will almost certainly reveal an alternative or surprising view of that person in the classroom. You have everything to gain by giving observation a try!

A few points to consider

Use observation to answer these questions:

1 Are there any differences between high and low achievers' behaviour during reading, or maths, or a practical art activity?
2 Do all children receive the same amount of praise and negative feedback from the teacher?
3 What strategies could you use to allow yourself short periods of time to observe the children?
4 What are three advantages and three disadvantages of structured over open-ended observations?

References and further reading

Ashton, P., Hunt, P., Jones, S. and Watson, G. (1980) *Curriculum in Action: Block 1: An Approach to Evaluation.* Milton Keynes: Open University.
Burton, L. (1984) *Thinking Things Through: Problem-Solving in Mathematics.* Oxford: Blackwell.
Croll, P. (1986) *Systematic Classroom Observation.* Lewes: The Falmer Press.
Flanders, N. (1970) *Analysing Teacher Behaviour.* New York: Addison Wesley.
Galton, M., Simon, B. and Croll, P. (1980) *Inside the Primary Classroom.* London: RKP.
Hopkins, D. (1993) *A Teacher's Guide to Classroom Research,* 2nd edn. Buckingham: Open University Press.
Moyles, J.R. (1989) *Just Playing? The role and status of play in early childhood education.* Milton Keynes: Open University Press.

Oates, J. (1991) The competent adult. In Open University *Working With Under Fives*, (Resource pack). Milton Keynes: The Open University.

West, N. (1992) *Classroom Observation in the Context of Appraisal: A Training Manual for Primary Schools*. London: Longman.

Wragg, E.C. (1994) *An Introduction to Classroom Observation*. London: Routledge.

4

You don't know what you know 'til you know it!
Competence-based teacher education

Neil Kitson

Cameo I

Claire is a young student teacher. Throughout her training she and her colleagues were asked to reflect on their practice and consider in what areas they felt proficient and then what they wished to develop and improve. She wrote: 'I think we captured the children's interest during the time in school with our theme of "pirates", particularly with the drama work, when I dressed up and took on the role of a pirate and the children asked me questions. I have become aware that, in order to engage the children, the activities have to be interesting.'

Cameo 2

Jackie expressed an all too common anxiety relating to classroom control when she wrote: 'I am still a little unsure about maintaining order and discipline. I managed it in the first teaching placement and I know that I can be firm with the children but I think I am maybe a little apprehensive about the next teaching practice and a new group of children. I do feel that I am capable of it — I just need to prove it to myself.'

Introduction

Using a list of statements relating to the task of teaching known as 'competences', both of these students were able not only to take stock of their developing role as teachers but were also able to see where best to direct their energies during the following weeks. Jackie goes on to say:

Through the next few weeks of the course generally I intend to concentrate on developing my ability to:
- plan long term, to develop a progression of understanding in children;
- review and evaluate my own work regularly and realistically;
- maintain discipline and order through positive reinforcement.

What can be recognized is that Claire and Jackie are both making statements about what they want to achieve and, in Jackie's case, how she intends to set about it.

Much has been written about the use of such statements of competence within teacher education (McNamara 1990; Baird 1991; Bennett *et al.* 1992; Carter *et al.* 1993). What Houston and Howsam describe in the following quote has become increasingly significant for today's beginning teachers as schools, and the educational system in which they operate, experience major changes:

> In changing times, unchanging schools are anomalous. Competency based [teacher] education promises the thrust necessary for adaptation to meet the challenge of a changed and changing society. The emphasis in competency-based teacher education on objectives, accountability and personalisation implies specific criteria, careful evaluation, change based on feedback, and relevant programs [of learning] for a modern era. (1972: 2)

This chapter will examine the rationale behind the idea of 'competency-based teacher education' and show how it can help all teachers within the profession, but particularly beginning teachers. I will do this by considering:

- what is meant by competence?;
- competences within teaching and teacher education;
- how this approach can help you;
- a model for a competence-based approach to teacher education;
- case-study examples of how the model has been used.

What do we mean by 'competence'?

The notion of competence was originally developed by industry and the world of employment from the ideas developed by behavioural psychologists. What they attempted to do was break down specific activities relating to a job into basic component parts – the basic skills, if you like, which will enable an individual to successfully carry out the job. It initially considers all the elements that would be needed and then groups them into specific manageable skills. By working through these skills the individual learner, be they a surgeon or an electrician, can assess what they have already achieved, what they have still to do, and then what they must begin to work on next. It means that learners can focus upon those areas which are important to them and pay less attention to those where improvement has already taken place or those areas individuals bring with them from aspects of their previous learning. In this respect it is more like real life learning as opposed to traditional, academic learning where all students must follow the same set of instructions and be presented with the same body of knowledge to ensure that they have all received the same and equal instruction. This 'traditional' method clearly fails to take into account the fact that everybody is different and life experiences vary considerably. (Maurice Galton discusses this in Chapter 1 in relation to children's learning.) Competency-based learning attempts to be more efficient by acknowledging the strengths of individuals and allowing the greater expenditure of energy on those areas where development is needed.

Unlike the traditional models of teaching and learning which concentrate on the transmission of a body of knowledge kept 'secret' until the point of transfer, here the skills needed to complete the task are presented at the outset. The individuals have knowledge of the range of skills and understanding required. They are able to become active participants within the learning process, no longer the passive recipients. They are enabled to identify their previously acquired strengths and their areas of deficiency and then engage in the process of selecting new skills which they wish to develop. In this way not only are they aware of what needs to be covered but they also have a responsibility for their learning. No longer can they blame the tutor alone for being ineffective! If competence-based learning has been correctly established, the learners have the responsibility to ensure that they are gaining access to the knowledge, skills, and understanding they require.

How do you think this way of learning can help you develop your skills as a teacher? Think about it for a moment before we move on.

Competences within primary teaching and teacher education

Teacher education is the process intended to prepare those individuals who want to practise in the profession of teaching. In common with the majority of professions, this preparation involves:

- acquisition of knowledge and the ability to apply it;
- the development of a specific repertoire of critical behaviours and skills.

To the extent that knowledge, behaviours and skills can be identified, these become the competence objectives for the training of teachers. Learning objectives are commonly classified according to one of five criteria which can be applied in the assessment of performance which, in this case, is teaching. These criteria are:

- cognitive objectives;
- performance objectives;
- consequence objectives;
- affective objectives;
- exploratory objectives.

But what are these objectives and how do they relate to teaching?

1 *Cognitive objectives* specify knowledge and intellectual abilities or skills that are to be demonstrated by the learner. In teacher education such objectives need to include aspects such as the knowledge of the subject matter to be taught, knowledge of pedagogy and the ability to analyse the curriculum area being taught and how to assess children's learning.

2 *Performance objectives* require the learner to demonstrate an ability to perform a given activity – one must not only know what should be done but also how. For intending teachers such an objective might be identified as, for example, the development of higher-order reading skills, controlling children within a PE lesson or taking the register.

3 *Consequence objectives* are seen as the results of the learners actions. For us in teacher education these are usually seen in the resulting work done by the children in the class under the care of beginning teachers. The teacher may need to develop a programme of phonics to help an individual's reading progress, or demonstrate the ability to get the class to engage in independent collaborative group work. New teachers need to be able to demonstrate the *effect* of their teaching and not simply to have *knowledge* of it.

4 *Affective objectives* deal with the area of attitudes, values, beliefs, and relationships. These are quite difficult to define but normally relate to the social health of the group – that is the way the children interact with, and relate to, each other.

5 *Exploratory objectives* can be viewed as self-learning or investigation. In teacher education the beginning teacher might make a visit to a local place of worship or watch an experienced teacher working with a class. Such experiences may lead to the realization that you need to find out more about the community prior to working with children from a minority group and, in so doing, further competency objectives are set up.

All five of these sets of learning objectives are important in the development of professional teachers who are flexible enough to meet the challenges of today's teaching. When we look at competences for teaching we must make the greatest possible use of the *consequence objectives*. The knowledge alone of how to do something is of only limited use (McNamara 1990). What one must strive towards is the *knowledge* of appropriate action, the *skill* of being able to put it into practice and the *ability* to evaluate its effectiveness through the results seen in the children's and teachers' activities.

Characteristics of competences for teaching

'Teaching acts are an observable performance' (McDonald 1974). Such performance is linked to situations that vary in terms of the underlying purposes of the teaching, the materials used, the children being taught and how they are responding to the specific situation. Such 'performance' has two main elements:

- a behavioural component;
- a cognitive component.

The first of these, the behavioural component, is a set of observable actions; the second is a combination of perceptions, interpretations, and decisions. Proficiency in both areas is needed in order to produce a competent performance.

Any set of competences that might be established needs to take these components into account. Learning to teach is an ongoing process and not one which can be achieved in a single year nor by attending a number of lectures – to the chagrin of many students! Rather it is a developmental process of evolving knowledge, skills and understandings, set in a context of appraisal and continual self-evaluation and re-evaluation. Teachers need constantly to examine their practice, assess and alter their approach with every new child and every new situation they encounter. To this end, teachers must become 'reflective practitioners' (Pollard and Tann 1993). This sense of reflection is built into the competence model for it looks at the education of teachers as an ongoing process which has begun before student teachers start their course and will go on for an extended time after the course has ended. Individuals will bring with them a wide range of knowledge, skills, and understanding into the training situation and this needs taking into account. While you might never have formally stood in front of a class in order to teach them, you may have had experience of running a swimming club or been responsible for running a department with a sales team. In both of these you will have acquired skills which will be of great use to you in the classroom. It is important that we begin to recognize those transferable skills which are brought to the learning situation in order to extend them in the teaching context. Credit needs to be given for those things which you can already do and you can feel good about before considering those areas where extra effort is needed. As a result, a greater degree of ownership in the new professional learning will be created. It is you who will set the agenda for learning and you who will evaluate what progress has been made. (Morag Hunter-Carsch explains some of the many ways of doing this in Chapter 12.)

For this process to be effective the point of entry into the professional training needs to be recognized and the competences which the individual already possesses should equally be acknowledged and valued. Learning development can then be indicated and plotted against certain 'markers'. The learning will be gradual and focused so that specific aspects can be considered, questioned, and developed. As McNamara (1990) shows, it is not enough just to have the facts necessary to teach: one also needs to know the best ways of putting those facts across to others. In order to help children learn effectively we need to set attainable goals (as Janet Moyles discusses in Chapter 6). Like children, we too need to feel success in our efforts; not made to feel that we are constantly being de-skilled by discovering that there is more and more we do not know. When using a competence approach, the range of skills is clearly established at the outset and it is the responsibility of the learner to select those areas on which to work. It is then clearly implicit within the structure of the competence approach that the *learning will never be complete, but a higher level will have been achieved.*

A compentence-based model

Over recent years the government has become increasingly interested in this competence-based approach to teacher education and in 1993 it published a list of competences for newly qualified teachers. This has been adapted by many involved in teacher education and, at Leicester School of Education, this has resulted in a concept which links competences with individual action planning. In order to explore the ways in which you can take advantage of this process, we first need to look at this model as described in Figure 4.1.

How are these competences used by students?

Throughout the year of training, PGCE students are given a number of opportunities to make formally recorded statements relating to their perceived level of competence. This is done through discussion with a tutor or with a 'critical friend', someone with whom one feels comfortable in talking through the situation and who will give constructive feedback. Having identified where students feel they need to develop their own knowledge, skills, or understanding, decisions are made as to *how* to improve on these competences – a very critical feature as progress is never made without an identification of how it is to take place.

When does this identification of competences take place?

There are three significant stages to the process of identification of competences and the development of an individual action plan.

1 *Entry phase*   Here one is looking directly at the individual's starting point on the course.
2 *Intermediary phase*   As new experiences arise so the competences will need to be re-appraised. This will constantly be changing and evolving as one develops as a career teacher. For example:
   • what was seen as 'effective management of behaviour' in one class may not be effective in another;
   • 'communicating with parents' may not be possible until later in the course so will not be relevant until then;

70 *Neil Kitson*

University of Leicester
School of Education

PGCE Primary

Professional Development
through Individual Action Planning (IAP)

Student: _____   Tutor: _____

Throughout the course you will be developing in professional confidence
and competence. This development will build upon the organisational,
managerial, social and professional skills you already have.

The purpose of this folder is to focus your attention on the processes of self-
evaluation. It is intended to lead to greater awareness of 'self-as-professional'
and help you understand the benefits of regular self-assessment as a student
teacher and beyond.

To help you achieve an overview of your development as a teacher through the
P.G.C.E. year, there will be opportunities at different phases in the year to
discuss your progress with a tutor. This record (and the accompanying
duplicated sheets) will form the basis of those tutorials. It will, of course, also
be informed by your partnership and teaching practice experiences.

Because you have ownership of this document, you can include reflections and experiences from your own professional experiences. *Do remember, though, that the evidence
of all these competences can be found in the answers to the question "How?"*

It is vital in making comments that you give both evidence of competency and devise a
plan for future action for discussion with your tutor. These are the two key elements in
Individual Action Planning.

Likely initial emphasis of each competency overleaf is indicated by:-
a) PARTNERSHIP   b) FIRST T.P.   c) FINAL T.P.

**Through the process of Individual Action Planning you should
develop an understanding of the concepts of balance, progression,
continuity and differentiation within the primary school
curriculum.**

On the following pages you will find general
headings & specific statements of competence ▶

Figure 4.1

1. Planning and preparation

Effective planning and preparation underpins a successful classr oom climate and helps promote purposeful learning.

A competent student teacher shows ability in:

1.1a. including in initial plans information about the school ethos, policies and organisation;

1.2a. incorporating suitable aims and objectives within a programme of work;

1.3a. ensuring that all materials, resources and aids are well prepared and checked;

1.4b. producing plans that sustain children's interest, attention and involvement;

1.5b. co-ordinating the work of a wide range of children with different interests and abilities;

1.6c. planning for the use of all available physical and human resources to meet the needs of the children;

1.7c. recognizing and providing effectively for children's individual needs (including those of gifted pupils and those with Special Educational Needs).

2. Management and organisation of the classroom

The atmosphere and environment of a classroom should be interesting, exciting, purposeful and attractive, inviting active participation.

A competent student teacher shows ability in:

2.1a. being aware of safety aspects at all times;

2.2a. matching classroom organisation to meet different needs in respect of:
activities
groupings of children (whole class, group, individual)
teaching strategies
curriculum areas

2.3b. selecting equipment, resources and I.T. appropriate for learning;

2.4b. promoting independence by making resources easily accessible to children;

2.5c. using displays effectively to enhance learning;

2.6c. making effective use of any additional adult support.

Figure 4.1 (cont.)

3. Presentation and management of activities

The presentation of the learning activity is about promoting the children's interest, attention, enjoyment and involvement.

A competent student teacher shows ability in:

3.1a. presenting 'self' confidently, generating interest and enthusiasm;

3.2a. involving children in purposeful discussion of activities and outcomes;

3.3a. giving clear explanations and instructions to children;

3.4b. engaging children in real-life, first hand experiences;

3.5b. establishing clear expectations of pupil behaviour in the classroom and securing appropriate standards of discipline;

3.6b. beginning and ending sessions effectively;

3.7c. listening to children and questioning them effectively;

3.8c. maintaining high expectations of all children;

3.9c. pacing sessions appropriately.

4. Children's progress and achievements

Recording the progress and achievement of children is about considering their social attributes and personal qualities as well as measuring any improvement in their development of concepts, skills and knowledge.

A competent student teacher shows ability in:

4.1a. giving sensitive and shared feedback within recorded and practical tasks;

4.2b. establishing and recording evidence of actual learning from activities;

4.3b. fostering children's own assessment of their activities and progress;

4.4c. monitoring and assessing children's progress;

4.5c. involving children in decision-making processes;

4.6c. using assessment as a means of reporting on children's progress.

Figure 4.1 (cont.)

5. Reflection, analysis and evaluation

For future planning in every area of teaching and learning, reflection, analysis and evaluation are essential entitlements.

A competent student teacher shows ability in:

5.1a. identifying and reflecting on experiences;

5.2a. presenting all information clearly and concisely in written form, as required;

5.3b. reviewing and evaluating regularly and realistically:

   planning and preparation
   presentation and management of sessions
   classroom organisation
   children's progress and achievements;

5.4c. developing strategies and techniques for better management of time both for self and children;

5.5c. developing strategies and techniques for dealing with sources of stress;

5.6c. reviewing and evaluating the balance of curriculum areas.

6. Professional relationships

Schools are about people and people have one thing in common: they are all different.

A competent student teacher shows ability in:

6.1a. fostering positive and encouraging support to the children;

6.2b. communicating and negotiating effectively with colleagues and children;

6.3c. communicating with parents.

7. Further professional development

Newly qualified teachers should have acquired the necessary foundation to develop:

7.1   the competencies identified in this document throughout their teaching career;

7.2   vision, imagination and critical awareness in educating children;

7.3   a readiness to promote the spiritual, moral, social and cultural development of children;

7.4   their professional knowledge, understanding and skills through in-service training and development;

7.5   a working knowledge of their contractual, legal, administrative and pastoral responsibilities as teachers;

7.6   contributing to the life of a school outside the classroom.

Figure 4.1 (cont.)

- 'fostering children's own assessment of their activities and progress' may well be possible in one school whereas in another school it may be necessary to start all over again.
- conversely 'identifying and reflecting on experience' is a skill which can be developed over time and is not dependent on a teaching situation.
3 *Exit phase*   This marks the transition from training to newly qualified teacher status. It is the time to take stock, to identify what learning has occurred, to think about what learning will need to take place in the first appointment and ways to ensure that access to such opportunities is created by the individual.

Students engage in these three stages with a growing degree of confidence. What is at first a rather tentative approach to the activity becomes a powerful tool which enables the students to assess their own strengths and plan for their own professional development.

Let us now look at a few *entry phase* responses to the competences. These students were only a few weeks into their course and had just begun to realize what was going to be required of them as teachers and what they had to offer the profession. In this first example, Anna quite naturally focuses on what she *cannot do* but begins to identify some of her potential strengths:

> There are two particular areas under 'presentation' and 'management' on which I wish to concentrate:
> 3.2a. Involving children in purposeful discussion of activities and outcomes – I have had only very limited experience in this area and then only with small groups. Consequently, I wouldn't describe myself as being competent in this area.
> 3.3a. Giving clear explanations and instructions to children – I often struggle to find the basic wording which I think is due to three years of University training in, essentially, pretentious writing!
> At the moment I assume I am able to fulfil most of the basic competences but more time and responsibility in school might disprove this! I have chosen to put the preparation section aside for the moment as this is the area in which I feel most confident as a result of the work I did for my first degree.

Another student, Cathy, again starts off with a positive approach but quite clearly she is fully aware of what she can do and what she finds difficult. This honesty and self-appraisal is very typical of initial responses.

> I'm a fairly well organized person and bringing up a young family has made me more so. I think I will be OK in planning, preparation and record keeping. I have chosen 3 main areas of competence to look at.
> 1   Management and organization of the classroom – Matching classroom organization to meet the different needs concerned with how to cope with a slow worker, or a non-worker. How do I develop a non-nagging approach?

2   Presentation and management of activities. Giving clear explanations and instructions to children – I think I can usually deliver clear explanations, but I need to develop adaptability and quick thinking to enable me to offer alternative explanations and different methods of answering questions and solving problems.
3   Reflection, analysis and evaluation – I find evaluation hard. I'm much more a 'Well that didn't go very well but tomorrow's another day' sort of a person!

Another student, Gill, had previously worked in marketing before deciding to train as a teacher. In her job she had acquired a wide range of professional skills which she was able to identify and relate to the teacher role in relation to competences 3.1a, 3.2a and 3.3a when she wrote:

> I had experience of making presentations to groups of people numbering from 2 to 200. Through the presentation an agreement usually had to be made, so it was vital that the presentation was correctly focused, professionally presented, and covered all possible aspects and eventualities. I feel that this will greatly help when I am working in a whole class situation and working in the class generally, as it is important that one makes oneself clearly understood. Also useful for working with other teachers and parents.

How readily the prior experience of another student matches 2.2a, 3.6b, 3.9c and 5.4c of the Leicester document! This student writes:

> I am used to working in a highly pressurized environment and under strict time deadlines and know the importance of prioritizing my work. These skills are easily transferable and, as teachers are under increasing pressure in and out of the classroom to produce work within time constraints, this skill will be useful. Also, time management with respect to classroom organization. Preparation and planning – my previous work taught me that success within any environment depends on it.

Item 6.2b was considered by another student:

> I used to work within a team to reach common goals as quickly and efficiently as possible. When in school, especially as a new teacher, it is essential to co-operate with other members of staff to tap into their experience. Don't be too proud to ask!

As the course progresses and you gain a range of experiences so your perception of yourself will change and your response to competences will alter. Some things will no longer seem so important – you now feel competent in them! Some skills originally not an issue may well have assumed a much greater significance as you find yourself in different teaching situations.

In the *intermediary phase*, as in Rachel's example below, with one teaching experience behind her, she expresses her very real and understandable concerns as she reflects upon her focus for the next few weeks in school.

I need to look at giving children more ownership of tasks, e.g. monitoring work covered, checking maths work using calculators, increased self-esteem and confidence. I gave praise and recognition where appropriate and tried positive management techniques, e.g. to gain class control praising those paying attention; those not, took notice and listened, rather than shouting.

Careful planning with clear expectations from each party produced a good working relationship during teaching practice. Communication with children: need to make what is implicit more explicit. Need to work on aspects of my personality.

Influence others and assert myself in an indirect manner, e.g. prefer to resolve conflicts through diplomacy and harmony, prefer to negotiate rather than to argue/debate and tend to ask rather than tell. Therefore I found open displays of conflicts in the school situation, especially situations of open intimidation, stressful.

In responding to people I tend to be reserved. I need to express my enthusiasm and energy. Open up body language, eye contact and express feelings more readily.

Pace of action and decision-making tends to be steady. Therefore, I find frequent interruptions stressful.

I need to be more precise in dealing with details: there is some ambiguity, lack of organization and poor planning. Therefore I must make sure that I continue to plan effectively and discuss my plans with the teacher.

Using the statements of competence she identifies areas for focus and then sets a clear plan of action in order to address these issues.

It would be helpful now to look at some examples of how the students used the competence statements to improve their teaching. The following are examples of competences that students have wished to develop, strategies for action and, finally, illustrations of what was actually done.

Competence:
1.1a. Including in initial plans information about the school, ethos, policies and organization.
Strategy:
Seek out an individual teacher within a school, the subject co-ordinator for example, or a tutor to help with a specific question.
Example:
If you're not sure about the school plans for History or the ethos relating to PSE then ask!

Competence:
2.2a. Matching classroom organization to meet different needs in respect of groupings of children (whole class, group, individual).
Strategy:
Use relevant literature in order to extend understanding.

Example:
If you are unclear as to what is meant by 'collaborative group work' use the library (or others) and find out.

Competence:
3.4b. Engaging children in real life, first-hand experience.
Strategy:
Set up specific situations within the classroom in order to gain experience not yet covered.
Example:
If you haven't been able so far to engage the children in real life, first-hand experience, arrange a visit, bring the resources into school or invite someone to come into school to talk to the children.

Competence:
2.6c. Making effective use of any additional adult support.
Strategy:
Examining classroom strategies which are used and evaluating their effectiveness.
Example:
Look again at how you are making use of the adults within the classroom in order to extend the children's learning.

Throughout the course individuals have the responsibility to take from those experiences being offered – from either formal learning opportunities (lectures and seminars), informal learning opportunities (tutorials and discussions with teachers) and individual learning opportunities (library study and personal research) – what is needed to acquire the knowledge, skills and understanding necessary for them to become competent teachers. It is the statements of competence that help them know what is required and against which they can plot their development.

This brings us to the final stage of the process, the exit phase. This is the transition between the teacher education course and the first appointment. Decisions on needs at this stage become an action plan for individuals to take with them into their first post and sets in place a process of critically appraising one's practice which should continue throughout the professional career of each teacher. As Early (1991) shows, there is growing interest by schools in the competence approach for staff development.

In this final extract, Simon not only looks back at what he has learnt but he looks ahead to where his learning will take him next.

. . . I feel that I have developed considerably during the past year. I didn't realize just how much there was to learn about teaching but I feel that I have begun the process! In terms of planning and evaluation I am aware of my own short-comings and also aware of what needs to be done. I still feel uncertain or rather unconfident about aspects of the maths curriculum but I've already talked to the Head of my new school about this and we have set up some meetings with the maths

Photo 7   What kind of competences are needed in this situation?

co-ordinator. It looks as if I'll be taking on some responsibility for music and drama so feel that I need to find out what courses are on offer in the LEA and see about getting on them. The Head has said she will try too . . .

Conclusion

What about those students who have gone through the process? How do they feel about using competences? The overwhelming response is always extremely positive. Quite clearly what is offered is not the open-ended behaviourist model alluded to at the beginning of this chapter but what has resulted is a positive approach to the individual's learning. Having used this process, the students at Leicester were asked what advice they would like to pass on to others wishing to use the competence model and it is fitting to end with their comments.

Using competences let us know what was expected of us and gave us something to work towards.

Identify the positive skills within yourself. Say what you can do and don't concentrate on what you can't do.

Using the statements helped me to focus on what was important for me to learn and build upon my strengths.

Take responsibility for your own learning. At the end of the day only you will really know what can be achieved.

The skills of self-evaluation that I learned as part of the competence process will set me up for my ongoing professional development. I think it's more effective in the long run.

References and further reading

Baird, J.R. (1991) Individual and group reflection as a basis for teacher development, in P. Hughes (ed.) *Teachers' Professional Development*. Melbourne, Australia: ACER.
Bennett, S.N., Wragg, E.C., Carré, C.G. and Carter, D.S.G. (1992) A longitudinal study of primary teachers' perceived competence in, and concerns about, National Curriculum implementation. *Research Papers in Education*, 7 (1): 53–78.
Carter, D.S.G., Carré, C.G. and Bennett, S.N. (1993) Student teachers' changing perceptions of their subject matter during an initial teacher training programme. *Educational Research*, 35 (1): 89–95.
Department for Education (1993) *The Initial Training of Primary School Teachers: New Criteria for Courses*, Circular 14/93. London: DfE.
Early, P. (1991) Defining and assessing school management competences. *Management in Education*, 5 (4): 31–4.
Houston, W.R. and Howsam, R.B. (1972) *Competency-Based Teacher Education*. Chicago: Science Research Associates.
McDonald, J.F. (1974) The rationale for competency based programes, in W.R. Houston (ed.) *Exploring Competency Based Education*. California: McCutchan.
McNamara, D. (1990) Reaching into teachers' thinking: its contribution to education student teachers ability to think critically. *Journal of Education for Teaching*, 16 (2): 147–60.
Pollard, A. and Tann, S. (1993) *Reflective Teaching in the Primary School*, 2nd edn. London: Routledge.

Part 2

LEARNING TO TEACH

5

Take some notice of me!
Primary children and their learning potential

Roger Merry

Cameo 1

Julie is six. She is working through a sheet of basic addition problems, using Unifix cubes. Given '3 + 2' she confidently takes three cubes from the box, counting each one aloud as she removes it, then counts out a further two in the same way. She then counts the total, reaching five, and writes '2' on her worksheet. The next problem is '5 + 2', but instead of beginning with the five cubes already in front of her, she returns them to the box and starts again from scratch. Nor does she notice that her figure 'five' is different from the five printed a few centimetres away.

Cameo 2

The teacher has gathered the children together to explain the next task. Each of them is to write their name on one of the large, white pieces of paper available, then take a small piece of coloured paper and fold it in the way demonstrated. They will then unfold the paper, cut it in the way the teacher has shown them and finally stick the coloured paper on to the white sheet. The teacher demonstrates each step again, then asks if anybody has any questions. No-one has and the children return to their seats. Immediately Martin's hand goes up: 'What do we have to do?' he asks.

Introduction

Such incidents are so much a part of hectic, everyday classroom life that busy teachers normally have no time to stop and think about them. Yet they raise many questions which could be of interest to psychologists as well as to teachers themselves. For instance, why doesn't Julie use the five cubes already in front of her, or correct her own figure when she sees a five written correctly? What do her actions suggest about her concept of number, her perception of the problem and her strategy for solving it? Why does Martin need to ask what to do when it has been explained and demonstrated so carefully and the children have been asked if they understand? What does his behaviour suggest about his attention, memory, understanding or motivation? In brief, what's going on inside these children's heads and how might teachers try to help them? These two basic questions lie at the heart of this chapter.

The first part of the chapter presents a brief outline of what cognitive psychologists have to say about attention, perception and memory, along with some implications for teachers. The second part of the chapter focuses more on cognitive development.

Attention, perception and memory

Cognitive psychologists propose a view in which learners are not merely taking things in in a passive way but are, in fact, highly active, often making use of fragmentary and incomplete information by supplementing it with past experience and predictions which they then check and modify in the light of new data. For example, research on *attention* has shown that, although we can scan the complex events going on around us, we can really only concentrate on one thing at a time in any depth. If you are driving along a familiar route, for instance, you may occasionally have had that sudden and frightening thought 'how did I get here?'. Experienced drivers sometimes unintentionally let their attention drift after a while, scanning the road ahead only very lightly while they concentrate on something else in their minds. However, a red light or pedestrian stepping off the kerb is picked up immediately and their attention returns to their driving . . . hopefully.

Even when we do manage to attend to something, our attempts to perceive or make sense of it rely on equally fragmentary information. Look up and glance around the room. It may seem that your eyes are moving smoothly around and that you are taking everything in but, in fact, you focus on one small area for a fraction of a second, then jump rapidly to another spot, all the time. The information received by your brain is, therefore, very piecemeal and fragmentary and you rely on your past experience and knowledge to fill in the gaps. *Perception* is not a passive taking-in of our surroundings, but a highly active process in which the information supplied by our brains is at least as important as the information received by our senses.

Similarly, remembering something does not simply involve retrieving it from storage. As with attention and perception, what we have available to

Photo 8   We can really only concentrate on one thing at a time!

us from memory is usually only partial and fragmentary so that we again have to supplement it by using our knowledge of the world – *memory* too is partly a creative process. For instance, you could not possibly remember every single word of this chapter so far, but if you were asked if it had contained the word 'custard' you would be able to answer with a confident 'no' because you *know* that such a word would not occur in this context. However, if you were asked if the word 'car' had appeared, you might answer 'yes' because you recalled a paragraph about driving earlier on, guessing that the word had appeared. (To save you checking, it didn't!)

What might some of the implications of such a view of human learning be for teachers?

Paying attention

Teachers are highly aware of the importance of attention because some children seem to have real problems with it. It's very tempting to blame Martin's problem on his inattentive behaviour, or to see Julie's reversed figure 5 as the result of a lack of attention to detail but, as we shall see, there could be other explanations. Some of the points below will suggest ways of trying to get through to these children but we should also be careful about interpreting poor attention as a problem entirely 'within the child'. We need to be aware of the difficulties we can inadvertently create for children – in a piece of writing, for example, expecting a child to concentrate on being creative, neat and grammatically correct all at the same time is actually making cognitive demands that many professional writers, let alone 6-year-olds, would find a challenge (Martin Cortazzi takes up this aspect in Chapter 11 and for further reading, see Smith 1982).

Attention and distractions

Picture in your mind a 'good' primary classroom. The children are working in several groups on a range of lively activities discussing the tasks with each other. The walls are festooned with colourful displays. A gerbil thrashes round in its wheel inside its cage. A computer screen flashes and makes funny noises. Although many children will thrive in and enjoy such a setting, for some children this 'good' classroom may, in fact, be a very difficult learning environment, full of distractions. Not surprisingly, a lot depends on the nature of the task and the potential distractions – given 'verbal interference' like other people talking, it is harder to perform a task requiring lots of language than one requiring only a little. This is not to say, of course, that teachers should rip down their displays, unplug the computer and have the gerbil put down. But it does mean that some children, some of the time, might learn better in a less stimulating environment. This need not be impractical or expensive – one early years teacher, for instance, set up an 'office' consisting of a large cardboard box fastened to the wall like a phone booth, and found that her children actually competed to spend a few minutes working in this seemingly boring but 'grown-up' environment, relatively free from distractions.

Attention and failure

Unfortunately, it is not always that simple. Understandably, as teachers we tend to see learning failure as a *result* of not paying attention but it could sometimes in fact be the other way round. Children who find it hard to cope with failure (as many of us do) may deliberately 'switch off' when confronted with a task at which they expect to fail on the grounds that if you do not try, you cannot fail. In the second cameo, Martin may well have deliberately only half-listened to the teacher's instructions, knowing that he will get the extra one-to-one help he likes simply by asking what he has to do. 'Learned helplessness' is a phrase sometimes used to describe such behaviour and it can appear to the child that deliberately not paying attention is a good strategy for avoiding failure and getting extra help. In such cases, trying to encourage children to feel more positive about themselves as learners will be at least as important as using lively, attention-grabbing materials, and the aim of this chapter is certainly not to suggest that cognitive processes and strategies should be emphasized at the expense of attitudes and feelings. See Sylvia McNamara's comments and advice in

Chapter 10 and Sotto (1994) for a discussion of how attitudes and cognitive skills interact.

Attention span

It is difficult to get an accurate idea of the length of time that an adult can go on attending to the same stimulus without letting attention wander. It is quite likely that, fascinating as this chapter is, your attention may well already have drifted away at least once, perhaps without you really being aware of it. For most children, the span of attention will be even shorter, probably only a few minutes at a time. This does not mean that we can shorten the school day to ten minutes, but experienced teachers are well aware of this potential limited span of attention and take measures to get around it. Variety and change are the key here. If good teachers are reading a story, for example, they will automatically build in some variety: a range of voices or gestures to avoid monotonous delivery; stopping to ask a question or pausing to show an illustration. They may well bring in discussion so that, although the activity is still 'reading a story', the children will be presented with different sorts of input and will be actively involved in different ways all the time.

Attention grabbers

What sorts of things 'grab' your attention? If you made a list, it would probably contain specific items such as 'a fire alarm' or 'my name' and more general ones such as 'bright lights' or 'something unexpected'. In fact, 'attention-grabbers' can be roughly divided into two categories. Some things grab our attention automatically – sudden loud noises, movements or pain, for example. Others are things which we have learned about and which involve our experiences, expectations or interests, like hearing our own name or seeing something bizarre or new to us, just as you probably noticed this row of xxxxxxxxxxxxxxxxxxxxxxxxxxxxxxxxxxxxxxxxxxxxxxxx well before you actually got to them in your reading. If you watch an hour or two of children's television, you could probably learn something from other experts in grabbing children's attention, even if it is rather disheartening to see what you are in a sense competing with as a teacher. This is not to suggest that you dress up as Batman (though that would capture the children's attention!) but that you note how children's cartoons, for instance, make use of bright colours, rapid movement, bizarre events and very short scenes in order to grab and maintain children's attention. Similarly, if you want to quieten a whole group of noisy children, it is usually better to call out a few names of the noisiest individuals rather than just say 'shh' to the whole class in a vague and optimistic way. Teachers also develop lots of techniques like 'hands-on-heads' to grab a whole group's attention, perhaps turning it into a game so that the children actually want to be among those who are attending to you.

Teacher's attention

One of the greatest compliments I was ever paid as a classroom teacher was by a child who told me, 'You must have eyes in the back of your head, Mr Merry!'. Experienced teachers have actually developed different attentional skills in order to manage a group of children and such skills can sometimes be difficult for beginners to learn. A new teacher, going round helping individuals or groups, may get commendably involved with them only to realize ten minutes later that the other children have demolished the furniture. An experienced teacher, on the other hand, will constantly glance around the rest of the room, particularly at individuals or activities which their experience tells them could become disruptive, nipping likely problems in the bud, and letting the children *know* that they are being watched. Such monitoring of the rest of the room would, of course, be highly inappropriate, if not downright rude, in a staffroom conversation but in the classroom it is a vital attentional skill which often marks out experienced and effective teachers.

Seeing is believing

If perception involves a great deal of 'imposing meaning', using our past experience to supplement fragmentary information, it follows that when children's experiences do not match those of the teacher, they will literally perceive things differently. The classic 'visual illusions' like the two heads/candlestick show how two people can look at the same thing and actually see something totally different, and one of the biggest problems for teachers may be to see things from the child's point of view. Such different perceptions help to explain Julie's behaviour at the beginning of the chapter. If her notion of the symbol '5' was something like 'that's the one with the two straight lines at the top and the curly bit at the bottom', she simply would not notice that hers was the wrong way round because her 'internal model' would describe her version just as well as the correct one. Watching how children actually write letters and numbers can sometimes give a clue to their perceptions – if a child forms both a 'b' and 'd' by drawing a 'ball and stick', for example, they are likely to get the two symbols confused. In such cases, teachers obviously need to draw the child's attention to the different orientation and encourage them to form the symbols in a different way, avoiding them becoming mirror images of each other.

'Advance organizers'

Apart from being aware of such different perceptions, teachers can sometimes actively intervene by preparing the children beforehand, especially if the material is complex or introduces new ideas. The idea is to tell them what they are going to see and direct their attention to the important bits even before they see it. In one classic study, for example, Bransford and Johnson (1972: 68) gave students a rather odd passage which began:

A newspaper is better than a magazine. A seashore is a better place than the street. At first it is better to run than to walk. You may have to try several times. It takes some skill but it's easy to learn . . . Birds seldom get too close. Rain, however, soon soaks in . . .

Although they understood each sentence, people found the passage difficult to comprehend and remember, but if they were told beforehand that it was about flying a kite, it was much easier. Hopefully, similar 'advance organizers' can make children less likely to concentrate on irrelevant features or to jump to faulty conclusions which then have to be corrected. Building up curiosity is also a strong attention grabber in its own right and can help arouse children's interest in the first place.

Modality preferences

Although we are not usually aware of it, adults differ quite dramatically in their preferences for having information presented in some ways rather than others and in the way they tend to process that information. Visual imagery is a good example. For instance, try to picture a car in your mind's eye. What colour is it? Which way is it going? Can you imagine Long John Silver driving it? People vary considerably in the vividness of the images they can form, including ones they could never have actually seen and are often surprised when they compare notes with friends. This, too, has important implications for teachers, who will understandably present material in ways which *they* find interesting or easy to use, not realizing that their children may have different preferences (Janet Moyles takes up this point further in Chapter 2). Some teachers of dyslexic children (who can be seen as having particular processing problems), therefore, deliberately use 'multi-sensory' presentation; we should all consider using, for example, pictures, diagrams, writing and speech in combination wherever possible, to get across the same message in different ways, rather than automatically choosing the one that *we* think is easiest because we prefer it.

Understanding and remembering

It will have become clear that 'attention' and 'perception' are inexplicably linked, and the same thing happens if we go on to consider learning and remembering. If we can perceive something in a meaningful way, it will be much easier for us to remember it. Take, for example, this series of letters:

ecnetnes a etirw ot yaw ynnuf a si siht.

Once you have recognized what it is – in other words, once you have 'perceived' it – you would be able to remember it and write it down quite easily. However, you would not simply be recalling what you had seen, but would use your understanding to re-create what was there. You would, for instance, probably start at the right-hand end and work towards the left. If the same letters had been presented in a random sequence, such as:

ehiyw iwtfo nrte iau e asnye nnsta stc

the task of remembering it would have been virtually impossible because you would not have been able to make sense of it in the first place. A major implication for teachers is, therefore, simply to recognize that children's perceptions, in differing from ours, often mean that the material we give them may be much harder for them to remember than it is for us.

Learning strategies

Although it is very difficult to find out exactly what strategies children might be using, this has been a popular topic for psychologists to study. Later in the chapter, we will consider briefly how strategies may develop but, as teachers, we understandably tend to concentrate on content – on *what* is to be learned rather than exactly *how* children should learn it. Even when we do try, we may still not give enough help. A popular and effective spelling technique, 'look, cover, write, check' for example, does seem to provide children with an overall strategy for learning spellings but many young children still are not sure what exactly to do when we ask them to 'look at' something in order to learn it. Very simple strategies, which adults take for granted, can be surprisingly effective. For example:

- shut your eyes and try to picture the word in your head;
- repeat the letters several times over;
- actually practise writing it out a few times;
- see if the word reminds you of any others which you can spell;
- compare your version with the correct one and, if yours is wrong, concentrate on the bit you got wrong;
- if you haven't got access to the correct spelling, write your version down and see if it looks right;
- if the word is familiar but spelled in an unusual way (for example with a silent letter) try deliberately mispronouncing it in accordance with the way it is spelled.

In general, research suggests that even very young children or those with quite severe learning difficulties, can improve their learning dramatically by being taught appropriate strategies, though they often do not spontaneously continue to use them for themselves. (For a review of research into 'educationally relevant' mnemonic strategies, see Levin 1993.)

The first part of this chapter has looked briefly at what cognitive psychologists could suggest to teachers about processes such as attention, perception and memory. Such processes are not static but are developing in children and this next section looks at some of the major ideas of psychologists interested in how these changes occur.

Cognitive development

For those who trained to be teachers some time ago, one name more than any other will still be associated with their notions about cognitive development – Jean Piaget has had a huge influence not only on developmental psychology, but indirectly on what goes on in the classroom. Certainly when I was a psychology undergraduate in the 1960s, he was accorded an almost god-like status equalled at that time only by Eric Clapton. A detailed summary of his theories is clearly beyond the scope of this chapter but almost all standard educational psychology texts will have a summary of his work. (See, for example, Gage and Berliner 1992; Fontana 1988.) Very briefly, Piaget proposed that there were several discrete *stages* of development which all children pass through, rejecting previous concepts as they came to realize that they were inadequate or misleading. He used demonstrations to show how children have to learn, for example, that the amount of liquid is unchanged even if it is poured into a different container, or how young children find it hard to see things from a different perspective. From Piaget's work, many teachers took the idea that a child needs to be cognitively 'ready' before new concepts can be introduced, though this does not mean that they should sit around doing nothing in the meantime!

There were criticisms of his theories and research, however, with a particularly important contribution made by Margaret Donaldson in 1978. Her book, which includes a summary of Piaget's work, reviewed evidence suggesting that some of Piaget's ideas were faulty and that, for example, some of the results he obtained were because children had not understood the situation or the questions asked, or were unable to relate them to their own experiences. (A view of the continuing debate is given in Adey and Shayer 1994.)

A few other alternative 'general theories' about cognitive development have also been proposed. The American psychologist Jerome Bruner was much more interested in education than Piaget: his ideas about how children 'represent' the world were actually embodied in some learning materials which he helped to produce. For teachers, one important idea was the 'spiral curriculum', in which the same topic could be re-visited in increasingly sophisticated ways as the child developed. Another was the notion of adults providing 'scaffolding' or temporary support to help the child move on to more complex learning. (For a collection of a wide range of Bruner's earlier work, see Bruner and Anglin 1973.)

The work of the Russian psychologist Vygotsky has also come to be more recognized in the West, long after his death. Vygotsky was particularly interested in social factors in children's development, emphasizing adult intervention to move the child on into what he called the 'zone of proximal development' so that his work is also of interest to teachers. (A detailed comparison of these three major theories is given in Wood 1988.) Since about the mid-1980s, however, there have not really been any new major 'general theories' attempting to explain all cognitive development. Instead, psychologists have tended to concentrate on gathering evidence for particular trends. This next section outlines some of the trends which it might be useful for beginning teachers to be aware of.

In terms of attention and perception, there seems to be a gradual shift towards greater control and awareness. The attention of very young babies seems to be grabbed by many things that we also attend to as adults but also towards the human face, for instance. As they grow older, children generally exercise increasing control, selecting on the basis of experience what will be most relevant for them. Such control also enables them to concentrate for longer on the same thing if they wish. As children's concepts become more sophisticated, they are increasingly able to make up for inadequacies in what is available to them from their senses.

General changes in their whole approach to solving problems usually accompany these developments (Tina Jarvis discusses investigations in a practical sense in Chapter 7). Many young children tend, for example, to react 'impulsively' by accepting the first solution that looks more or less right, often on the basis of what has worked in the past, whether that response is actually relevant or not. Older and more successful learners are more reflective: they are able to hold several possible ideas in order to consider them, at the same time accepting that they do not yet know the answer because the problem may be a complex one and there may not be one simple answer anyway. Resnick (1987) describes the characteristics of such 'higher order thinking' in which the children are able to regulate their own mental activities, analyse complex situations and impose meaning using nuances of judgement (in the arts situations this is exemplified by Martin Wenham's example of Liam's painting in Chapter 8).

Similarly, children become increasingly able to 'de-centre', to see the problem from different points of view and, in a sense, to step outside themselves and to suspend their previous assumptions. The capacity to think in terms other than just the 'here and now' goes hand in hand with the growing ability to deal with more general and abstract ideas rather than simply with concrete objects and events in the current context – another term used to describe this development is that their thinking becomes more 'de-contextualized'. Going back to the first cameo, Julie will become increasingly able to recognize that the five cubes she ended up with in the first sum represent the same number that she needs for the second problem.

To put Bruner's idea very basically, children can be seen as developing through three different ways of 'representing' the world around them. Their earliest thinking involves what he called '*enactive representation*', where they have to have the physical objects and manipulate them. Thus Julie needs to 'enact' the problem by taking the cubes out of the box and counting them out loud. Later, she will be able to deal with '*iconic representation*' when simply seeing a picture of five cubes will be enough, though she may still have to touch the picture and count aloud at first. Finally, she will be able to deal with abstract concepts or '*symbolic representations*' like the arbitrary symbol '5' which has absolutely no visual similarities to five objects at all.

At the same time as they are developing the ability to think at different 'levels', children are also developing a range of strategies – ways of dealing with information. It has already been suggested that young children simply often do not know what to *do* when presented with a learning task and that any form of instruction can help, at least to solve the immediate problem. So how do such strategies develop?

Children's developing strategies

Once they have realized that they do actually need to do something in order to learn (itself a major step), the earliest strategies to emerge involve simply trying to prolong the information. To understand this, look at the random digits below for five seconds, then shut the book, wait for ten seconds, then try to repeat the numbers:

4 8 5 2 7 0 3 9 1

What strategies did you use? For a start, you almost certainly repeated the numbers to yourself, in your head. Adults do this because we know that the information will rapidly 'fade' or disappear but many children simply are not aware of this basic fact, so that simply discussing such basic 'rote' or 'rehearsal' strategies can sometimes be helpful, even with children at the top end of the junior age range.

Even on such a basic task, however, you probably did other things too – perhaps without even realizing it. You may have tried to picture the numbers in your mind's eye, bearing in mind from what has been previously said that some people find this much easier to do than others. You perhaps repeated the numbers but in groups of twos or threes rather than one at a time, cutting down the load from nine single digits to three or four larger 'chunks' (you may even have said 'forty-eight, fifty-two', etc). Even though you were told that the digits were random, you may also have expected some kind of trick (this chapter is about psychology after all!) and spent your five seconds desperately looking for some sort of system. (If you did this, it is also likely that you 'cheated' by spending longer than five seconds!) This 'search after meaning' has already been discussed as a crucial factor in human thinking, and we do it as adults because we know that if we *understand* something, it will be far easier to *learn* and remember. Again, children need to be helped to recognize this in order to improve their strategies.

What do all these strategies have in common? They all involve some form of transformation or elaboration of the initial information presented – not just looking at it passively or even repeating it but actively changing it and adding to it in ways to make it easier to learn. These 'elaborative' strategies are a major hallmark of children's cognitive development. We should also note that such strategies probably involve a growing awareness of our own thinking. We learn, for example, what sorts of materials we find easiest to deal with, to correct our mistakes, or to predict what strategy will be most effective, and then plan accordingly. This ability to think about our thinking is referred to as 'metacognition' and it is very much in keeping with the other general trends outlined in this section.

Conclusion

An understanding of such processes as attention, perception and memory, and of how they develop in children would appear to be very useful to teachers. Yet cognitive psychology seems to have had very little direct impact on classrooms: Sotto (1994 – a very readable text) discusses why teachers can be very aware of psychological principles but still decide not to apply them. Richardson (1992) notes that even those who actually teach cognitive psychology to students make little use of its principles to inform their teaching! Perhaps part of the problem is that these processes are so much a part of us that we are rarely even aware of them, let alone willing to consider changing them: we are unlikely to decide to try a bit of 'perceiving' because we have a few minutes to spare! If so, then even the brief discussion in this chapter may help to raise that awareness a little and to give some insights not only into our own minds, but also into the minds of the thousands of children like Julie and Martin whose problems confront teachers every day.

References and further reading

Adey, P. and Shayer, M. (1994) *Really Raising Standards: Cognitive Intervention and Academic Achievement.* London: Routledge.

Bransford, J.D. and Johnson, M.K. (1972) Contextual prerequisites for understanding: some investigations of comprehension and recall. *Journal of Verbal Learning and Verbal Behaviour,* II (7): 17–26.

Bruner, J.S. and Anglin, J.M. (1973) *Beyond the Information Given.* London: Allen and Unwin.

Donaldson, M. (1978) *Children's Minds.* Glasgow: Fontana/Collins.

Fontana, D. (1988) *Psychology for Teachers,* 2nd edn. Basingstoke: British Psychological Society/MacMillan.

Gage, N.L. and Berliner, D.C. (1992) *Educational Psychology,* 5th edn. Dallas: Houghton Mifflin.

Levin, J.R. (1993) Mnemonic strategies and classroom learning: a twenty year report card. *Elementary School Journal,* 94 (2): 235–44.

McNamara, S. and Moreton, G. (1993) *Teaching Special Needs.* London: David Fulton.

Resnick, L.B. (1987) *Educational Learning to Think.* Washington DC: National Academic Press.

Richardson, J.T.E. (1992) Cognitive psychology and student learning. *Psychology Teaching Review,* 1 (1): 2–9.

Smith, F. (1982) *Writing and the Writer*. London: Heinemann.
Sotto, E. (1994) *When Teaching becomes Learning: a Theory and Practice of Teaching*. London: Cassell.
Wood, D. (1988) *How Children Think and Learn*. Oxford: Blackwell.

6

What shall we do today?
Planning for learning – children's and teachers'!

Janet Moyles

Cameo 1

Response from a newly qualified teacher when asked by students what had been her most successful strategy for dealing with children's learning: 'Planning lessons thoroughly in writing over the day, week and half-term. This gave me the confidence to know where I was trying to head. It also meant I could let the children in on what they're supposed to learn and have learnt and that made it all suddenly much easier! It also meant that I could give the children some information to start and then add details later in the lesson – otherwise they would have got swamped and switched off.'

Cameo 2

Student teachers talking after a first visit to their teaching practice classes:

Student A: 'I've got a Year 4 class and the teacher wants me to cover time and shape in maths, Aztecs and explorers for history, weather in geography, colour and light for science, the Impressionists in art, tuned percussion in music, speech and quotation marks in English, teach them to play stool-ball for PE and introduce them to the new control technology stuff in school . . . and all in six weeks!'

Student B: 'You should be so lucky! All I've been told to do is think of something based on the topic of "Stories" with my Year 2 class and I haven't got a clue where to begin!'

Cameo 3

The beginner teacher had just finished reading a story to a reception class about some children going to the seaside. To engage the children in reflection about the story he asked, 'Why do you think the children enjoyed going to the seaside? Who can tell us some of the things they did?' Several children put up their hands as was the custom and the teacher chose Melanie who immediately exclaimed, 'My Gran's cat got a bird in the garden and ate it!'. In jumps Gita with 'There was a dead dog outside my house tomorrow [sic]!', at which point several children joined in gory tales about deceased animals. The teacher tried again: 'Yes, that's very interesting but what about the children in our story. They were at the seaside doing all kinds of things. Tell me about some of them.' By this time, few of the children had any interest in the seaside story but had plenty to say about... guess what?!

Cameo 4
From a student's journal: evaluation of a history lesson, Year 5.
David T. is convinced that our present Queen Elizabeth was born in the 1500s when she was called Elizabeth 1st. When pointing out the differences between the two, I mentioned that Elizabeth 1st had red hair, to which David replied, 'Yes but it's all grey now, isn't it! I saw her on tele yesterday'.

Introduction

Although the NC determines *what* children should learn in the Key Stages, it is still very much the prerogative of the class teachers, within the frameworks decided in the school as a whole, as to what children *do* each day. Written planning is required of all teachers, particularly those new to the profession, and, although time-consuming, is eminently worthwhile for teacher and child purposes as the new teacher in cameo 1 explains.

Primary teachers usually plan the programme of activities (or lessons) with three specific things in mind:

• children's individual and collective learning opportunities and interests (often specific to the age group);
• curriculum intentions (both the NC and the school's guidelines and policy documents);
• the teacher's own interests, motivations and professional responsibilities.

These are closely linked, as is evidenced in the cameo situations. Each operates to both support and yet equally constrain the others. For example, whatever the teacher's curriculum intentions, the children often have their own agenda, as both cameos 3 and 4 show, and making as good a match as possible between them is a crucial yet challenging planning feat. It involves teachers in:

• having a good knowledge of a particular class of children as well as understanding children generally;

- detailed and thoughtful planning and implementation of activities based on knowledge of children and curriculum;
- undertaking interpretation and analysis of children's experiences/responses and evaluating outcomes.

These three areas are the focus of this chapter and they are approached from the main practical angle of offering a range of different kinds of documentation for planning. First, however, it is worthwhile identifying what is meant by 'curriculum'.

Curriculum

Very broadly, it could be said that the curriculum is everything the child experiences in the context of schooling which is intended to foster learning. The 'subject' curriculum, therefore, is only a part of the broader overall curriculum. Schools also have a 'hidden' curriculum, which centres around those aspects which children and teachers cultivate within their more informal relationships but which contribute to the general ethos of the school.

Curriculum processes should involve the children in many learning experiences of which knowing, thinking, doing, communicating and remembering are some main features. We know that any curriculum 'works' when, as Bennett *et al.* (1984) suggest, children can give evidence that they are:

- acquiring new knowledge and skills;
- using their existing knowledge and skills in different contexts;
- recognizing and solving problems;
- practising what they know;
- revising and replaying what they know in order to remember it.

What you will be attempting to do as a teacher is to ensure that all of these processes are engaged in by children during most of the school day. This will be achieved through planning activities around a topic (sometimes called a theme or project) or around individual subjects. Either way in state schools you will be working within the framework of the NC. (Bennett and his colleagues found that, unfortunately, most curriculum tasks in maths and English, presented to 6 and 7-year-old children only required them to give evidence of the latter two processes.)

Planning for learning

In the belief that primary children's learning is holistic, many teachers plan curriculum activities through cross-curricular 'topics' – a typical starting point is shown in Figure 6.1.

Topic-based work has the added advantage of seemingly covering all required subjects and the wider curriculum. Unfortunately, too broadly-

T O Y S 🚚🚂👜🚗

△ Science from toys, e.g. energy, forces, movement
△ History of toys
△ Design and making of toys
△ Data collection and classification of toys
△ Materials used to make toys
△ Technology toys, computerized toys
△ Toys from different parts of the world
△ Where toys are made
△ Movement patterns of toys
△ Moveable parts of toys
△ Sharing and caring for toys
△ Reading and writing about toys
△ Talking about favourite toys
△ Musical toys – music about toys
△ Aesthetic qualities of toys

Figure 6.1   Example of cross-curricular topic plan

based or too many areas can lead to the kind of situation found in the first cameo for Student A, where the teacher was finding himself overwhelmed by *content* matters. Student B had quite the reverse problem and required more information about children's past and present story knowledge in order to make sensible decisions. With nine subjects, the overall curriculum and assessment procedure, there is a great danger that the children's understanding will be very shallow and superficial. This has occurred despite teachers' best efforts to make the curriculum manageable for children and themselves (Webb 1993).

There is a need for primary teachers to challenge these subject-centred curriculum practices, particularly in the early years, lower and middle juniors, as it is both oppressive of good primary practice (DES 1989) and antithetical to the way children of this age learn. It is worth noting that the NC does *not* require teachers to work in this way; in fact the curriculum document (SCAA 1994: 7) states that a 'key factor contributing to [teachers] perceptions of overload is over-interpretation of requirements'.

Many schools attempt to make sense of the curriculum by specifying topics for particular year groups across the school, balancing out subject and other curriculum aspects, for different ages of children. Primary age children bring their own perceptions to bear on learning (as we saw in Chapters 2 and 5); therefore, the *processes* through which they acquire experiences assume greatest importance. This is part of the reason for the children's response in cameo 3 where something (or nothing!) in the story suddenly triggered a quite different train of thought. It is interesting to speculate on how *you* would have reacted to this situation.

In cameo 4, the child's current grasp of the concept of time – notoriously difficult (what do *adults* really understand of times past?) – means that comparing the two Elizabethan periods is beyond his present level of under-standing. He will need many more process experiences of, for example, ordering pictures of distant past, recent past and present objects or events plus many stories and role play opportunities about other times in order to develop his understanding.

A topic, if carefully planned, can provide many good curriculum experi-ences for children *but* it is vital that the starting points are manageable for teacher and children. A science topic on 'Colour and Light', for example, is much too broad and offers no suggestion as to where one might begin to teach children. Planning such a topic web generates the need for a whole series of mini-topics which get further and further away from any specific learning experiences (see Moyles 1991). There are a few 'golden rules' for topics:

1 Start with something from which children can have an immediate experience – something to *do*. (Torches and a darkened area of the room or a 'Colour Walk' around the local area could lead into 'Colour and Light'.)
2 Children must be given opportunity to offer their suggestions to the planning – it gives them some responsibility from the outset and the teacher has the security of knowing that activities will be within the children's interests and experiences.
3 Relate the topic to children's lives and experiences as far as possible. The 'Aztecs' will require a great deal of work *from the teacher,* yet who is it who is supposed to be learning? At the very least, children need to see plenty of pictures of Aztec people and places and have drama/role play opportunities.
4 Include within topic plans:
   • content – subject and wider curriculum, including reference to pro-grammes of study (PoS) and attainment targets (ATs);
   • skills and processes children should use and develop;
   • the main concepts to be covered;
   • points at which assessment will be undertaken.
   These may be done all on one large plan, or different smaller plans done showing how areas integrate with each other.

Photo 9   Planning for active learning also means planning for tidying away!

5 Pin topic plans on the wall – this constant reminder to children and others who enter the classroom, often prompts relevant books, pictures, artefacts, etc. being brought to school.

6 Try to introduce the focus of any new topic at the end of a week, then spend time talking over its potential with the children. Children may well use the weekend to hunt out useful topic-related items and talk it over with adults and older siblings. It is also your starting point for what children already know and can save a lot of unnecessary time and planning.

7 Involve the children in constantly *reviewing* progress: what they have learned and what more there is to do and understand in the time available. This not only ensures everyone remains focused but means that planning each day's activities is simpler.

8 Allow children with specific interests to follow these within the topic and mark these on your overall plan. This is particularly important where some children's interest in the topic may be waning and some personal motivation is needed.

9 Keep the time scale appropriate to the age of the children. With younger children perhaps a week or two, extending to a half-term for junior children, as concentration, knowledge and skills increase. Even at older

junior level, it is difficult to sustain a topic for a whole term, partly because of time but partly because children's interests still tend to ebb and flow.

An example of a topic plan is given in Figure 6.2. How far does it appear to meet the requirement of the list above? What might be added in order to make it more comprehensive?

Subject planning and specialist teaching

What has been said about planning topics equally applies to subjects – but in reverse! (For an example of subject planning leading to activities, see Figure 6.3.)

Some schools, particularly with children in Years 5 and 6, are now operating specialist teaching time, when the school's specialist teachers work with different classes or groups of children. Many primary schools operate practices such as 'setting' for maths, English or science, which is a way of ensuring that children of different abilities receive specific teaching. However, many primary schools still operate a one-teacher/one-class system with teachers being required to teach all subjects to all abilities.

Detailed planning and implementation

The emphasis on children 'doing' and playing is particularly vital with 3–8 year-olds, and for older children should only gradually be replaced by less active learning approaches (see Moyles, 1994). The active curriculum is well represented in Figure 6.4 which also gives clear guidance on what your detailed planning needs to include in relation to processes and skills.

Primary children occupying too much time being told or working at pencil and paper activities will soon get bored and may, at best, simply not learn and, at worst, may generate discipline problems. Children presented with too much too soon (as in the case of the travel agency cameo in Chapter 2) may be so busy exploring new materials that the teacher's intentions are, albeit temporarily, lost. The old adage 'I hear and I forget; I see and I remember; I do and I understand' is one well worth memorizing! Worksheet activities and continual exposition rarely enable children to be actively engaged in their own learning processes. Rather they often teach children how to fail; search for the 'right' answers; be passive recipients; hate written work; learn by 'rote' without understanding; be a spectator in one's own learning; wait to be told; find learning painful and/or boring and expect others to control their learning. Most teachers do not really want this for children and yet get drawn into this mode of working mainly to try to 'fit everything in'. There are other ways.

With previous planning for topic or subject and knowledge of the kind of processes and skills you are aiming for, it is vital to undertake some

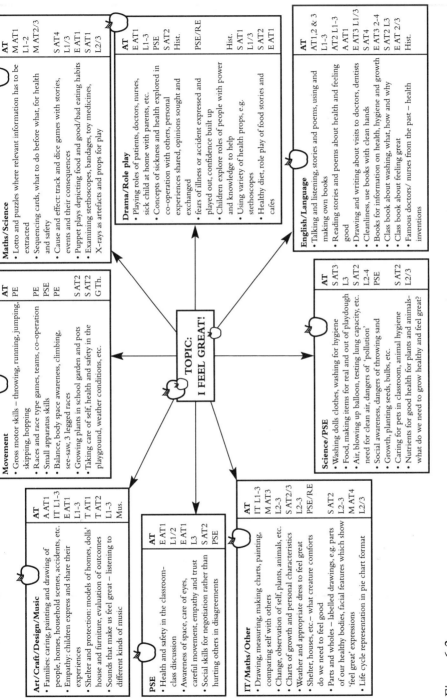

Figure 6.2

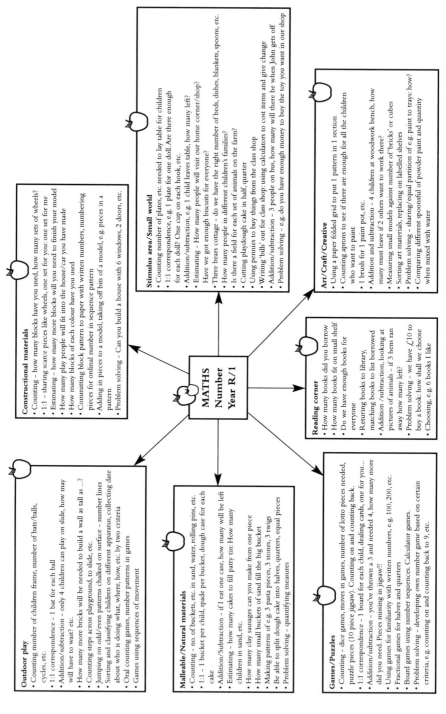

Outdoor play
- Counting number of children frame, number of bats/balls, cycles, etc.
- 1:1 correspondence - 1 bat for each ball
- Addition/subtraction - only 4 children can play on slide, how may will have to wait? etc.
- Counting steps across playground, to slide, etc.
- Jumping on odd/even patterns chalked on surface - number lines
- Sorting and classifying children on different apparatus, collecting date about who is doing what, where, how, etc. by two criteria
- Oral counting games, number patterns in games
- Games using sequences of movement

Constructional materials
- Counting - how many blocks have you used, how many sets of wheels?
- 1:1 - sharing scarce pieces like wheels, one set for you: one set for me
- Estimating - how many more blocks will you need to finish your model
- How many play people will fit into the house/car you have made
- How many blocks of each colour have you used
- Committing block pattern to paper with written numbers, numbering pieces for ordinal number in sequence pattern
- Adding in pieces to a model, taking off bits of a model, e.g. pieces in a pattern
- Problem solving - Can you build a house with 6 windows, 2 doors, etc.

Stimulus area/Small world
- Counting number of plates, etc. needed to lay table for children
- 1:1 correspondence, e.g. 1 plate for one doll. Are there enough for each doll? One cup on each hook, etc.
- Addition/subtraction, e.g. 1 child leaves table, how many left?
- Estimating - How many people will visit our home corner/shop?
- Have we got enough biscuits for everyone?
- Three bears cottage - do we have the right number of beds, dishes, blankets, spoons, etc.
- How many people in different children's families?
- Is there a field for each set of animals on the farm?
- Cutting playdough cake in half, quarter
- Using pennies to buy things from the class shop
- Writing 'bills' out for class shop: using calculators to cost items and give change
- Addition/subtraction - 3 people on bus, how many will there be when John gets off
- Problem solving - e.g. do you have enough money to buy the toy you want in our shop

Art/Craft/Creative
- Using a paper folded grid to put 1 pattern in 1 section
- Counting aprons to see if there are enough for all the children who want to paint
- 1 brush for 1 paint pot, etc.
- Addition and subtraction - 4 children at woodwork bench, how many must leave if 2 others want to work there?
- Measuring small models against number of 'bricks' or cubes
- Sorting art materials, replacing on labelled shelves
- Problem solving - sharing/equal partition of e.g. paint to trays: how?
- Comparing different spoonsful of powder paint and quantity when mixed with water

Reading corner
- How many books did you borrow
- How many books fit on small shelf
- Do we have enough books for everyone
- Retuing books to library, matching books to list borrowed
- Addition /subtraction, looking at pictures of animals - if 3 hens ran away how many left?
- Problem solving - we have £10 to buy a book: how shall we choose
- Choosing, e.g. 6 books I like

Malleable/Natural materials
- Counting - no. of buckets, etc. in sand, water, rolling pins, etc.
- 1:1 - 1 bucket per child, spade per bucket, dough case for each cake
- Addition/Subtraction - if I eat one case, how many will be left
- Estimating - how many cakes to fill patty tin: How many children in sand, etc.
- How many clay sausages can you make from one piece
- How many small buckets of sand fill the big bucket
- Making patterns of e.g. 3 pasta pieces, 3 stones, 3 twigs
- Be able to split dough cake into halves, quarters, equal pieces
- Problem solving - quantifying measures

Games/Puzzles
- Counting - dice games, moves in games, number of lotto pieces needed, puzzle pieces (10 piece jigsaw). Counting on and counting back.
- 1:1 correspondence - 1 board for each child, dealing cards, one for you...
- Addition/subtraction - you've thrown a 3 and needed 4, how many more did you need. Pieces missing in jigsaw!!
- Using games for familiarity with written numbers, e.g. 100, 200, etc.
- Fractional games for halves and quarters
- Board games using number sequences. Calculator games.
- Problem solving - developing own number game based on certain criteria, e.g. counting on and counting back to 9, etc.

MATHS Number Year R/1

Figure 6.3

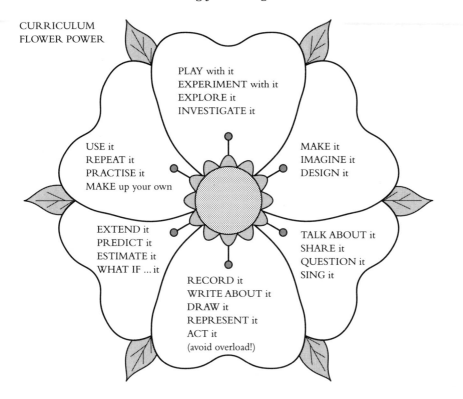

CURRICULUM
FLOWER POWER

PLAY with it
EXPERIMENT with it
EXPLORE it
INVESTIGATE it

USE it
REPEAT it
PRACTISE it
MAKE up your own

MAKE it
IMAGINE it
DESIGN it

EXTEND it
PREDICT it
ESTIMATE it
WHAT IF ... it

TALK ABOUT it
SHARE it
QUESTION it
SING it

RECORD it
WRITE ABOUT it
DRAW it
REPRESENT it
ACT it
(avoid overload!)

Figure 6.4

quite detailed planning of each particular activity to be undertaken by the children. The chart shown in Figure 6.5 is one found helpful by beginner teachers to structure their activities, giving as it does opportunity to comment on both the children's activities and also what the teacher will be doing. You must recognize a) that children can learn without your continual presence; and b) that you must plan to work with individuals or groups if it is ever going to happen. As indicated in the Bennett *et al.* model earlier, activities will need different levels of teacher attention:

1 teacher intensive – when children are undertaking new learning or the teacher is assessing existing learning;
2 teacher hovering – when children are engaged in applying knowledge and may need occasional teacher support;
3 teacher monitoring – when children are practising skills and knowledge in relatively familiar situations requiring little teacher involvement;
4 teacher available – when children are engaged in absorbing their own mastery and may need the teacher to tell or show an outcome at some stage.

Session:		Date	Time	Curric Area

PLAN	COMMENT
Aim	
Objectives	
NC links	
Resources	

Activity structure	Timing	Teacher activity	Children's activity
INTRODUCTION			
DEVELOPMENT			
CONCLUSION			

EVALUATION - continued overleaf

Figure 6.5

The planning chart also ensures that you remember that each activity will need a specific introduction, something which develops it further (as the new teacher found out in the first cameo) and a conclusion. The evaluation gives the basis (as explored by Morag Hunter-Carsch in Chapter 13) for making decisions on who has learned what and what is needed to progress to the next stage.

Remember with such planning charts that your *aims* are related to things you wish to achieve in the *longer term*, for example 'children should enjoy science and learn a number of key concepts'. In contrast, *objectives* are *short term* related to what the children should have learned and done by the end of that activity, for example 'children should be able to use their knowledge of light in order to explain how the beam falls on an object'.

Ready to teach?

The final level of planning is how you and the children are actually going to work together in the learning context. There are several phases in this interaction, summed up under the following headings and questions:

1 *Entering strategy*
   What will be your starting point(s)? Introduction?
2 *Exploration mode*
   What exploration will the children undertake? What materials/resources will be available? How/by whom would they be set up?
3 *Content*
   As in your planning but how will you tell the children what you intend them to learn as well as do?
4 *Ownership and responsibility*
   What level of ownership will the children have? What responsibilities? How will the children know what they are supposed to learn? How will these aspects be conveyed?
5 *Teacher strategies*
   What will your role be? How will you interact/intervene in the activities and sustain/extend them?
6 *Evaluation and analysis*
   How/when/who will you observe to see what children were learning in relation to concepts covered and the objectives set?
7 *Reflection/review mode*
   What opportunities will you provide for children to reflect on their learning and be part of its review/evaluation/analysis?
8 *Justification*
   What quality and standard of outcomes will you expect? How will the value of these be communicated to others (e.g. through display, records)?

Using the chart shown in Figure 6.6, plot how you would approach the task indicated in the light of the above statements. Doing this task will mean that you have had to consider different kinds of organizational strategies,

What will you teach?
How will you teach?
Who will you teach?

The children have been working on a topic about

F I S H

So far they have all had :
a story about fish
the chance to examine a real (but dead) trout in detail
identified the habitats of different kinds of fish
drafted a poem about fish
produced a class database on the computer about fish
begun a topic book on their favourite fish

<u>What will they do next?</u> How much of it will need to be 'teacher intensive'? Plan some activities which the children (and you) will do tomorrow.

<u>Fill in the timetable:</u>

9.00 a.m.

10.30 a.m.   Playtime

11.00 a.m.

12.00 noon Lunchtime

1.30 p.m.

2.30 p.m.

Figure 6.6

for example whether you introduce something to the whole class, give tasks to groups or pairs, or allow children free choice to explore materials for themselves. Figure 6.7 suggests a range of activities which might take place in the classroom and asks you to make decisions as to what you would organize in which way.

Having undertaken these activities with children, it is vital that you and

WHICH ACTIVITIES WOULD BE BEST ORGANIZED IN WHICH WAY?

Choice is:
- Whole class
- Ability groups, one focus/subject
- Groups – same focus, different activity
- Groups – different focus, different activity
- Rotated groups – same focus, different activity
- Single sex groups
- Paired activity
- Individual activity with or without adult
- Free choice from pre-determined list
- Free choice
- 'Other' (explain)

ACTIVITIES:

1.	Story	2.	Practical maths
3.	Science demonstration	4.	Clay/woodwork session
5.	Spelling session	6.	Working on a topic
7.	Home corner play	8.	Outside visit and follow-up
9.	Design technology	10.	P E /Movement session
11.	Floating and sinking exp.	12.	Religious education

You may qualify / determine other factors as necessary. But you MUST JUSTIFY YOUR CHOICE!

Why is this the most appropriate organization?
What are the alternatives?
Will you be able to assess learning in this context?
How would you explain your decision to •children,
•parents, •colleagues, •a curriculum adviser?

Figure 6.7

the children reflect on what you did and the success or otherwise of the outcomes.

Interpreting, analysing and evaluating children's experiences

What we are essentially assessing is to what extent the children (and you) have been able to:

- reach the objectives set for them in planning;
- develop appropriate attitudes and opinions;

- reach high standards and offer quality outcomes;
- deal with the rates at which they learn;
- find out about their strengths and weaknesses;
- understand what learning should take place next for children to progress;
- know what activities or experiences should now be provided or repeated and what differentiated experiences are needed for which children.

We then evaluate these against longer-term aims to see what adjustments are required in planning. This process involves us in much interpretation of evidence and collection of data for written evaluations and records. Be careful that your interpretations are as value-free and objective as possible. For example, look at the following two written observations, one highly subjective and the other much more objective.

> This went really well. Sam was having a wonderful time playing with the sand tray; she really enjoyed playing with Surekha and Amrit and they all seemed to get a lot out of it. They didn't communicate at all but just enjoyed playing alongside each other and doing things together.

> Sam was using a bucket and spade in the sand with Surekha and Amrit, filling and emptying the bucket for a full 10 minute period. There was no verbal interaction between the children but Surekha watched Sam on three occasions and then attempted to emulate Sam's actions. (Would Surekha benefit from more opportunities to learn from a peer model?)

It is quite obvious that the second written observation is a much more useful diagnostic tool for the teacher in working on the next phase of planning.

Finding out about children's learning

Another main strategy for finding out about children's learning has to be through talking to them or getting them to write down what they did and what they think they learned. However, in analysing, interpreting and evaluating learning competence in this way, we need to remember that children's ability to understand things is not always matched by their literacy performance, particularly in the early years. Children who can give an extensive oral explanation of an exciting science experiment often then write 'I put it in the cup and it disappeared. the end' [sic] (see Martin Cortazzi's examples in Chapter 11). This happens right across the primary school particularly where fine motor development is slow and a child actually finds writing really difficult if not actually painful! Just those very processes of *active learning* discussed in detail above, are nearly always more important to primary children than writing about tasks!

Photo 10   The playground is usually deemed part of the 'hidden' curriculum of schools

Finding other ways of analysing and evaluating what children know is vital, not least through planning classroom activities in such a way that you have time to *observe* in the many ways described by Linda Hargreaves in Chapter 3. It is in active situations that children frequently illustrate more of their knowledge. For example, I well remember a boy who stood on the edge of a group of children attempting to make a pulley out of various items of 'found' materials (sometimes called 'junk', though very precious in the primary school!). He chose to watch, despite the evident enjoyment of other children, and flatly refused to explain his reticence to become involved. After a half-hour the group had still not managed to produce a pulley. Almost at the end of the session, the boy walked up to the table, picked up three or four items and rapidly and ingeniously made a working pulley. It would have been easy to have thought of him as dull, lazy, insecure, sullen or downright obstinate! We must also be mindful that children's apparent knowledge is not always 'secure'. Children can, for example, readily declare that the earth is round but then draw a picture of it flat-topped in order to show themselves standing on it! Young children can 'parrot' information, such as counting from 1 to 10, but when asked what number comes after 6 they haven't a clue! (see Chapter 5).

Other ways in which children can demonstrate learning

As well as oral and written language outcomes, children could be expected to show different aspects of their learning in several other ways (though none of these should be overused – variety is imperative!):

• drawings;
• poems (and other different forms of writing, e.g. acrostics);
• diagrams and charts;
• mind maps (see Buzan 1993);
• making lists;
• photographs, with or without children's captions;
• making booklets about different activities – 'This is what we learned when we *worked* with the sand', 'This is what we found out about Ancient Egypt';
• explaining to other children what to do (see Chapter 10);
• video/audio recordings of activities;
• undertaking drama/role play;
• doing demonstrations for others.

However assessment is undertaken, you need to ensure that children are given opportunities:

• to make their own ideas explicit – starting from what children know is a must in ongoing planning;
• to produce an end result in different ways and with several alternative solutions – investigations and problem-solving activities allow children to show physically what they 'know';
• to explore ideas with peers – it is much easier to argue your points with peers than with adults, particularly as children get to Years 5 and 6;
• opportunities to actively question their own thinking and undertake explorations in order to learn about their own misconceptions;
• question their own outcomes through open-ended questioning 'What would happen if . . .';
• to be part of situations in which they need to generalize in order to use and develop concepts;
• to *observe for* rather than simply *look at* objects and artefacts and raise questions – help children to detect relevant similarities as well as differences;
• to achieve by setting goals for children which are attainable with just the right amount of effort – this means knowing the children's capabilities well – and telling them what they are intended to learn;
• explore materials before expecting them to do something specific with them;
• apply their knowledge in a situation where they can succeed;
• learn and use the appropriate vocabulary for each topic so that they have the means to explain their activities to you;
• to gather all the information they need in order to fulfil the demands of

the activity – we don't have to wait for children to re-invent the wheel every time but, having been told, children must be allowed to 'prove' whatever the concept is for themselves (Sotto 1994);
• to be genuinely praised for achieving learning.

The teacher's role

You should also give yourself plenty of opportunity for interpreting, analysing and assessing what *your role* has been in the children's learning. The following questions will act as a conclusion to this chapter and also serve as a reminder of the kinds of things important for you, as a developing professional, in planning for children's learning on a daily and weekly basis.

1 How positive or otherwise do you feel about the curriculum activities you provided?
2 Did you present activities with enthusiasm and vigour?
3 In what ways did the teaching and learning appear successful/unsuccessful to you?
4 What did you learn – about planning, curriculum, children and so forth?
5 Was the atmosphere generated in the classroom pleasant, task-oriented and positive?
6 How did you handle any challenges?
7 Were you more involved with the children in relation to supervision of *activities* or the management of *learning*?
8 Were your teaching strategies congruent with the objectives you set? Did you offer a structured sequence of experiences?
9 Were your interactions with children 'professional' and did you give and receive appropriate feedback?
10 How well did you communicate with children? Did you pace your talk appropriately and were your instructions (verbal and non-verbal) clear?
11 Did you make effective use of your time and energy?
12 Did you use a variety of teaching styles and strategies – exposition, different groupings, discussion, play and active learning, practice tasks, problem solving, investigations and so forth?
13 Have you marked, analysed and diagnosed children's learning errors and noted those who need help?
14 Have you made appropriate observations and evaluations of children's learning?
15 Have you and the children used the physical space and resources effectively?
16 Would you have enjoyed the activities if you had been one of the children?
17 Have you discussed your progress with a mentor and noted points for professional development?
18 Have you enjoyed the experience of teaching – and learning?

References and further reading

Bennett, N., Desforge, G., Cockburn, A. and Wilkinson, B. (1984) *The Quality of Pupil Learning Experiences*. London: Lawrence Erlbaum.
Buzan, T. (1993) *The Mind Map Book: Radiant Thinking*. London: BBC Books.
Department of Education and Science (1989) *Good Primary Practice*, HMI Report. London: HMSO.
Derman-Sparks, L. and the ABC Task Force (1989) *Anti-Bias Curriculum: Tools for Empowering Young Children*. Washington, DC: NAEYC.
Early Years Curriculum Group (1989) *Early Childhood Education: The Early Years Curriculum and the National Curriculum*. Stoke-on-Trent: Trentham Books.
Moyles, J. (1991) *Play as a Learning Process in your Classroom*. London: Collins.
Moyles, J. (ed.) (1994) *The Excellence of Play*. Buckingham: Open University Press.
Schools Curriculum and Assessment Authority (1994) *The Review of the National Curriculum: A Report on the 1994 Consultation*. London: SCAA.
Sotto, E. (1994) *When Teaching Becomes Learning: A Theory and Practice of Teaching*. London: Cassells.
Webb, R. (1993) *Eating the Elephant Bit by Bit: The National Curriculum at Key Stage 2*. London: ATL.

Acknowledgements

I am grateful to Barbara Garner for allowing me to use her diagram for Figure 6.4. Figures 6.2 and 6.3 are adapted from the EYCG booklet detailed in the references.

7

What shall we put in the fruit salad?
Developing investigative thinking and skills in children

Tina Jarvis

Cameo

The class had been asked to prepare afternoon tea for their parents. One group set out to design and prepare a fruit salad. They were told they could use three fruits from a choice of apples, clementines, bananas, melons and kiwi fruits.

During their work the group carried out investigations in mathematics, design and technology, and science. Investigative skills are important elements in each of these subjects, although they are used in slightly different ways and for different purposes. This can be illustrated by considering how the group went about designing their fruit salad.

Initially the children had to find out what combinations of fruits were possible in a mathematical investigation. At first they just wrote down different combinations in a rather disorganized way. After a while their teacher suggested a more systematic approach would be necessary if they were to find all the combinations possible. Eventually they saw a logical pattern of results emerging which they used to ensure that they had found all possibilities.

In design and technology, it is important to test the properties of different components and how they might be joined. Consequently the children also investigated different ways of cutting each fruit, examined their flavours and considered various colour combinations in order to create an attractive, tasty dish.

While engrossed in the task, one child noticed that the apple went brown very quickly making it less attractive. Someone commented that his granny said peeled apples had to be put in water. The group decided to test this out and placed some pieces of apple in water and some were left in the air. They discovered that only the uncovered apples went brown. The teacher asked the group if this always happened. After some thought the children recalled abandoned apple cores also went brown. When asked why they thought this happened, it was suggested that something in the air made the apple go brown and the water kept the air out. This was essentially a scientific investigation as it focused on explaining some physical or biological phenomena, albeit in very simple terms.

Introduction

It can be daunting to give children the freedom to try out their own ideas, as there is always the worry that they will become disruptive or that they may come up with a question that the teacher cannot answer! Children are usually highly motivated by the type of activity described in the cameo, so are less likely to be difficult, as long as the task is within their capability and every child in the group can be fully involved. In undertaking investigations, children are able to use the kind of 'higher-order' cognitive skills outlined by Roger Merry in Chapter 5 and you will be able to see evidence of thinking in the way children approach the tasks. In this chapter, therefore, I shall:

- examine what is meant by 'investigation' as a cross-curricular process but with examples particularly related to science concepts and skills, technology and mathematics;
- offer a range of examples of how these activities can occupy a major role in the primary curriculum and in classroom practices.

What is an investigation?

Investigations are activities in which pupils examine different ways of carrying out a task or explore the effects of making changes in situations. Although some investigations, as in the cameo, have a specific objective or solution, the means by which the goal is achieved is open-ended. Other investigations have no immediately obvious goal as in the case of the science aspect of the above investigation where the children had no specific aim or preconceived result in mind.

Why develop investigations in the classroom?

Investigations develop both creative and critical thinking that will assist subsequent academic studies as well as enabling people to cope more effectively with everyday problems. In order to think creatively, children need

Photo 11   A science investigation

to move beyond their first ideas to suggest alternatives. These ideas should be critically examined to make reasoned choices. Creativity involves taking a risk that one's ideas might prove foolish or inappropriate. Critical thinking requires an open mind that is prepared to make decisions based on evidence which may challenge deeply held personal views. Neither are easy. (In Chapter 8, Martin Wenham takes up these issues in relation to art-based activities.) Children will only develop creativity and critical thinking within a secure, supportive environment provided by the teacher. As investigations are an integral part of science, mathematics and design technology, these subjects can provide both appropriate contexts, which are in the experience and interest of the children, and a structure to enable children to develop strategies for critically examining their imaginative ideas. That said, investigations offer a wide, cross-curricular experience for both children and teachers.

Science investigations

The way young children are expected to develop science investigatory skills in the NC provides a useful structure for developing investigations in a wider context, as they provide a way to test the applicability of different ideas. However, it is important to realize that teaching science investigative skills alone is not sufficient as these skills are the means to create and test scientific concepts, explanations or hypotheses.

Science concepts

The whole purpose of science is to explain the existing physical and biological world. Scientists attempt to create ideas or generalizations that fit all situations, anywhere in this world or even the universe. Scientific generalizations are being changed and refined all the time. For example, until the time of Galileo and Newton there was a general belief that the Earth was the centre of the universe. Scientific knowledge is still tentative, so even the most cherished theories can be challenged by new evidence. Therefore, the scientist must be creative in order to suggest new theories as well as able to test them logically. Scientific investigations provide one approach to evaluate existing ideas and test the value of new ones. Children can follow similar procedures to test and explain their own ideas and if necessary adjust them.

Even very young children have ideas to explain what is happening around them (see Chapter 6). In many cases these explanations are not the same as those given by today's scientists. For example, many children think that light comes out of their eyes when they see objects (Osborne *et al.* 1990); only one wire from a battery is necessary to make a bulb light (Osborne *et al.* 1991); and large blocks of ice are colder than small blocks because of their size. Therefore, the teacher should encourage children to articulate their own ideas, raise their own questions and test their ideas logically and, if necessary, adjust them. A practical investigatory approach not only develops the children's thinking skills, it also gives them a taste of scientific discovery and helps them to recognize that they can have a role in revising and improving current scientific ideas.

Example: Saving the kittens – a class scientific investigation

A practical investigation was used to help children explain some of the factors that influence whether materials are good or poor insulators. It is important that the children's activities have relevance to them, so a story about some kittens provided the context of the lesson.

A student teacher told her class of 7-year-olds that a cat had given birth to kittens in a mountain cave. As the kittens needed to be brought down the hillside before the weather got too cold, it was important to wrap them up in a warm material. The children were asked to test different materials to find out which would be the best insulators for carrying the kittens and to explain why some materials were better than others.

The children were given a variety of materials including wool, fur fabric, cotton, foil and plastic. They observed the fabrics carefully and then predicted which they thought would keep the kittens warm the longest. The children were asked to give reasons for their predictions. Some thought the wool would make a good insulator because it was thick, whereas others thought the foil would be best because it was used when heating meat in an oven.

With guidance the teacher helped the children to make the test fair. Five plastic bottles of the same size were covered with the same amount of material and placed in a milk crate to stop them falling over. For safety reasons hot water was put into the bottles by the student teacher. A thermometer was placed in each bottle and the height of the fluid was recorded every quarter of an hour. A kitchen timer was used, as this was easier for the children to use than reading a clock. The fur fabric and wool were found to keep the water hot longest. The foil was the poorest insulator. This appeared to confirm the explanation that thick materials made better insulators. Those children who had predicted foil would be a good insulator had to rethink their ideas.

When talking about their findings the teacher drew the children's attention to the fact that the fur trapped a lot of air which improved its heat retention capacity. She also told the children that the metal in the foil was not only thin but that the metal conducted heat away from the bottle. To help the children understand this idea, she reminded them that metal spoons become hot quickly when left in hot water, unlike wooden or plastic spoons which did not let heat move through them easily. Finally the more able children wrote about the experiment, while the less able produced a series of annotated drawings. (Martin Cortazzi, in Chapter 11, gives stimulating examples of several ways in which children can record the results of investigations of all kinds, while Jane Hislam, in Chapter 9, shows how storying can operate as the basis of children expressing their imagination and learning.)

Developing science investigatory skills

In the fabric investigation the children used several skills including observation, measurement, setting up a fair test, predicting and explaining. In order to develop such skills, children will need some activities that focus on one or two skills only, as well as having the chance to carry out whole investigations. The teacher needs to help children to make their own choices about when and how each skill should be applied and to encourage them to raise and test their own questions. How can these skills be developed with young children?

Observation

In the kitten experiment, the children had to choose which observations were significant for their test. The way the light reflected on the water might have been interesting but not relevant in this case. On other occasions, a more open-minded approach is necessary where as much detail as possible is collected to stimulate new questions and discoveries. Before the class carried out the kitten investigation, their teacher wanted the children to look at a variety of fabrics carefully. She gave pairs of children two squares of fabric to find as many differences and similarities between them as possible. The discussion and comparison prompted a wide range of creative ways of examining their samples, including whether they felt or looked different when wet, could be cut or creased easily, were transparent or woven. This experience not only developed into learning about insulation but also provided the foundation for finding out why some materials were waterproof and others absorbent. (Observation is emphasized as a crucial factor in children's and teachers' learning in several of the other Part 2 chapters.)

Classifying and organizing data

Phenomena need to be sorted in different ways to help identify significant relationships. If children make a collection of things that stick to magnets they should find that these are all metals, although some different metals belong to the non-magnetic set. This activity should help them to recognize that iron-based metals are magnetic.

To help children make appropriate classifications, teachers will need to suggest criteria for sorting. When the children were examining fabric they could have been asked to sort fabrics into those that are elastic (can be stretched but go back into their original shape) and those that are not. On other occasions the children can be asked to suggest factors for themselves. One group of children thought of sorting toys according to colour, presence of wheels, material and type of energy used. Subsequently each individual grouped the toys according to a self-chosen criteria. One child sorted them into those she liked and those she did not like, which justifiably prompted the remainder of the class to complain that this was not fair! The teacher was then able to talk in general about appropriate ways of making sets, including the fact that some classifications needed measurement; for example dividing the toys into big and little would be too vague.

Recording and measuring

Observations should be systematically recorded. Tick sheets, charts and graphs are useful but have to be introduced carefully as very young children find them difficult to fill in. It helps to start with very simple charts which only record one feature, such as 'Does the toy have wheels – yes or no?'. Once the children have mastered this they might be presented with several columns but which still only focus on one criteria. They might record the type of energy used by different toys, for example battery, spring, elastic, people's push or pull or wind. With experience more complicated charts can be used. In all cases it is helpful to design the chart *with* the children so that they can see how it works and they are given the knowledge to draw up their own charts later. Although this may seem time-consuming it pays off in the end.

Measuring equipment is often needed to distinguish between phenomena or actions. Initially children will require help to know how and when to use equipment like thermometers and force meters. Before any activity, it is important that you check whether the children are able to use the equipment for its intended purpose. For example, some children do not realize that the fluid in the thermometer rises as it gets hotter and falls when cooled. Without this basic understanding measuring temperature will be meaningless. In this case the children could place a large clearly marked class thermometer in different locations to watch and talk about the changes.

As many thermometers have scales extending over 100 degrees, the numbers and related calculations can be too advanced for some children. It may be possible to avoid the use of the thermometer at all by letting the children feel differences by hand (remember to make sure that it is safe). Another approach is to use a matching technique. In the kitten experiment, the less able children drew around their thermometer and coloured in the height of the liquid at each reading. When they compared the series of drawings for each material they could see which was the best insulator. If a matching technique is used, you can use the experience to introduce mathematical skills such as reading scales and showing the children how to carry out the calculations involved. This will be facilitated if the more able children have had the opportunity to make the more accurate readings as their work can be used in the explanations.

Carrying out a fair test

As the children start trying out different investigations, the teacher should introduce the idea of fair tests. In the 'kitten test' it would not have been 'fair' if a lot of fabric was wrapped around some bottles and only a little around others. With guidance, the children will be able to identify the variables that might influence a result and recognize that they must only change one. Only the variable that is being tested must change, i.e. the type of fabric. Everything else should be kept the same – size of bottles, amount of water in the bottles, the way the fabric is fixed to the bottle and so on.

Prediction and hypothesizing (generalizations and explanations)

Prediction is an important skill to help plan an investigation. When the children think about what might happen in a test, they will be helped to know what to observe and what to measure. Children (as well as teachers!) are often reluctant to predict in case they are wrong. You will need to provide a supportive atmosphere which encourages children to take 'risks'. Initially it is often helpful to ask the children to predict orally rather than writing their ideas down as this is less threatening. By asking children to give reasons for their predictions they can also begin to hypothesize, which is the ultimate aim of all science activity.

A scientific hypothesis explains why something happens by suggesting a cause for an observed effect: in the 'kitten experiment' the children hypothesized that materials were good insulators if they were thick. They could have tested this idea further by comparing a set of thick and thin fabrics of the same type. On another occasion, a class noticed some plants dying on a window sill. The teacher encouraged the children to suggest why or how this happened. The explanations included: the plants had been in too much sun, they had not been watered enough and the soil was poor. All of these are *causal hypotheses* and are scientific because they can be tested by experiment. To test their first idea the children grew some plants in direct sunlight and some in a more shaded area.

Evaluating and drawing conclusions

The children need to describe and explain what has happened during their experiments but, do remember, it is not always necessary for them to do this *in writing*. You will need to introduce a range of reporting methods, such as oral reports, drawings, tables, graphs and model-making, so that children (many of whom may come from different first language back-grounds) can make their own decisions about how they can communicate their findings most effectively. The children should also evaluate their experimental procedure, suggesting improvements and commenting on the limitations of their results, so that they can carry out further investigations more effectively.

Applying knowledge acquired during investigations

In order to help children to consolidate new ideas it is useful to ask them to apply their knowledge. This may be in the kind of technological investigation now described.

Technological investigations

Technology is involved with changing products and environments to satisfy human needs or wants, whereas science is concerned with explaining the existing world. Technology applies science concepts to make these products but also uses ideas from all other curriculum areas. Similar testing skills are used in technology as in science but they are not aimed at making generalizations. Rather, they are used for *testing* how good a product is, or which materials and methods would be best for making a new product. As examples, groups of children in different classes tested:

- a variety of mugs for stability, capacity, insulation properties, appearance, cost, comfort to hold and ease of cleaning in order to identify the best mug for a child;
- different ways of joining fabrics when they were making cloth shoes;
- various colour combinations in the process of designing a poster.

Testing products and methods is only a part of design and technology: it is also concerned with *identifying needs and opportunities, making products and evaluating* them. The procedure of investigating and producing a product to solve a specific need can be applied to other problems. Consequently, design and technology provides practical, relevant and manageable contexts to enable children to develop the expertise to tackle many kinds of problems. Occasionally, the children will suggest a project but most design and technology tasks will be introduced by the teacher. However, in all cases there should be an open-ended element to allow for differentiation and individuality. For example, young children can be shown the skills in making a lift-the-flap book but the story line and illustrations should be individualized. Although children should be given this opportunity to be creative, they will need to be taught basic technological skills, such as using saws and cooking implements correctly, as well as strategies for clarifying and solving problems effectively as in the following example.

Example: Rescue from a well – a class technological investigation

A class of junior children were challenged to build a model of a simple pulley system to rescue a 'child' who had fallen down a well. The model was to be made to lift a doll which was placed at the bottom of a large cylinder, approximately 10cm in diameter and 20cm deep. The cylinder had a small platform around the top which could be used to rest the model on. The teacher guided children through the design and making process as outlined below. (These are simplified as, in practice, there is a tendency to go backwards and forwards from one step to another.)

Clarifying the task

The children needed to be sure they understood the task. Children often rush into an activity without looking at the whole problem, so have to make adjustments later. In this case they had to solve two main problems: building a framework with a pulley that fitted on to the platform; and finding a way of picking up the doll.

Review of existing knowledge that may be helpful and how similar problems have been solved by them or others in the past

When making the model pulley system, the children were helped to recall how to join wood using cardboard squares and ways of making pulleys.

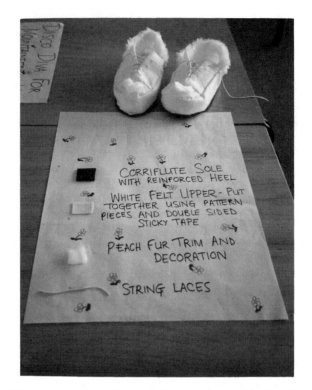

Photo 12   The outcome of a technology investigation undertaken by student teachers

They were also given a variety of books showing simple models and actual examples of pulleys. Using others' research is an important stage of the investigation. It is foolish to 're-invent the wheel' when it is more appropriate to build on existing inventions.

Collection of different solutions

In order to promote creativity, groups were encouraged to brainstorm several solutions. Brainstorming gives an opportunity to collect many ideas in a short time without evaluation, criticism or discussion. Some of the ideas may well be impractical but, at this stage, creativity is more important. For example, one group suggested using respectively a large magnet, a scoop and a crocodile as a way of lifting up the doll!

Comparing and evaluating different approaches

All the solutions were evaluated and a few chosen for detailed exploration. This stage may involve testing different materials and combinations of components. The testing approach should be carried out in a logical and fair way along the lines of scientific investigations. In this task, many of the groups wanted to use a cotton reel on a piece of doweling as a pulley but it fitted too loosely so several methods of joining were tested.

Choosing an approach, identifying the different tasks, deciding on an order for action and carrying out the plan

Eventually each group decided on an overall approach bearing in mind the time limit and available materials. A few groups drew plans but this was unusual. If children are unfamiliar with the materials and techniques it is very difficult to produce detailed, drawn plans but all the children had done a lot of oral planning and testing. Each group made their models which varied enormously: some were triangular structures, others rectangular; some were made of wood, others of corriflute; some had winding gears whereas others did not. Inevitably, unanticipated problems arose which involved going through this same series of steps again, albeit briefly, applying the same imaginative and investigatory approach.

Evaluation and review

First and foremost each group had to demonstrate that their model could 'rescue the doll' as this was the problem to be solved. They were then asked to identify their successes and problems and to evaluate both the final product and methods used. Finally the class were asked to suggest improvements. If the children are not clear about the original purpose of the product and the criteria to be satisfied, the evaluation is likely to be very superficial. It is important to give time to the evaluative process as this reflection is significant in enabling children to become independent creative problem-solvers.

It does take time for the class to build up all these skills. Therefore, initially you will need to take a leading role by using class or group discussions to help the children through the problem-solving process. As the children become more experienced they can be increasingly left to work through their projects independently.

Mathematical investigations

When young children come to school their mathematics may reach high levels of independence as they sort objects into different categories and investigate how to fit shapes together in order to come to their own conclusions. As they grow older, this independent thinking should not give way to a formula-based method of learning which is based wholly on the assimilation of received mathematical knowledge and whose test of truth is 'this is the way I was told to do it' (Cockcroft 1982: para 321).

Mathematical investigations which promote independent thinking can be exploring mathematics within itself. The children might be asked to investigate the possible patterns that can be made out of five squares, such as pentominoes, or ways of dividing a square into halves. Other investigations relate to exploring the range of possibilities for solving a problem, such as ways of making a fruit salad or finding different layouts of a classroom. As can be seen below, the stages of a mathematical investigation are similar to those in design technology but the emphasis is on using systematic strategies for finding *patterns* in phenomena. Here the creativity tends to come towards the end of the investigation when the child sees the possible relationships and suggests ways of describing them.

Understanding the task

You will need to make sure that the child has a clear grasp of the intended task, what they need to do and how it will be evaluated.

Exploring the possible outcome

Initially, the children may have a disorganized approach but, by encouraging them to look for patterns and relationships, they may come up with a logical way of tackling the problem.

Developing a systematic approach

This will involve finding a methodical approach to ensure all possibilities are covered and recording ideas so that the same ideas are not repeated.

Recognizing a pattern in order to predict unknown or untried cases

For example, if children are investigating triangular numbers or growth in a staircase, they should find the cubes needed to make the stairs produce the following pattern 1, 1+2, 1+2+3, 1+2+3+4, etc. They may be able to predict that the next number will be 1+2+3+4+5 and the ninth step will need 1+2+3+4+5+6+7+8+9 cubes. Of course if their prediction is not correct they will need to rethink their ideas.

Coming up with an explanation or pattern or generalization

In the above example, able children may be able to make the generalization that the *nth* step will need 1+2+3+ . . . +n. They then need to decide whether it will always work. If not their ideas may again need to be revised.

Concluding and evaluating

The value of an investigation can be lost unless the outcome and process is discussed by and with the children. Such discussion should include talking about not only the successful approaches but also reflecting on the false trails so that the whole experience can enhance children's ability to tackle later investigations and to improve their thinking skills in general.

Making it all happen – classroom management and ethos

Although slightly different, investigations in science, design and technology, and mathematics all enable children to be both creative and logical. To develop these thinking skills it is important that children have the opportunity to make decisions for themselves in a secure positive environment. This means that you will need to:

1 *Involve pupils in some of the decisions* regarding how they set up their investigations and in what they will make or do.
2 *Provide easy access to mathematical and scientific equipment, tools and a variety of materials* so that the children are able to make choices for themselves. Ideally the children should be able to see what is available. Being able to scan the possibilities can help to stimulate the children's ideas.
3 *Encouraging small group discussion* as articulating ideas and negotiating procedures promotes creativity and provides mutual support (see Chapter 10).
4 *Providing time for children to make, and correct, mistakes in a supportive atmosphere.* There is a temptation to provide only those materials which are directly needed and give such detailed instructions that the children are guaranteed a good 'end product'. However, this will *not* be in the children's long-term interests in developing their ideas and imagination. The timing of the teacher's intervention is very significant, as children need to learn from their mistakes but must not become excessively disheartened. If children become stuck after trying, questioning by the teacher or sharing other children's solutions are useful ways to assist without actually giving the solution, although the latter may be necessary sometimes.
5 *Valuing a range of outcomes.* If the children have the opportunity to respond in different ways, their final products will range in quality and creativity. Therefore each piece of work should be assessed with respect to the ability of the child concerned.
6 *Accepting some noise and mess is inevitable.* Working and talking in groups may well be noisy but this does not necessarily mean that children are being disruptive. The teacher needs to monitor the activity and conversations to check that the children are on task (Linda Hargreaves describes several ways this can be done in Chapter 3). Although there will inevitably be some mess, this can be managed if the children are aware of the responsibility of using materials economically and of cleaning their working areas after use. If this expectation is developed by adults from the nursery and reception years, the children gain by having increased responsibility. It also has the advantage of releasing teachers to concentrate on *teaching* rather than on organizing and preparing materials.

7 *Answering the unanswerable question*! If the teacher has tried out activities that are presented to the children, it is unlikely that many unanticipated questions will arise, even if a child tackles the investigation in an unexpected way. However, occasionally questions will crop up which the teacher cannot answer. Some can be investigated later or researched by looking in books. But if this fails, the teacher should feel able to admit to not knowing. This is itself a good model for the children, who also need to develop the confidence to acknowledge when they do not know and need help.

Conclusion

Teachers will usually find that very young children, or even those identified as having special educational needs, are able to surprise them with the variety and imaginative approaches to problems, once they understand that the teachers want them to be independent. 'Standing back and watching groups of highly motivated children using their own initiative and resources to extend their experiences and capabilities significantly is an experience that few teachers forget in a hurry' (Shepard 1990). Do try to ensure that you have this experience yourself.

References and further reading

Cockcroft, W.H. (1982) *Mathematics Counts*. London: HMSO.
Fisher, R. (1990) *Teaching Children to Think*. Oxford: Basil Blackwell.
Garrard, W. (1986) *I don't know: Lets find out: Mathematical Investigations in the Primary School*. Ipswich: Suffolk County Council.
Harlen, W. and Jelly, S. (1989) *Developing Science in the Primary Classroom*. Edinburgh: Oliver and Boyd.
Jarvis, T. (1991) *Children and Primary Science*. London: Cassell.
Jarvis, T. (1993) *Teaching Design and Technology in the Primary School*. London: Routledge.
Johnsey, R. (1986) *Problem Solving in School Science*. Hemel Hempstead: Macdonald Education.
Johnsey, R. (1990) *Design and Technology through Problem Solving*. Hemel Hempstead: Simon and Schuster.
Kincaid, D., Rapson, H. and Richards, R. (1983) *Science for Children with Learning Difficulties*. London: Macdonald Educational.
Osborne, J., Black, P., Smith, M. and Meadows, J. (1990) *Primary SPACE Project Research Report: Light*. Liverpool: Liverpool University Press.
Osborne, J., Black, P., Smith, M. and Meadows, J. (1991) *Primary SPACE Project Research Report: Electricity*. Liverpool: Liverpool University Press.
Osborne, R. and Feyberg, P. (1985) *Learning in Science: The Implications of Children's Science*. Auckland: Heinemann.
Shepard, T. (1990) *Education by Design: A Guide to Technology Across the Curriculum*. Cheltenham: Stanley Thornes.

8

Not by bread alone
Developing thinking and skills in the arts

Martin Wenham

Cameo I

Liam is an artist. He stands in front of his easel, on which there is a painting, almost complete. Like many twentieth-century artists, Liam radically simplifies the subjects of his paintings and uses colours quite different from natural ones in order to achieve the effects he wants. His latest painting is of his house, which he has reduced to a green rectangle with a blue border. Smoke from the chimney is shown by a single brush-stroke, curling and changing direction with great boldness, in a delicate pink. Liam stands quite still, head slightly to one side, looking at his painting. He is clearly not satisfied with it and is considering what to do next. Suddenly he picks up a brush, loads it with paint of a vivid red and, with a single, swift twist of his hand and arm, adds a red disc to the centre of his green house. He looks again and nods, satisfied. The painting is finished and can be left to dry. Liam walks away from his easel, across the room . . . to the play area, where his friends are playing shops.

Cameo 2

Mrs Black is lecturing on children's art. Mrs Black is the headteacher of a successful primary school which has a deservedly high reputation for the quality both of the artwork produced by its pupils and the way this is displayed to create a stimulating visual environment. Mrs Black has been invited to share her experience and enthusiasm for children's art with about fifty graduate student teachers and has brought a selection of children's work with her. She speaks fluently and vividly about the creativity of children, their spontaneity and the extraordinarily high standard of the work they achieve.

Mrs Black knows that many of her audience feel unsure about their ability to teach art in the early years primary classroom and her aim is to help them to see that, given appropriate opportunities, children's art has qualities which, all too often, are lacking in the work of adults. She also wants to communicate the idea that art in the primary school can and should be a lot of fun, but most of her audience seem unable to share her enthusiasm or respond to the paintings she has brought for them to look at. Subtle but unmistakable changes in facial expressions and body language show that, far from feeling more confident, the students are confused and becoming more anxious. How, they are asking themselves, can they know whether and when a child is being creative, and what is creativity anyway?

Introduction

Liam is not quite 5 years old, but he is an artist. He knows what he wants to do and how to do it. He uses materials with skill and decision. He concentrates totally on what he is doing and at every stage interrogates his painting visually, to work out how it is progressing and what should be done next. Above all, he knows when to stop. Will Liam still be an artist when he is 15 or 25 years old?

In the second cameo, what is it that leads Mrs Black to think that these paintings and drawings are so good? Above all, how can beginning teachers help their pupils to develop the skills and abilities needed to produce work of a comparable standard?

This chapter sets out to explore ways in which to accept these challenges and begin to answer some of these questions. Firstly, however, we need to look carefully at some ideas about learning and views on the nature of aesthetic activities such as painting, sculpture, music, dance and poetry.

Learning in the arts: inspiration or exploration?

Learning for most people, and especially for children, is most effective when it takes place through the interpretation of first-hand experience (see Chapters 2 and 6 particularly). This is perhaps most clearly seen in science education, where children's knowledge and understanding grow as they investigate changes and use scientific ideas to interpret what they have observed (see Tina Jarvis, Chapter 7). People with only limited experience of art, music, dance and poetry usually regard them as being very different from science but what science and the arts have in common is that, as activities, they are all based on *investigation, exploration and communication* (Swanwick 1988: 88).

A group of people with a range of knowledge, understanding, skills and intentions could, for example, experience and observe a thunderstorm (or a house being built, or a football match) and use their experience as the basis for a wide range of work. The events could be:

- written about in scientific terms;
- made the subject of a drawing or painting;
- used as the basis for a musical composition;
- used as the theme of a poem;
- provide ideas for a dance sequence or drama.

Exploration and investigation in a variety of ways is the basis for theme- and topic-based work in school. It is also the basis for all the so-called 'aesthetic' areas of the curriculum, just as it is the basis of the sciences – and for the same reason. In order to *learn about the world* we live in and its possibilities, including imaginary ones, we have to *experience the real world* at first hand.

Popular views on the arts have been formed by image-makers rather than by artists themselves; by spectators rather than participants. The result is that writing and ideas about painting, sculpture, music and the other arts is based entirely on their products. The processes by which these products are arrived at are largely hidden from spectators, but are of great importance, not only to the artists themselves, but also to the teacher whose aim is to develop the skills and understanding of children. In order to achieve this aim, we need to recognize clearly, and then discard completely, the artificial spectator language with which much writing about the arts has become encumbered. As Sausmarez (1964: 10) put it, education in art 'needs to develop personal enquiry on the basis of practice . . . seeking always the individual solution to each problem'.

The conventional Western view of the artist (in the broad sense) is a spectator's view: artists are seen as specially gifted individuals who are inspired to create original works which express emotions and inner states of being to a degree impossible by any other means. Inspired, creative, original, expressive: this is the language of art dealers' catalogues, popular magazines and weekly columns by second-rate critics, but when we try to find out what it really means the answer is, not much! Anyone participating in the arts, whether as an artist or a teacher, is likely to find views couched in this kind of emotive language very unhelpful, because the ideas it represents neither describe what artists aim at and intend, nor open a way into understanding and effecting learning. The reason for this is simple: *it is quite absurd to set out with the intention of being inspired, creative and original, or of expressing one's innermost feelings and emotions.* These qualities come, if they come at all, as gifts unasked. They can neither be predicted nor commanded and deliberately aiming at them only makes it less likely that they will be achieved. All an artist can do is set out to *investigate* thoroughly and *communicate* clearly. As T.S. Eliot (1969: 31) put it: 'For us, there is only the trying. The rest is not our business.'

How do artists view themselves? Apart from self-styled, solitary geniuses like Wagner, artists of all kinds are, in the main, very social: art, for

Photo 13   Developing thinking and skills in the arts

the most part, is very far from being a solitary activity. Painters and sculptors need galleries, playwrights and composers need performers, even poets need publishers and everybody needs patrons. How do the processes of art look from the inside? Artists do not, in general, see themselves as inspired but rather as people whose knowledge and experience helps them to recognize and be receptive to ideas which can act as the basis for future investigations. As the Swiss painter Paul Klee (1953: 7) put it: 'For the artist, communication with nature remains the most essential condition. The artist is human; himself nature; part of nature within natural space.'

Neither are working artists likely to see themselves as 'creative'; a term much too vague and woolly to be useful to a working professional. Artists investigate the possibilities suggested by ideas and experiences in a thorough and rigorous way. When an able painter works on a landscape, she or he is exploring and interrogating the landscape visually and the painting is, in part, the result of this investigation. Nor do artists, if they are wise, set out with the intention of expressing their inner emotional state. The most deeply-felt poetry, for example, is rarely directly written about the poet. (In writing of time and love, Shakespeare, in Sonnet 65, writes of everything except his real subject until the second half of the last line.)

The work which an artist produces, like a scientific research paper, is a report on progress so far. Work in the arts, like research in the sciences, is undertaken not to express what is already felt or known but to find out (see Bennett 1994: 351). The landscape painter, Kees Beerman, observes that, in his work, he wants to 'make something with a mystery in it – is it a burial mound, is it a monument, is it a sign? I don't know, therefore I make it' (quoted in Grant and Harris 1991: 78). Working in this way requires the artist, like the scientist, to use a balanced combination or synthesis of imagination, reason and skill. The Romantic view of art and artists tends to over-value imagination and undervalue reason, but an artist's view is likely to be very different. The Spanish painter, Goya, for example, observed that 'Imagination deserted by reason creates impossible, useless thoughts. United with reason, imagination is the mother of all art and the source of all its beauty.'

Teaching and learning in the arts

If we can discard the spectator's idea that artists are inspired, creative and expressive, and substitute the participant's view that they are receptive investigators and communicators, effective teaching and learning in all the arts becomes much easier to perceive, understand and practise. Painting, sculpture, crafts, music, drama, dance and poetry can all be seen as ways of exploring, investigating and communicating. To learn to do any of them effectively it is necessary, as in any activity, to learn how to interpret experience. Gaining experience, interpreting it and communicating what emerges involves a bringing-together of knowledge, understanding, skill, imagination and reason. To adapt an old proverb: *Without understanding, experience is blind; but without experience, knowledge and understanding are empty. And without skill, all of them are dumb.*

The need for children (and teachers!) to engage in activities such as drawing, painting, sculpture, weaving, music, dance and the writing of poetry is obvious: actual doing for oneself is the only way to gain first-hand experience. What may not be so obvious is that such first-hand experience cannot, on its own, form the basis of effective learning and teaching. There are two reasons for this. Firstly, we can observe that when undertaken on their own, making, performing and writing may sometimes yield effective results, but in almost all cases this comes about more by good fortune than by design and intention. Only in the context of a growing knowledge and understanding are these activities likely to result in a consistently high and increasing level of achievement.

Secondly, it is only through knowledge and understanding that anyone, whether child or adult, can learn from what they have done and so extend their skill and ability. It is, of course, possible for exceptional individuals to be self-taught and virtually re-invent whole art forms for themselves but it is a woefully inefficient way of learning, and one at which very few people succeed. Teaching and learning in the arts, or indeed any part of the curriculum, can be fully effective only when *first-hand experience is guided* by a teacher who understands the activity sufficiently well to be able to perceive the needs of pupils and satisfy them.

Spectators and participants

The differences between Liam painting and the students' response to Mrs Black's lecture can now be understood more fully. Liam was a participant, engaged in an investigation through painting. What he was investigating is impossible to say exactly but the painting itself shows that he would probably have been learning more about the placing of colours, their balance and relationship to shape, the properties of brushes and paint, their action on paper and the effectiveness of gestures. The evidence that he was actively investigating lies not in the painting he produced but in the way he carried out an intense visual scrutiny and interrogation of it before adding his final touch of contrasting colour. The only unusual thing about the episode was that he knew when the painting was finished and didn't carry on over-painting it until it turned into something resembling river-mud, as 5-year-old children so often do. Liam in fact was learning as every artist learns: by doing *and thinking*, the combination of imagination and reason which Jane Hislam also explores in Chapter 9. As Aaron Scharf (1967: 37) remarked: 'Every good work of art . . . communicates the sense that something in it has been newly tried. The artist is always in training.'

In contrast, Mrs Black was speaking to the students in conventional spectator language about children's painting, although she herself is an accomplished artist-designer. Her attempt to communicate failed because her audience had neither the first-hand experience nor the knowledge of painting which might have given meaning to her interpretations. The students could not connect the ideas and information with their experience and understanding but felt that they should have been able to do so. The result was that the majority ended up feeling inadequate, de-skilled, more baffled by children's art than ever, and so more reluctant to try out art activities for themselves. It is this kind of experience which encourages so many teachers to use the well-known escape hatches labelled 'can't draw' and 'tone deaf' to avoid art and music in the curriculum. Actual inability to co-ordinate vision and hand movement does exist but, like genuine tone-deafness, is very rare. Feelings of inadequacy are almost always the result of a lack of learning and opportunity to gain experience in childhood. The remedy is to work with children as much as possible: to become a participant in their designing, making, performing and writing, rather than a mere spectator (further ideas on the latter are given by Martin Cortazzi in Chapter 11).

Roles and relationships in the arts

At this point it may be useful for you to review the role of the artist as investigator and communicator. To do this, it is necessary to make clear distinctions between three ideas which are often confused:

- the subject of art;
- the object of art;
- the work of art.

The relationship between these ideas is illustrated by Figure 8.1.

The *subject* of art is, simply, what is being investigated: those parts of the world, real or imaginary, which are being explored and enquired into. The *object* of art is the immediate product of artistic activity, and therefore the means by which the artist communicates. This could be a physical object such as a painting or sculpture, written language as in a poem or musical composition, or a performance. The *work* of art is the ultimate product of artistic activity. It is the result of the response of the viewer, listener or reader to the object of art.

The potential of an object of art, which gives it its value, is that it can enable those who experience it to enlarge and develop how they see, hear, feel and understand (see Swanwick 1988: 88). Encountering any object of art under favourable circumstances may mean that a person will never perceive the world in the same way again. So-called 'great' art is simply that which does this in a very profound way for a large number of people but lesser works, including the art of children, can be equally effective in developing understanding and awareness for those who are prepared to set aside prejudice and experience them with an open and receptive mind. It is the work of art, just as it is the work of science and history, to change and develop how people perceive and understand the world and it is a major goal of art education to help pupils enlarge and deepen their knowledge and understanding not only through actual practice but also through positive interaction with objects of art. It may also be noticed that once a viewer, listener or reader begins to interact with objects of art and develop a changed perception through doing so, she or he ceases to be a mere spectator and becomes, at least to some degree, a participant.

As Figure 8.1 also shows, the relationship between an artist and both the subject and object of art is an interactive one. The processes of designing, making, rehearsing, performing, composing or writing are based on enquiry,

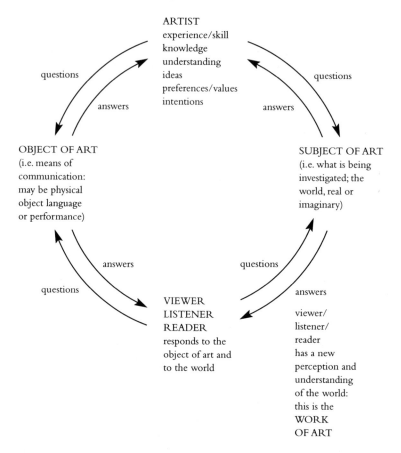

Figure 8.1   Roles and relationships in the arts

on a continual interplay between the artist and the world, the materials and resources used to communicate through the object of art, and of the object itself as it grows and develops. A sculpture, for example, is the result not only of an investigation of forms and their relationships, but also of the physical properties of materials and the methods by which they are shaped. The resulting object of art represents not only the progress of the artist's investigations, but also the degree to which skill, knowledge and understanding have developed as a result of the process.

Routes into education and the arts

Working with the idea that all the arts are based on processes of enquiry and communication makes it much easier for beginning teachers to find effective ways of developing activities and skills. There can be little doubt that in the arts, as in any other part of the curriculum, the most effective teaching is done by participants rather than spectators. Particularly for less confident and experienced teachers, two kinds of activity are likely to be particularly productive:

1 Developing skills and knowledge through first-hand experience.
2 Acquiring the knowledge and understanding needed to interpret the work of children, other artists and oneself.

Developing skills through first-hand experience

If the teacher is already skilled in any activity (playing an instrument, making clothes or producing plays, for example), it is almost always productive to take this skill into the classroom and use it as at least part of the basis of work planned with the class. If the teacher has no developed skills in the arts, it is helpful to participate as much as possible in the children's activities, while still observing how they are working. When a teacher engages in an activity with pupils and openly treats it as a shared learning experience, the children usually see much more value in the work than when the teacher remains aloof. To do this requires a close and positive relationship between the teacher and the class, in which the children are prepared to take at least some responsibility for their own learning (see Janet Moyles discussion in Chapter 2). It may not be possible for student teachers to develop such a relationship but, where it does exist, the role of the teacher as participant can be extraordinarily effective.

Sharing skills, participating in children's work, planning and teaching are all likely to be even more effective when teachers can themselves engage in exploratory learning, for example in evening classes, which in many cases do not involve a long-term commitment. Skills such as simple printmaking and the use of dyes and resist on fabrics, learned on short courses, can often be transferred directly to the classroom and developed further through teaching.

Developing knowledge and understanding

The second kind of activity in which teachers need to engage is an acquisition of the knowledge and understanding needed to interpret and carry forward their own activities and those of their pupils. This knowledge and understanding is likely to be of three kinds:

• a practical knowledge of materials and equipment;
• an understanding of the elements of an activity and of how these are combined into patterns;
• an appreciation of the objects produced by a range of artists, cultures and periods.

Knowledge of materials and equipment
Knowledge of this kind, which both grows out of and informs the development and sharing of skills, is needed mainly in art and music. In order to teach effectively, teachers need a first-hand, practical knowledge of the properties and potential of the materials and equipment used in the activities undertaken. In art, these would include paper, paint, pencils, crayons and pastels; brushes, sponges and other implements for applying liquid colour; dyes, fabrics, threads and resists; simple sticks and blocks for printing; card, glue and other materials for construction; clay, playdough and mod-roc for modelling, together with simple equipment for using them. In music, teachers need to be acquainted with as wide a range of simple instruments as possible, particularly percussion both tuned and untuned, concentrating on the quality and variety of sounds which each instrument can produce.

In both areas, a great deal of knowledge can be gained simply through exploratory play (see Chapter 6), but for adults especially, learning is likely to be much more efficient if a systematic investigation of properties is undertaken. What, for example, are the properties of ready-mixed, water-based paint on off-white sugar paper? These can be investigated by painting a square 10×10cm on a large, flat sheet with unmixed and undiluted paint, then repeating this with increasing amounts of water added. The procedure can be repeated with paper on a slope, mixed colours and with colours allowed to mix on the paper. Such investigations not only yield a lot of information about colour, texture and the use of paint, but also are likely to suggest activities in which children can productively engage.

Investigations of musical instruments are much easier if they are undertaken in small groups, because it is often impossible to hear what a listener hears when playing an instrument oneself. One useful strategy is to play all the available instruments in pairs, using different rhythms, to hear how their sounds blend or contrast with one another. This will show at least some of the possibilities for using them in different combinations. Here again, the results not only enable teachers to use instruments with children more confidently because the sound quality of each is known or can be predicted, but also suggests ideas for such activities such as sound-trails, accompanying songs or providing rhythms for dance. The experience and learning are likely to be even more productive when teachers and children make instruments for themselves (see, for example, Sawyer 1977).

Elements and the development of pattern
In activities such as art, music, poetry and dance, the results of investigations are communicated in characteristic ways. In order to understand what is being communicated, it is necessary to be able to 'read' objects of art such as paintings and sculptures, performances in music, dance and drama, and the language of poetry. In the visual arts this ability is given the special name of 'visual literacy'. Although teachers and children need to develop the same kind of ability in all the arts if teaching and learning are to be

Photo 14   Pattern is one element in arts education

effective, attention is concentrated here on a basic understanding of the visual arts and music, as the areas with which you are most likely to be concerned.

If communication in the arts is analysed, it is found that it can be understood in terms of patterns, forms and structures, which are built up and elaborated from elements which, as their name suggests, cannot be reduced to simpler component parts. For example, the visual elements into which a painting, drawing or graphic design can be analysed are:

Colour: the quality of light (resulting from its frequency or wavelength);
Tone: how light or dark a line or shape appears;
Line: a mark having length and direction, but (theoretically) no width (Figure 8.2a);
Shape: an area distinguished from what is adjacent to it by a boundary (Figure 8.2b).

To these, some observers would add:

Space: the empty area or 'ground' which contrasts with the 'figure' placed on it.

Colour and tone form a pair of related elements, as do line and shape. Combining one or more elements from each pair makes it possible to build

a. Lines have length and direction; which may remain the same (straight line) or change in a variety of ways.

b. Shapes may be bounded by lines, or by edges (in this case, of tone).

c. Textures may be built up from tone (or colour) combined with line, or shape, or both.

d: Patterns of lines, and of shapes bounded by lines, with texture added.

Figure 8.2 Some visual elements

up a quality of surface known as texture (Figure 8.2c). Any of the visual elements, whether combined to form texture or not, may be arranged to form pattern. Pattern in the visual arts is rather different from pattern in the mathematical sense, which is simply any arrangement having some degree of order. To an artist or designer, 'pattern' usually means repetitive pattern (see Proctor 1990), in which a component or motif, built up from visual elements, is repeated in a more or less predictable and regular way (Figure 8.2d).

Once visual elements can be identified, it is possible to begin an appraisal not only of paintings, drawings and prints but also of one's whole visual environment, and to begin helping children to see in the same way. The aim of this activity is firstly, to be able to identify which visual elements, together with texture and pattern, are most prominent in a particular piece of work. Having identified these, it is usually possible to begin observing how these interact with each other and the subject (see Itten 1975; Sausmarez 1964). How does the placing of colours make them interact, for example, and how far do they resemble the actual colour of the subject, if this is real? In doing this, resource packs (such as Clement and Page 1992d) can be useful, but the discussions in them tend to be cultural and thematic (see below) rather than analytical, whereas both approaches are needed in order to understand the visual arts.

In sculpture, another element, that of *form,* has to be added. Form is three-dimensional, whereas shape is two-dimensional. The texture of a sculptural surface may appeal to touch, as well as sight, and tone (as shadow) may assume added importance, but colour, line and shape may not contribute at all. It is always important to explore sculptural objects from different directions and observe how the elements interact to create an overall effect as one moves in relation to the object. This is as true of a small sculpture by a child as it is of a large and famous one.

In music and dance, patterns are built up out of elements in an analogous way, but with an important difference: the patterns are perceived in a sequence through *time.* In music the elements are:

Pitch: how high or low a sound is;
Duration: how long it lasts;
Dynamics: how loud or soft it is, and whether this changes;
Timbre: the distinctive quality of different instruments, voices and ways of playing or singing.

These elements may be variously combined to form musical patterns such as:

Rhythm: a repeated pattern of sound and silence;
Tempo: how fast or slowly the rhythmic pattern is repeated, and whether this changes;
Melody: a sequence of sounds with varying pitch and/or duration.

Musical patterns may be combined to form more complex structures, such as the beginning, middle and end of a piece, or the verses of a song. In dance, the elements of movement can similarly be thought of as being combined into more complex patterns and structures (Laban 1956).

As in developing skills and knowledge of materials, first-hand experience is essential when seeking to identify elements and perceive how these are being combined into patterns and structures. It is useful to think of elements and patterns as 'advance organizers': ideas which can direct attention and promote observation, but effective learning can be achieved only when they are used to interpret observations of children and their activities in the classroom. Once the teacher has developed a measure of confidence in observation and interpretation in terms of elements and patterns, children can usefully be introduced to these ideas and encouraged to use them in evaluating and communicating about their own work and environment.

Learning from the work of others
The need to learn from the work of other artists arises because all the arts are social activities, and artists rarely work in isolation. Artists are communicators who work within a tradition, even though many attempt to tear tradition down and some, like Picasso, succeed, although in doing so they only establish a new 'tradition' to replace the old. Artists can communicate only with those who understand the conventions within which they work: the 'rules' of the artistic 'game'. If children and teachers are to become effective participants in the arts, it is essential that they study objects of art from their own and other cultures in such a way that the knowledge and understanding they develop informs their own activity and helps them to evaluate it and develop it further (see Morgan 1985: 93–9, for some useful strategies).

Objects of art in any medium may please us when we know nothing of their origins, but they are not self-explanatory. We can open effective communication with them only when we understand at least something of the societies and conditions in which they were produced, as well as the personalities, beliefs and intentions of those who made them. There are two main ways in which this can be done, and ideally both should be used:

1 Studying acknowledged masterpieces with the help of expert critical commentary, which in recent years has been made easier by the availability of very high quality sound recordings and reproductions of paintings with detailed notes (see, for example, Clement and Page 1992d). It should be appreciated, however, that it is impossible adequately to reproduce sculpture in flat images and that this art-form has to be experienced at first hand to be effective.
2 By personal encounter: music, drama, poetry and storytelling have for many years been taken into schools by professional performers, many of whom not only welcome children's questions but also their participation, sharing with them the experience of performance. Local crafts people and visual artists can also provide, through day visits or residencies, opportunities for children to observe and question working artists and to work alongside or in collaboration with them. This is an experience which is likely to be as rewarding and thought-provoking for the artist as it is for the children and teachers.

Conclusion

Certainly, as a teacher, you will never cease to learn from and with the children.

Questions

1 How would you respond to Liam's artistry? What are your perceptions of yourself as an 'artist' in any medium?
2 What are your perceptions of yourself as an 'artist' in any medium?
3 From where and under what experiences have these perceptions evolved?
4 What will you need to consider in order to begin to explore elements of the arts with children with whom you will teach and learn?
5 What will you need to consider and develop within yourself in order to begin to explore elements of the arts with children with whom you will teach and learn?

References and further reading

Bennett, A. (1994) *Writing Home*. London: Faber.
Clement, R. and Page, S. (1992a) *Principles and Practice in Art*. Harlow: Oliver and Boyd.
Clement, R. and Page, S. (1992b) *Investigating and Marking in Art*. Harlow: Oliver and Boyd.
Clement, R. and Page, S. (1992c) *Knowledge and Understanding in Art*. Harlow: Oliver and Boyd.
Clement, R. and Page, S. (1992d) *Picture Resource Pack and Teacher's Book*. Harlow: Oliver and Boyd.
Eliot, T.S. (1969) *Four Quartets*. London: Faber.
Grant, B. and Harris, P. (1991) *The Grizedale Experience*. Edinburgh: Canondale Press.
Itten, J. (1975) *Design and Form: the Basic Course at the Bauhaus*. London: Thames and Hudson.
Klee, P. (1953) *Pedagogical Sketchbook*, trans. Sibyl Moholy-Nagy. London: Faber.
Laban, R. (1956) *Principles of Dance and Movement Notation*. London: MacDonald and Evans.
Morgan, M. (ed.) (1985) *Art in the First Years of Schooling*. Suffolk County Council Education Committee.
Proctor, R.M. (1990) *Principles of Pattern Design*. New York: Dover.
Sausmarez, M. de (1964) *Basic Design: the Dynamics of Visual Form*. London: Studio Vista.
Sawyer, D. (1977) *Vibrations: Making Unorthodox Musical Instruments*. Cambridge: Cambridge University Press.
Scharf, A. (1967) *Geoffrey Ireland; Poet with a Camera*. London: Lund Humphries.
Swanwick, K. (1988) *Music, Mind and Education*. London: Routledge.

9

A story in your head
Developing oracy and imaginative skills in children through storytelling

Jane Hislam

Cameo I

Craig sat with his mouth wide open and his eyes wider still. When the teacher finished telling the story there was a small silence and then Craig drew in his breath and asked: 'How did you *do* that?'.

Teacher: 'Do what?'
Craig: 'Say it without a book. Where did it *come* from?'
Teacher: 'Where do you think it came from?'
Craig: 'From out your head?'

Cameo 2

A Year R class are clustered around professional storyteller, Roberto Lagnado, as he tells them an Aladdin-like story. When he had finished a child asked: 'Is there a book in your head?' (see Figure 9.1).

Cameo 3

Joe, aged 4 years, is playing alone in his sandpit at home with a pile of bricks, some Playpeople, an upturned wastepaper basket and a toy fire engine with a ladder. The game is about a wolf who wants to eat people, so the people decide to put him on a roof until he can be trusted to come down. Joe narrates as he plays:

We can get rid of him. How will we get him down? They pushed the button and the ladder lowered. Then out came the hose, right through the holes. He shouted I promise I will not eat anyone. But the people would not listen they put their hands over their ears. Right if you promise never to eat anyone we will let you down. They heard the engine coming neee-naaa-neee-naaa-neee-naaaa.

Figure 9.1 'The man with the book in his head'

Introduction

Many teachers, when first telling stories to a class, remark on the fact that children expect stories to come from books and are surprised when they do not. This is quite understandable since, in many children's experiences, the word 'story' is often closely related to the written word.

In the first two cameos there *was* no book and the children were at first mystified and then intrigued. Previously, whenever teachers told them to gather round for a story, a book appeared. In these situations the teacher acts as mediator for the writer who is the creator of the story. The writer-storyteller is absent, almost invariably an adult and probably regarded as someone with special and creative gifts.

In cameo 3, Joe shows that even the youngest children are capable of producing imaginative commentaries to accompany their play. His narratives form part of an imaginary world which is already rich with images

Photo 15   Is there a book in your head?

from books, television and his own life experiences. The fact that he has already heard many stories read and told has almost certainly assisted in the process of his own story making (Wells 1986).

This chapter explores ways in which primary children's imaginative powers can be valued and expressed through storytelling. Beginning with considering the experience of listening to oral stories and their sources, it then moves on to examine the role of imagination, language play and children's talk. The teacher's role in this process is crucial. If children are to be encouraged and challenged imaginatively and linguistically, then teachers have to show them the way. The model provided by the teacher, therefore, constitutes the second main focus and includes storytelling work-shops, using poetry and rhyme and how stories can be chosen. Finally, I examine the children's involvement as storytellers.

The experience of listening to an oral story

Craig's teacher described him as 'not easily motivated'. At story time Craig would often work his way outwards from the story circle to the edge of the room where he proceeded to see how many pencils he could snap or how quickly he could destroy Christopher's 'best ever' model. But, on this occasion, Craig sat absolutely still and 'spell-bound', as is often said about the experience of storytelling. It seemed that, for those few minutes, he had entered the world of the story itself.

The story he had heard the teacher tell was 'Sapsorrow' (a version of Cinderella). Craig was hooked from the moment the teacher, with no book in sight, began:

> There was once a king whose wife had died. He had three daughters. Two were bad. One was good.

What is more, Craig was able to hold the story so clearly in his mind that when, several days later, he was invited to retell a story of his own choice he picked this one. With an uncharacteristic degree of accuracy, he elaborated on the story using elements of his own. He also talked about the story with confidence to his teacher and then to his 'talk partner'. He even told the story at home.

Why this story had such an effect on Craig, it is impossible to know. The story experience is highly personal and individual. Perhaps traditional fairy and folk stories have lasted so long precisely because they *do* engage our imaginations and emotions so powerfully. Reading a story aloud can also create a powerful imaginative experience, but the fact that this story was *told* rather than *read* seems to have played an important part in its effect on the listener. This is an experience worth creating as frequently as possible in the classroom.

Story sources and story links

Craig was impressed that the story just seemed to come from nowhere, 'from out your head'. The particular retelling of this story, whilst personal and unique in that moment, was far from the work of an individual imagination. The teacher acknowledged and talked explicitly to the children about how her version of the story stood alongside countless others across time and other countries. The teacher read and told them other stories with similar themes and familiar objects – rings, shoes, rags to riches, joy to sorrow and back again. She brought in books and told more stories so that the children began to appreciate that there are versions of the Cinderella story in oral and written form right around the world.

In cameo 3, Joe's story, whilst unique and spontaneous, also draws on a range of linguistic and literary influences. The language and imagery of television were apparent, especially in the different voices and intonation which he used to enact the story. It was also obvious that he had listened to many stories read and told from the language he chose to use, for example, 'But the people would not listen. They covered their ears.'

Joe's story arose without the involvement of adults. When we create an imaginative experience for children in the classroom and invite children to enter a story, we are inviting them to draw on all the experiences and language which connect and relate to it, including all the other stories they may know. The effect can be dramatic as the following experience demonstrates.

In my first year of teaching, I told part of the story of Sir Gawain and the Green Knight from the Arthurian legend, not because I had any particular appreciation of the value of oral storytelling, but because I could not find a suitable version of the story to read to my class. I remember feeling terrified that I would forget the story and also that the children would think it an odd thing for me to do. There was also a sense of vulnerability as I sat there with no book between me and the children. It turned out to be a risk worth taking! Somehow, the story itself seemed to take over. Strong visual memories of all the King Arthur stories I had read and heard came flooding back and my own imagination was stirred in a profound way. I began to recognize that stories can act on the imagination in ways that are forever remembered, something that I already knew but had not consciously transferred to my teaching. I had gained an insight into the powerful role teachers can play in that process.

The role of imagination

Words can seriously affect your heart. (source unknown)

These moments when the story 'takes over' give great shared pleasure to children and adults alike. The storyteller and the listeners act together to create the story: for each participant the story takes shape in an unique way. This must be why Bob Barton (1986) talks about the active involvement of the listeners. It is at these times, that we are reminded of the power that we hold as teacher-storytellers. When children listen to a story with eyes open wide, they experience the fact that language has the power to make the impossible happen.

Not only must we choose stories with care but we must encourage children to feel that they are active participants in the imaginative process. If you are prepared to take the risk and tell a story without the aid of a book there will inevitably be rich rewards. When we tell stories we are reminded that language can have magical as well as practical purposes and that language learning can be fun at the same time as it is purposeful. Small children already know this as they practise and experiment with language in their play. By encouraging children to re-create stories orally after hearing them told, teachers are often surprised at how creative they can be and how much imagination some children express. Paley (1981) explains why retelling stories so often allows children to express themselves more fluently than normal. She argues that this is partly because of the dependability of the story and partly because of the fully formed nature of the language in which the story has already been heard. Retelling stories seems to release children to put language together in ways which are often remarkable in their complexity and vitality, using structures, vocabulary and voice which are much extended from normal usage in the classroom. Some children who are reserved and even silent in other contexts have been observed to become animated and competent language users in storytelling (Aylwin 1992).

Stories from books, pictures and oral sources can provide daily enrichment for the imagination but these need to be chosen with attention to quality of the story itself. Too often, stories are seen as useful pieces of resource material which can be used to stimulate interest or lead into classroom topics – often quite separate from the central themes of the story and only tangentially or superficially connected with the emotional core of the story. To overlook the imaginative power of the story itself is to deny that very aspect which children will most naturally want to explore and reflect upon.

Playing with language

Young children are naturally inventive with spoken language in their play. Very young children who have heard stories told and read, demonstrate strong evidence of narrative competences. Echoes of the stories they have experienced appear in their play and children try out language in new ways and take risks with language which they would not do in routine settings. This symbolic, playful use of language draws on all kinds of experiences, including stories and advertising jingles on television, nursery rhymes and playground games, as well as their own first-hand experiences. Sadly, at school, there is often such a strong emphasis on the use of conventional language that these opportunities for language play can be overlooked or squeezed out. It is important for teachers, parents and other adults to continue to allow children scope in their searching for new ways of expressing early experiences through experimenting and playing (as Janet Moyles discusses in Chapter 6).

The status of talk

Many writers (Booth and Thornley-Hall 1991) recently have emphasized the importance of developing children's oral skills in the context of collaborative work. Whilst many thousands of classroom hours have been given to children writing, their talk has traditionally been given lower status, with less time spent organizing for talk to happen and less thought given to how children develop as competent users of spoken language. The National Oracy Project (1987–93) has had an important role in highlighting talk and giving practical examples of ways in which teachers could extend the talk repertoire in the classroom. Developing children's spoken language is now recognized as an important part of the curriculum with widespread recognition that *talk is central to learning*. It is important to provide children with plenty of opportunities to work in pairs and small groups, exploring and retelling stories and exchanging personal anecdotes. In this way they will recognize that you value their talk. They will be encouraged to respond to each other building personal confidence and increasing their linguistic competence as speakers and listeners.

Teacher as model

There are countless practical ways in which you, the teacher, can create a positive learning model for young children in the classroom:

- Make apparent your own pleasure in the written and spoken word and talk to children about the images which language creates for you.
- Share with the children through reading aloud, storytelling, drama and language play a wide variety of imaginative genres. In your first years as a teacher, this may involve you in consciously extending your own repertoire of stories by browsing in book shops and libraries, reading, listening to storytellers and identifying the kinds of texts that give you special pleasure.

Your first step has to be to rekindle in yourself that freshness of enthusiasm which young children experience when they first encounter stories and poems which are meaningful for them. This may involve you in deliberately remembering your own childhood experiences, or you may have to make a fresh start if these memories are not particularly positive ones for you. Many student teachers have discovered their delight in children's books quite late in life! Share your enthusiasm by recounting personal childhood memories, reading or reciting favourite pieces of poetry, or simply talking with the children about the things you like best. Above all, children need as much opportunity as possible to hear you reading aloud and telling stories with pleasure and increasing skill. In making a beginning, be prepared to take some risks, experiment and spend time finding the stories that you like yourself since these will always be the ones which will work best for you. By this means you are providing opportunities for children to respond to a rich variety of language and literature and helping them become aware of their part in creating stories both as listeners and tellers. As Bob Barton (1986: 9) says:

> Far from being passive, the listener is extremely busy participating in the recreation of the story; for a successful listener needs to be a storyteller too. And this becomes an important reason for presenting stories out loud to children: it helps them to comprehend the role they are expected to play in the story game.

Being a positive model for children also means recognizing and acknowledging that the imagination is not a commodity which some children lack but a human quality which we all possess and which can be strengthened and enriched in a safe learning environment. By engaging children's minds through story and creating a language context in which children can talk and play imaginatively, even those children whose imaginations may have already become dulled, fearful or obsessive (Mellon 1992) can experience moments when the imagination gives personal confidence to their lives. In the face of a barrage of images which overwhelm children through different media and the world around them you may feel that there is a greater need than ever for children to experience oral stories and poems which reaffirm the value of their *own* imaginative powers and which encourage them to express their thoughts and feelings in words.

A storytelling workshop

Storytelling is probably the most comfortable and accessible way of promoting children's meaningful talk in the classroom. Apart from anything else, it is cheap on resources, is highly flexible and can take place practically anywhere. Key features of storytelling are:

• it is a personal and individual act of imagination;
• it is essentially social and participative;
• it works for all age groups.

Storytelling can be particularly valuable in the bilingual classroom. The universal qualities of story mean that cultural traditions from home and school can be brought together on an equal basis. Storytelling provides a natural context for the use of home languages. Stories with repeating patterns, call and response, and active participation will be particularly valuable additions to the bilingual classroom repertoire.

For all children, stories immediately provide a shared and generally pleasurable experience, allowing them to talk in a non-threatening way about experiences, draw on aspects of their own lives and respond individually to the story. The context of the story should enable everyone's contribution to be acceptable. Teachers should resist a prescriptive approach to stories and be open to children's own responses. The experience of making a story your own, by thinking about it, discussing it, picturing it in your mind is part of what invests the story with imaginative life and is what Bob Barton (1991: 42) calls 'communal wondering' which 'encourages children to discover that the heart of storytelling lies in the ability to project oneself imaginatively into the story and to determine what is important about the story for oneself'.

A good starting point is to develop a small repertoire of short stories, rhymes and games, as well as songs.

Poetry and rhyme

One for sorrow. Two for joy. Three for a girl. And four for a boy . . .

Although it is undoubtedly true that the oral tradition in this country is weaker than it once was, it continues to live strongly through songs, rhymes and sayings, many of which link with memories of early childhood. There may be favourite family stories told on long journeys or rhymes and songs at bathtime. My grandfather always used to exclaim the rhyme above with great joy whenever we saw magpies on our visits to the country; now, when magpies arrive in my city garden, I repeat the words to my daughter so the saying passes from one generation to the next as it has in many other families. It is both personal and communal, a tradition which is culturally specific but also similar to many others across the world. Nowadays television acts as the carrier for many of these sayings, rhymes and songs, and children will probably need little encouragement to share some of these with you.

Try trawling back through your personal repertoire to see how evocative people, places and past events in your life can be. It is likely to be personally pleasurable as well as professionally useful to find ways to link these memories with children's present-day experiences. This may be a good place for you to start without a book because these rhymes are easily memorable and will act as an invitation for children to tell you their own.

Choosing stories to tell

Move from personal stories into short tales that you already know quite well. The traditional fairy tales make good choices for two reasons:

1 Their familiarity will help you avoid the trap of feeling you have to memorize the story. Try reading several different versions and allow your own preferred way to emerge, perhaps the version you had read to you or heard told as a child.
2 Traditional tales lend themselves particularly well to oral retellings, the way they have been transmitted for centuries before printing began. Also, the archetypal nature of the stories leaves freedom to change and reinterpret parts without damaging the basic story fabric. As you think about the story, picture it in your mind, imagine the woods, the little house, the chairs and tables. Think about the shape of the story rather like humming a tune, or tracing the outline of a picture with your finger. Then have a go!

A student teacher told her version of 'Stone Soup' during her first teaching experience. Although she was very nervous beforehand, she found that she was carried along by the simple structure of the story and the children's keen participation. When they realized she was going to *tell* them the story she quickly gained their attention. She involved the children by asking them to come and 'throw' a potato, a leek, some salt into the pretend cooking pot. Afterwards she told me how the process of telling the story helped her make the story her own. This is often the experience of storytellers. She also found that the children's participation in the story led to a rich discussion of stories they knew, drawn from different cultural backgrounds. As Paley (1981: 122) suggests: 'Fairy tales stimulate the children's imagination in a way that enlarges the vocabulary, extends narrative skills and encourages new ideas.'

Once you have gained some confidence, actively work at developing a personal story repertoire and start looking for good sources of stories. Often this will be from written collections. My favourites at the moment include Pie Corbett's *Tales, Myths and Legends* and Mary Medlicott's *Time for Telling*. I especially like these collections because they are firmly rooted in an oral culture, being the written versions of traditional stories told by contemporary storytellers.

As storytelling becomes more popular amongst adults as well as children, there are increased opportunities to hear professional storytellers at work, many of whom are available to work in school. From them you can not only learn new stories but also observe different storytelling styles and techniques and gain a greater awareness of the way you want to tell stories. Storytelling is, first and foremost, an act of communication but it is also a performance art and practice will improve your ability to 'perform' even at a very informal level.

Involving children as storytellers

Right from the start of your storytelling programme you can encourage children to participate in the stories you tell and organize them to tell stories to each other. Some examples follow. Many such ideas are developed in books about storytelling and I would especially recommend any book by Bob Barton as well as the National Oracy Project book entitled *Common Bonds*.

1 Get them to retell the story they have just heard in pairs (talk partners, NOP 1992) or tell each other personal stories.
2 Involve a large number of children in the early stages through *circle stories* where each child in the circle takes it in turns to add a piece to the story.
3 To follow up a storytelling session, children can be asked occasionally to:
   • write or draw main events of story;
   • arrange the main events of the story in a time line;
   • use puppets to act out the story;
   • paint feelings and relate these to particular parts of story;
   • make comic strips;
   • develop a storyboard (see Figure 9.2 as an example from a Year 3 child)
   • retell it in different ways;
   • write their version of the story.
4 Create for children small story places or bays which are separated in some way from the main areas of the classroom. (June Peters, a storyteller from London, created the idea of 'story tents'. Children who were normally shy and unwilling to participate demonstrated their storytelling ability in their own quiet place behind a makeshift curtain. Such stories can sometimes be tape-recorded and listened to later.)
5 Artefacts can be used as stimuli for the invention of stories or to bring to mind story themes. Children can work in pairs to develop a story which they then tell to a different pair.

wolf	2 Nasty Wolf	3 wolf B·H·D	4 the pig@	5 But the
3 Pigs	Freezt.	P.g.S	Gets Stot	wolf kiiier
Leav Home	S.w.B	Pig ring on	By the	was the
Bild house		teliphon	wolf kiiler	cat eoter
				fat and
				cat ecter
				.mr tirRoller

S.W.B. = straw, wood, bricks   B.H.D = Blows house down

Figure 9.2

Creating a story collaboratively

After a storytelling session at college using artefacts, a student teacher decided to use a 'storybag' with a Year 2 class. Each time he told a story he would begin by drawing an object from the bag – a ring, a shoe, a mirror. (There was unanimous recognition of what the story was going to be the day five beans were pulled out of the storybag!) Later, he gave a set of storybags to the children who, in pairs, invented their own stories using the objects they found inside: powerful symbols – rings, bottles, containers of all kinds, mirrors and locks of hair. There may be surprises in children's responses for adults who have certain preconceived and culturally-based ideas about the story objects. The children make their own associations: a storybag which contained three objects – a mirror, a brush, and a shell – gave rise to a story in which the shell sent messages to Power Rangers, the mirror was a strong ray deflector and the brush a secret weapon!

On another occasion the student teacher asked the class how they would feel about making up a story together from the storybag. The children looked a little bewildered at first and Gurjit asked whether it would come from *everyone's* head. Michael looked around at the group and then said: I suppose really we could make up stories about anything if we wanted to! The student felt enormously encouraged at this public recognition of the potentially limitless possibilities of the creative imagination. He was aware of how difficult it often is for children to *write* a story 'out of their heads' and wanted to see whether the collaborative making of an oral story would provide a secure context in which everyone's ideas could be pooled. Out of the bag he drew a tiny remnant of faded carpet and began: 'What if . . . this carpet were a magic carpet . . . and carried us out of the class-room, above the school, hovered over Sainsbury's, began to glide across the city . . .'.

He began the story, taking the main narrative role himself and stopping at points in the story where decisions about characters, places and events could be offered by the children. It was therefore quite distinctly a piece of storytelling and not drama or role play, since the narrative voice remained an essential feature of the story throughout. The carpet took them over the land to the coast and Skegness, across the sea (some interesting insights along the way about the children's geographical understanding!) and at last to a giant's castle where they were deposited at the door. There was a feeling of high expectation about what was behind that door even though not a single person, at that point, appeared to have decided on what it might be. The story had taken on a life and direction of its own, and seemed almost tangibly to fill the circle of space between the children. Michael became rather agitated and the teacher decided to use his authority as main narrator to inject lightness and humour into the telling and so reduce the suspense. Not one child asked how it could be that everyone fitted on the carpet, or expressed any scepticism about the storyline or about the process of creating the story itself. Their story, like the magic carpet, had succeeded for those few moments in transporting them to other places and times in their imaginations.

For the teacher the magic carpet was rather a clichéd image. However, in the collaborative creation of the story, his own imagination seemed to draw on pictures from a variety of sources. Half-remembered picture books, a version of the Arabian Nights perhaps, a carpet hanging in an expensive store, the sensation of flying from childhood dreams, the captivating moment from book and film when the Snowman and the small boy rise above house and field. This amounted to a distillation of experiences from real life, books, television and dreams. For each participant child, the images would, of course, be different. The imagination grows from direct experiences of our senses but crucially too from the received experience of literature and from hearing others talk and describe what they hear and see.

As the young child learns more about the world and its possibilities through play, so we gain greater understanding of ourselves and our feelings through stories. We make sense of new kinds of information, imagination leading us into new possibilities. Children also grow with a need to express themselves imaginatively and, as teachers, we can gain much by providing them with the opportunities to do so.

In conclusion

What you can do personally:

- think back over your own childhood experiences of story and what gave you particular pleasure;
- build up your story repertoire starting with personal stories, well-known traditional tales and broaden your range to include stories of different kinds and from different cultures;
- seek opportunities to hear storytellers.

What you can do in the classroom:

- provide opportunities for children to hear lots of stories;
- talk about stories;
- give children time to talk to each other in pairs and small groups and to retell stories;
- be an attentive listener;
- provide audiences who value children's talk;
- recognize and acknowledge relevant sources of imaginative material for children (e.g. television, family stories, stories from different cultural backgrounds);
- if possible, invite in professional storytellers to work with the children.

References and further reading

Aylwin, T. (1992) Retelling stories in school, in P. Pinsent (ed.) *Language, Culture and Young Children*. London: David Fulton.
Barton, B. (1986) *Tell me Another: Storytelling and Reading Aloud at Home, at School and in the Community*. Ontario, Canada: Pembroke Publishers.
Barton, B. (1991) Bringing the story to life, in D. Booth and C. Thornley-Hall, *The Talk Curriculum*. Ontario, Canada: Pembroke Publishers.
Booth, D. and Thornley-Hall, C. (1991) *The Talk Curriculum*. Ontario, Canada: Pembroke Publishers.
Colwell, E. (1991) *Storytelling*. South Woodchester: Thimble Press.
Corbett, P. and Moses, B. (1991) *My Grandmother's Motorbike: Story Writing in the Primary School*. Oxford: Oxford University Press.
Corbett, P. (1993) *Tales, Myths and Legends*. Leamington Spa: Scholastic Publications.
Medlicott, M. (1991) *Time for Telling: a Collection of Stories from around the World*. London: Kingfisher.
Mellon, N. (1992) *Storytelling and the Art of the Imagination*. Massachusetts: Element Books.
Minghella, A. (1988) *The Storyteller*. London: Boxtree Press.
National Oracy Project (1992) *Common Bonds: Storytelling in the Classroom*. London: Hodder and Stoughton.
Paley, V.G. (1981) *Wally's Stories*. Cambridge, Mass: Harvard University Press.
Rosen, B. (1988) *And None Of It Was Nonsense: The Power of Storytelling in School*. London: Mary Glasgow.
Wells, G. (1986) *The Meaning Makers*. Sevenoaks: Hodder and Stoughton.

Let's co-operate!
Developing children's social skills
in the classroom

□ **Sylvia McNamara**

□ **Cameo 1**

Some Year 1 children are learning through play in the infant corridor of a primary school. They have formed into clusters around particular activities as is usual. Within each cluster of children are some 'best friend' pairings. A group of girls are playing with play-dough wearing aprons. There is a reluctance among a certain group of boys to don aprons and choose 'messy play'. This group of boys are playing with some toy cars, trucks and a ramp construction they have made, linking with the science work they have done earlier on 'forces'. One girl tiring of the play-dough walks over towards the 'boys' group. As she comes near one boy calls out 'Go away! We don't want girls here! Anyway you're too fat to play with us.' He and his friends giggle. The girl blushes, turns away and sits on her own in the reading corner.

□ **Cameo 2**

A group of Year 5–6 children are organized into random groups of five or six people. They are then set the task of building a platform from newspaper strong enough to take the weight of a book. This has been a science SAT task for KS1 and is being used to see how well the children in the groups co-operate with each other, and whether they can do the task. The children and task are put on video. No group completes the task but the videos are played back to the children, who immediately realize, as one child puts it, that 'everyone was talking and no-one was listening' – an accurate summary of what happened. In one group a child crawled under the table and was ignored by the rest, in many groups useful suggestions were repeated several times by individual children but had been ignored by the rest. In most groups there had been serious squabbles over the sticky tape.

Cameo 3
A group of Year 3–4 children working in random groups of five are set the task of designing their own Saxon house and devising a name for it in runes. When observed they are seen to be systematically including everyone in the group by name, inviting contributions from everyone, and are heard to make comments like: 'You haven't said much Rema – what do you think?' and 'That's a good idea, Mark'. When one child with behavioural difficulties threatens to withdraw from the group, they are all involved in coaxing her back. 'It won't be any good without you, Katie' and 'Don't go mardy on us, Katie' and even 'Katie, you know we need to work together'.

Introduction

What makes children behave as they do towards one another? Do we just accept it and shrug it off as 'children being children'? The view taken in this chapter is that all children, regardless of age, should be *taught* the social skills needed to work with one another in the classroom, and that such skills need to be included throughout the day-to-day curriculum not as a separate aspect.

From my own and other practising teachers' evidence, the skills rarely appear to be taught in an explicit and systematic way often because teachers do not know how to. What I will set out to show is that the benefits to everyone of actually *teaching* children the requisite skills are enormous. The acquisition of these skills means that children are less likely to need adult help in dealing with issues loosely termed as 'discipline'. Such skills help the children to:

- manage their own friendship squabbles;
- resolve more major conflicts themselves;
- work more independently of the teacher by utilizing the skills, strengths and knowledge of the other children in the class;
- work effectively and co-operatively in problem-solving groups.

The biggest challenge for you in engaging in this work is to acquire the skills yourself! This is necessary both to model the skills and to adapt the ideas offered in this chapter. Adaptation requires an understanding of the processes behind the skills: once you have a conceptual understanding of the theory you will be able to look at the ideas in the books referenced at the end of the chapter that both teach the skills and help implement the curriculum. Incorporating the social skills training into activity planning should be a natural consequence, as will be an idea of what to do if things do not go according to plan – which is not to blame the children!

This chapter aims to help you consider the means by which you can help children to co-operate more effectively in the primary classroom. All the time you read, try to relate the ideas about children to yourself and your experiences of situations in which you co-operate with others. Firstly, however, we return to the examples of interactions given in the earlier cameos.

Setting appropriate attitudes for learning

What can be seen in the first of these cameo portraits is the way in which some children can be excluded by other's thoughtless, hurtful comments. If these children are already feeling inadequate at school work then such feedback will confirm their sense of low *self-esteem*. Self-esteem is the sense of worth that children feel about themselves and is the gap between their 'ideal' self and their perceived current performance, explained more fully later in this chapter. One of the important benefits of work on social skills is that it encourages children to think about how they feel about themselves.

A classroom where social skills training is happening in a systematic and organized way allows discussion about how we feel when others make hurtful comments. This practice will become 'normal' and what will probably emerge during such discussions is both the sense of low self-esteem that the perpetrators of such comments have themselves (such as the boy in the first cameo) and the prejudices they hold, for example about 'girls work and play' as opposed to 'boys work and play'. In such classrooms it will not be uncommon for a boy in the group to say, 'Oh come on, Dean. You're only saying that because you got a low mark in your spelling test. You know it's not fair to say she's fat.'

In the second cameo there is evidence of a task not being completed which often gives rise to teachers feeling that group work is a waste of time, that it takes up teacher time in sorting out squabbles and that it does not work. The cameo indicates another way of using the data: the video of the children working gave an indicator of how badly the children worked together before a group work skills training programme was put into place. Seeing themselves 'in action' enabled the children to reflect on their current performance and work towards improving it.

Hopefully, by now, you will have recognized that the third cameo is an indicator of how things can be! It shows what to look for in terms of effective group work and the power and importance of peer support for 'on-task' behaviour with children who have behavioural difficulties. It also shows that the ability of children to acquire social skills is not age related. Many teachers assume that young children cannot work in groups or be considerate towards one another because developmentally they are not 'ready' for it. The research evidence gathered by practising teachers on in-service courses indicates that this is not true. In fact, in many cases the reverse is true. It can be very difficult indeed to get older aged children to work in a 'new way' that demands self-restraint, initiative, self-responsibility, reflection and accountability for group ventures. I have often wondered whether the way in which we teach at the moment means that schooling is responsible for a 'dependency' culture where children rely on the teacher to initiate, arbitrate, organize, assess and set the pace for learning. When working with very young children the responsiveness is immediate, they get themselves organized into pairs, carousels and whole circles far more quickly than either older children or adults!

So what should the beginning teacher do?

There are a number of aspects to deal with in setting co-operation in place. These are now outlined and guidance given on specific things you should do.

There are specific skills to teach

In order to work with others, which is what 'co-operate' means, there are skills which children need. These include:

- how to listen to each other and value each other;
- how to talk about feelings so that they can clearly state their own problems and then try to solve problems and build trust;
- how to show empathy;
- how to give feedback – positive and negative;
- how to be friends with others – this includes encouraging others, helping others, peer tutoring (teaching others);
- how to negotiate;
- how to reflect on their own learning process, their own and others' performances and contribute in groups;
- how to self-organize, including assessing their own strengths and weaknesses, target setting and action planning;
- how to break things down into small, manageable steps.

There is a model for skill training

This model is a useful guide for all teachers. In reality it is the same model used for teaching basic skills in reading and writing, but it is unusual for us to think in these terms for social skills.

Model the skill in action
In other words if you want the children to look at you when they talk to indicate they are giving you their full attention (and to do this to each other) then you have to do it to them. In a busy classroom this is often

Photo 16   Children need many skills to work collaboratively in groups

difficult and requires a conscious effort on the adult's part. A classroom rule which helps here is that children should always ask someone else on their table or nearby first if they do not understand something, before they ask the teacher and the teacher should always check that they have done this before giving them full attention. This encourages independence and helps the next point.

Teach the skill

Sometimes this is only a question of drawing the children's attention to the skill. For example in a 'back-to-back' listening exercise, the children sit back-to-back and both have a piece of paper, clipboard and pen. One child draws a picture with two or three clear shapes, then gives instructions to the other to enable that child to draw the same picture. If you ask the children afterwards if this was easy or difficult, and what it was that made it so, they will usually say difficult because you could not see the other person. This can lead to the 'knee-to-knee' rule: when children do pair work they sit either on chairs or on the carpet in a knee-to-knee position. They take it in turns to be the speaker and the listener, the latter putting into practice the skills they have identified and practised. The skills training of the listener can be supported and reinforced using a third child as an observer.

Provide opportunities for practising the skills
Initially the practice should be in the context of social information. The children can be asked to take it in turns to talk about their favourite food, television programmes, holidays or out of school activities. This is important because it gives the children the opportunity to find out things they have in common with children they may initially categorize as being 'not like them'. This is particularly important for children at both ends of the ability spectrum. The research by Smith and Thompson (1994) on bullying shows that it is children with special educational needs and quiet children who are 'brainy' who are usually subjected to low-level bullying, such as name calling. Experience shows that regular 'sharing' times, in pairs and in circle time can help to reduce such bullying, especially when combined with open discussion about 'what it feels like to be picked on'. Once the skill of 'looking like you are listening' or 'encouraging others to talk', has been established, it needs to be practised as part of regular curriculum time.

Praise and use positive feedback when the skills are used
This can take the form of 'Good Listener' certificates, based on teacher observation, speaker feedback or peer observation (through the use of 'spotter checklists' – see Figures 10.1 and 10.2), or a 'Friendly Person of the Week' award, based on self audit sheets, such as a 'Friendly Deeds' chart signed by the people for whom they have carried out the friendly deeds. This might be after a few weeks on 'friendship skills training' (see McNamara and Moreton 1995).

The skills needed to work effectively in groups are hierarchical

Whilst the aim is for the children to be able to work productively and get the best outcome they can in terms of solving curriculum related problems, the skills needed for this are very sophisticated. Some authors have identified two sorts of skills needed for effective group work. One set is *task skills*, which include:

• setting targets;
• ensuring the task will be done on time;
• clarifying the problem;
• generating alternative solutions;
• discussing relative strengths and weaknesses of various solutions.

These are skills which many adults, especially teachers, possess in abundance. The other set is *maintenance skills*, which include the skills of:

• ensuring that everyone is included;
• inviting people to talk;
• ensuring that a contributor has been heard and understood by paraphrasing their contribution and making links between different contributions through linking statements which look for common elements;

Listening Skills

When your partner was listening did she/he:

1. Keep still ☐

2. Keep quiet ☐

3. Look at the speaker ☐

4. Remember what their partner said ☐

Figure 10.1   Spotter checklist 1

• encouraging group members to make contributions by smiling at them, praising useful contributions, nodding.

These are the skills which many adults including teachers would expect chair people and leaders to do. If children are to develop group work skills and social skills they need to learn how to do all the functions separately. This model of group work sees children switching roles many times from one maintenance function to another to a task function and back to a maintenance one, based on need within the group at any one time and not based on having only one skill (Johnson and Johnson 1985, 1986, 1987).

Tuckman (1965) and Stanford (1990) have identified that groups go through different stages in developing relevant skills. Since it is difficult to carry out skills such as paraphrasing, in a group, because several things are happening at one time, it is better to start group work training in pairs (see Kingsley Mills *et al.* 1992).

Pair work is the safest place to start (random pairs are essential)

One of the problems often identified by student teachers and practising teachers alike, is the difficulty of getting high talkers to stop dominating

Working in a Group

Did I like working in this group?

Did others listen to me?

Did I listen to others?

Was everyone included in what we did?

How could I be a better group person next time?

_____

_____

Figure 10.2 Spotter checklist 2

discussion – and the difficulty of getting low talkers to talk at all. These two are of course connected. Our experience shows that when we give the high talker the role of encourager and reward them for demonstrating the skills of good listening, encouraging, supporting and summarizing, they act as a catalyst for the low talkers. Pair work means that it is a safe place for the low talkers to talk and for the high talkers to practice their new role.

Pair work has other benefits. It helps pupils to hear what is actually being said and not what they *think* has been said, which cuts down on disputes arising from mis-communication and allows children to know what they think – often we do not realize exactly what we think about a topic until we verbalize it. Pair work also allows the children to become comfortable sharing with more than one other peer group member, possibly someone other than their 'best friend'. Random pairs are essential if children are to reap the benefits outlined above. If the children are reluctant to use a random pair technique try pair 'cards' – give out cards with two matching symbols, words, pictures on them and get children to find the 'match'. At the same time, it is essential to explain clearly over and over again the reason for doing the random pair work like this.

You may have noticed that the same children tend always to work together. It is important in school and later in life to find ways of working with a variety of people even if at first you seem to have little in common with them. You can always draw a parallel with the other teachers in the school, saying that Mrs B and you are not best friends but you work together! Tell the children that they will not have to work in random pairs and random groups all day but just for certain activities and for other activities they can be in friendship pairs and fours. As time goes by their friendship groups will become wider and this will be less and less of an issue.

The recommendation in this chapter is to form your groups by having two pairs join together, and let them work in groups of four for quite some time; the larger the group the more skilful the children need to be. The children themselves can then work out a system for allocating roles in groups such as scribe, observer, encourager, goal setter. They can also be encouraged to rotate these roles, and to assess their own and others performance in the roles, based on a 'two things positive and one thing negative', feedback formula.

Speaking and listening skills need to be explicitly taught

While the NC stresses the importance of speaking and listening skills in all the core and foundation subjects, the assumption often made by many teachers is that the children will pick up these skills by being given tasks that require them. This is odd in the face of the carefully structured help that goes on to teach children to read and spell. The recommendation in this chapter is that it is necessary to audit the speaking and listening skills the children need for each part of the curriculum and to explicitly teach these skills. Children need to view a video of themselves reading out their piece in an assembly to see the need for them to practise the skill of 'voice projection', otherwise they will always do badly on the skill of speaking/ presenting to a large group (one of the ATs for English).

Small group work comes next

Although it is important to do pair work first and group work next, in reality this is a distinction for you to keep in your heads for it does not mean that there should be no group work before children have acquired pair skills first. What it may mean, however, is that the children only work in small groups of four for quite some time and that you can interpret the difficulties children have in working in groups in terms of skills yet to be taught, or practised or reinforced, rather than a problem with group work itself.[1]

There needs to be a clear understanding of the hierarchy of task. Problem solving in co-operative groups is the most difficult task. Children can use group work for 'jigsawing' first (see NOP/NCC 1990). *Jigsawing* is an information exchange exercise, where children are put into 'expert' pairs (for example during a topic on the Romans this might be villas, baths, gods, roads, soldiers). The children then find out as much as they can about their area of expertise, pool ideas in the expert groups, ensure they are all briefed and reform into new groups where one person from each area of expertise is present and all try to learn as much as they can from one another. The advantage of this approach is that the children stay with a high level of motivation for a large body of knowledge area of the curriculum such as history. They can gradually build up to working in groups from the safety of pairs and they can record information in any way they like as long as it helps them to pass the information on – they do not have to problem solve.

Circle work is important

Children need practice in talking in the 'high-risk' place of the whole circle. This can be made into an enjoyable experience for children if there is a clear turn taking structure and if there are sentence completion activities rather than a competitive sharing circle or a general discussion. The turn taking can include a 'thinking time' clause, where children can pass but the teacher will come back to them. With young children, passing round a teddy when only the person holding it can speak, helps to prevent 'shouting out'. Sentences need to be of a social nature so that the children are sharing information on which they are the experts and commonalities are set up: for example favourite foods, what makes me mad, things I find hard in class, or things I am good at.[2]

Talking about how you feel – the neglected part of the curriculum

The opportunity for children to say how they feel needs to be clearly provided in a systematic way. The 'affective domain' is often neglected and yet causes children blocks in their learning. The skill of saying how you feel helps children to learn the skills they need in order to empathize, negotiate, to settle disputes and to contribute in a meaningful way to records of achievement (discussed by Morag Hunter-Carsch in Chapter 12).

Boys – a special problem

The number of boys who are excluded in both primary and secondary schools is becoming alarmingly high and is in a totally disproportionate figure to the number of girls. This in itself mirrors the amount of time classroom teachers spend in dealing with discipline problems with boys as opposed to girls. In addition there is now widespread concern about the academic under-achievement of boys at secondary level and research evidence linking achievement at primary schools with achievement at secondary level. For both academic work and ability to function socially and resolve disputes in an institutionally acceptable, non-aggressive way, boys need the interpersonal skills that girls seem more easily to 'pick up' and develop. Boys need the social skills training outlined in this chapter urgently. They may even need special extra lessons taught by male teachers, particularly those boys at the top end of primary school. Again the argument put forward here is that while there are socialization influences on boys in society at large and in homes in particular, teachers should not assume that boys are 'like that'. They need to see aggressive behaviour for what it is: a skills deficit area.

Main features relevant to children's learning

Learning through talk

The work of Bruner and Vygotsky suggests that we actually come to understand what it is we think through talk (Roger Merry explains this in greater depth in Chapter 5). Pair work to start a new topic allows children to make the connection between the topic in hand and any prior learning. Talk to recall prior learning between sessions is helpful to prepare the children for the next step in their learning. In your teacher education course experiences, you will have appreciated the depth of understanding you need in order to explain things like science to the children – the younger the children, the more information you need. The verbalizing also provides an opportunity for children to check out their understanding of specialist words by using their own more common language to express the same ideas.

Self-esteem enhancement

One of the major blocks to learning is a child's self-concept.[3] There are three aspects to self-concept:

- the self-image – the way the child sees himself or herself;
- the ideal self – what the child feels he or she ought to be;
- self-esteem – the difference between these two.

Hence the smaller the difference between self-image and the ideal self, the greater the self-esteem.

Research by Coopersmith (1967) shows that the way children feel about themselves is determined by the way they interpret the messages received from 'significant others' who are usually parents, teachers and peers. Clearly, if all three work together then great progress can be made. Children who have a low self-esteem will often pick on another child with low self-esteem and make negative comments about them. This means the children need to be trained to observe the behaviour of each other and to praise one another whenever they can. In circle time, one child might pass a 'compliments slip' to another saying 'I am going to give this to Claire because she helped me when I fell over this week'.

Peer learning

Peer learning may occur as an off-shoot of the pair work which has been recommended in this chapter or it may be a logical extension of social skills training, and may embrace a structured cross-age tutoring scheme. There is powerful research evidence to show that there are academic and self-esteem gains for both the tutor and the tutee in peer tutoring programmes, but especially for the tutor (Topping 1988). Being a peer tutor can be helpful for those who have special educational needs and most especially for those children who have behaviour problems as well as learning problems. This is partly to do with the role of responsibility that peer tutoring gives to such children. Being treated as responsible increases the amount of responsibility shown. Peer tutoring is a structured form of friendship, and as such can be a helpful training ground for children who seem to have friendship and co-operation difficulties in their same-age classroom.

Differentiation by classroom organization for children with special educational needs

There is currently a debate as to what constitutes differentiation. One definition in vogue is that of differentiation by outcome, task and classroom organization. Social skills training for co-operative group work ensures that the latter is possible in the classroom, and that the children who do not have special needs will have the skills to include, increase the self-esteem, befriend, explain and scaffold at appropriate times with the child who has special needs. In such classrooms the student teacher may even find the children with special needs starting to carry out some of these functions themselves.

Curriculum implementation through group work

To ensure that all children reach their academic potential, there must be a clearly structured systematic programme of social skills teaching that is designed to equip the children with the skills they need for effective working in groups. In addition it is essential that opportunities for these skills to be practised are created across the curriculum, so that this way of working becomes in fact a pedagogy, a teaching method.

Race and gender

If race or gender issues threaten the efficacy of random pairs because it may result in girl/boy pairs, then allow the children to randomly select a partner within same sex/race groups then join two pairs together to make a mixed-sex/race four. Always explain the purpose of the exercise and the long-term aim which is for everyone to be able to *work with everyone else.* The cultural differences about personal space and eye contact will emerge in discussion and the student teacher can take their cues from the children.

Conclusion

Children can work co-operatively together in groups as long as they are taught the skills to do so. The sooner they learn these skills the easier it is for you as they have not acquired 'bad habits'. You need to practise skills training with children in small ways across the age ranges in order to acquire confidence in teaching the skills and practice in diagnosing which skills are used or needed. In this way you will build up a good repertoire of activities which are enjoyable and motivating for the children as well as being worthwhile in their own right.

Think about . . .

It would be a useful activity now for you to consider a few questions to see how far your own understanding is evolving – you might answer them in co-operation with a friend (pairing), in a small group or even with several others in a circle!

1 What is your understanding of the skills needed for co-operation?
2 Can you identify task and maintenance functions in a group – which do you do?

3 Do you think the skills for co-operative group work can be taught to *all* children?
4 Have you noticed children who seem to have a low self-esteem? Can you describe what they do which makes you think they have low self-esteem?
5 Why do you think so few teachers use pair work and skills training for group work? How and when will you try it out? (You will need to make plans.)
6 What do you understand by the term 'differentiation'?

Notes

1 The arguments for choosing the right activity for group work are put forward by Bennett and Dunne (1992), and more ideas for co-operative group work are to be found in Dunne and Bennett (1990).
2 Ideas for circle time can be found in White (1987) and in Mosley (1993).
3 Robinson and Maines (1989) define self concept as: 'A person's perception of his unique personal characteristics such as appearance, ability, temperament, physique, attitude and beliefs. These determine his view of his position in society and his value to and relationship with other people.'

References and further reading

Alexander, R., Rose, J. and Woodhead, C. (1992) *Curriculum Organisation and Classroom Practice in Primary Schools. A Discussion Paper*. London: HMSO.
Bennett, N. and Dunne, E. (1992) *Managing Classroom Groups*. Hemel Hempstead: Simon and Schuster.
Coopersmith, S. (1967) *Antecedents of Self-Esteem*. San Francisco: W.H. Freeman and Co.
Dunne, E. and Bennett, N. (1990) *Talking and Learning in Groups*, Leverhulme Primary Project. London: Macmillan.
Johnson, D.W. and Johnson, R.T. (1985) *Co-operative Learning: Warm-ups, Grouping Strategies, Group Activities*. Minnesota: Interaction Books.
Johnson, D.W. and Johnson, R.T. (1986) *Circles of Learning: Co-operation in the Classroom*. Minnesota: Interaction Books.
Johnson, D.W. and Johnson, R.T. (1987) *Learning Together and Alone. Co-operative, Competitive and Individualistic Learning*, 2nd edn. New Jersey: Prentice Hall.
Kingsley-Mills, C., McNamara, S. and Woodward, L. (1992) *Out From Behind the Desk. A Practical Guide to Groupwork Skills*. Leicestershire County Council.
Robinson, G. and Maines, B. (1989) A self-concept aproach to dealing with pupils, in R. Evans (ed.) *Special Educational Needs: Policy and Practice*. Oxford: Blackwell Education in Association with NARE.
McNamara, S. and Moreton, G. (1993) *Teaching Special Needs*. London: David Fulton.
McNamara, S. and Moreton, G. (1995) *Changing Behaviour*. London: David Fulton.
Mosley, J. (1993) *Turn Your School Around*. Wisbech: LDA.

NOP/NCC (1990) *Teaching Talking and Learning in Key Stage One, Two, Three.* London: NATE.

Smith, P.K. and Thompson, D. (1994) *Practical Approaches to Bullying.* London: David Fulton.

Topping, K. (1988) *The Peer Tutoring Handbook: Promoting Co-operative Learning.* London: Croom Helm.

Tuckman, B.W. (1965) Developmental sequence in small groups. *Psychological Bulletin*, 63 (6): 384–99.

Stanford, G. (1990) *Developing Effective Classroom Groups: A Practical Guide for Teachers Adapted for British Schools by Pam Stoat.* Bristol: Acora Books.

Vygotsky, L. (1987) *Thought and Language.* Cambridge, Mass.: MIT Press.

White, M. (1987) Circle time. *Cambridge Journal of Education*, 20 (1): 53–6.

11

Do we have to write about it now?
Developing writing skills in the primary classroom

Martin Cortazzi

Cameo 1

You are with a class of 5-year-olds in the role of observer. Most children are writing: labelling pictures of animals. The teacher is dealing with a queue of children near her table. From time to time she scans the room to gauge children's behaviour and whether they are working on task. You observe Nathan writing 'cat'. He writes the 'c' starting from the bottom; the 'a' starting from the right with an anti-clockwise movement; the 't' is written from below with an upward movement and is crossed right to left. Nathan shows his work to the teacher. She looks at it and says 'Well done, Nathan, that looks nice. OK.'

Cameo 2

A Year 4 class has a writing session with a beginning teacher. They have just had a drama and movement session on the theme of the story of Rama and Sita. This is often told during the Hindu new year festival of Diwali in early November, and the children enjoyed moving as the 'monsters' which were killed by Rama in the story. Now the teacher asks the class to make a list of words to describe the monsters. They read their lists aloud and with prompting they group them into categories and label each one (see Figure 11.1).

The teacher elicits which categories contain nouns, verbs or adjectives. In pairs, children use the words to give oral descriptions of imagined monsters. They then draw monsters and label their pictures using words taken from the lists. Finally, they write stories (including descriptions based on their drawings). Later the teacher will make a picture gallery of the drawings and children will read their stories to the class; other children will listen and try to identify the appropriate picture.

Movement		Eating	Looks	Body parts
stride	creep	bites	shiny	arms
tramp	slither	gulps	filthy	knees
stamp	slink	devours	awesome	legs
bound	slide	gobbles	disgusting	trunk
Personality		**Colour**	**Noises**	**Size/shape**
vicious		orange	scream	enormous
vile		navy	roar	bulky
cunning		peach	squeak	squat
mean		purple	grunt	towering

Figure 11.1   A list of words to describe 'monsters' compiled by a Year 4 class

Cameo 3

A Year 6 child, using English as his second language, writes a report following a visit to the zoo.

The Tiger got out from a zoo One day I went to the zoo with my father, and we got to there by bus. first we buy some drink and food to eat. then we go in the zoo. we saw many animals, we saw lion tiger and elephant. but one tiger was Missing. and than the people saw the tiger. they all run away. and my father call the police and the police have come. they fire the gun and the tiger is die.

How do you respond?

Introduction and comments

Writing takes time. For most children it is a long-term labour to learn letter formation and to master spelling patterns. Apparently arbitrary writing conventions are often not discussed in the classroom. The final product is what counts – at least, this often is the hidden message given in the treatment of writing. From teacher's comments, from the way in which writing tasks are set, and in the manner in which writing is received, children come to believe that it is important to get it right first time. Errors may be penalized: directly when children are asked to copy out and correct their writing; indirectly when what is wrong receives more comment than what is correct, what is appropriate or what notably strives to create meaning.

This chapter will first discuss the three cameos cited above and will include teachers' and pupils' views about the purposes of writing in the primary school. Then three important approaches to developing children's writing skills in schools will be discussed: *process approaches* which emphasize the actual process of writing and stress the role of purpose and audience; *genre approaches* which pay particular attention to text structures related to social purposes; and the application of a framework of *knowledge structures* which emphasizes links between language and thinking, and using writing for learning. All three approaches are useful in developing writing throughout the primary curriculum.

Teachers' and children's views about writing purposes

Nathan has focused on the product – so has the teacher. He knows what the letters look like and has reproduced them to look right. In learning to write, however, children need to balance the product and the process. In this case, Nathan needs more instruction and practice with someone watching to check for the direction, movement and flow of handwriting. Teachers cannot observe all the children in this detail all the time, of course, but they should systematically observe each child at some time (as Linda Hargreaves examines in Chapter 4). The teacher could also point out the reasons for writing letters with specific movements, for example, to make it easier to join letters later. As an observer, you need to assess the seriousness of events like this before deciding whether to intervene or whether to mention it to the teacher immediately or later. You also need to ask yourself whether you are observing to see how children learn and perform unaided, or observing in the role of teaching assistant or team member.

In cameo 2, the beginning teacher has several important points about writing in mind. She is aware of the need to provide a clear context for writing and to develop written skills in all areas of the curriculum. This session has a religious education context and movement/drama have provided immediate experience of the particular words to describe the monsters.

The teacher is aware of the importance of balancing preparation with interest: the need for children to prepare for a writing task, while not having too much talk beforehand, lest everything has been said and interest is lost. Some writing tasks can become pure practice, tagged unnecessarily on to existing experience, so that children protest, 'Do we have to write about it afterwards?'. In this case, the teacher has focused on vocabulary and recycled relevant words from the initial elicitation, through categorization and labelling, to productive use. In doing so, some vocabulary and spelling problems have been solved in advance. No children are in doubt about what to write or how to write it. They have heard, read and said some new words several times before using them in writing.

The teacher is also aware of the importance of providing a realistic audience for children's writing; for example when older children write stories for younger ones. In this case she has set up a writing task with a clear focus and outcome. Children can see the point of writing the descriptions in order to play the Gallery Game. Each reader will have a reasonably attentive audience who have a clear purpose in listening to each text as it is read.

The teacher in cameo 2 is aware that the monsters have rather taken over the story at this point; she will come back to the religious theme later by focusing on Rama's character and actions and by examining the symbolism of light in Hindu, Christian and other religious celebrations. She may use a chart to help children plan some writing, comparing how light is important to different groups.

In cameo 3, the obvious problems in the text are to do with punctuation (confusion between commas and full stops, use of capitals) and grammar (inconsistency of tense, lack of some plural forms). Before rushing to correct these as a teacher, you might reflect on the need to balance accuracy with fluency, or correctness of form with meaning of content. In this case, much of the text is correct in grammar, spelling and punctuation. The story is simple, but has a clear narrative structure. The errors do not impede the communication of meaning. You might think of how to respond to the content and general form and how to encourage the writer, before drawing attention to some of the more systematic errors. Simply praising the writer is not enough; it would be a good idea to focus on teaching the tenses and raising awareness of the role of capital letters. You might consider how to help the writer develop the reporting and narrative elements.

But some background knowledge will also be helpful here. The 11-year-old writer in cameo 3 speaks Chinese and has been in Britain for only eighteen months. He arrived speaking no English. The shift from the simple past (went, got) to the present (buy, go) can be a problem for monolingual writers too. Usually children will correct this themselves if they read the text aloud, with a little prompting. However, with a user of English as a second language more attention may be worthwhile. Chinese, in fact, has no tense forms: the Chinese equivalent of 'go', 'goes', 'going', 'went', 'gone' is a single unvarying word. Some systematic teaching of the past forms of common verbs, linked with time markers such as 'yesterday' or 'last year' contrasting the meaning with the present, would be useful.

Again, Chinese has no capital letters: Chinese characters do not change at the beginning of sentences. However, there are full stops (actually, small circles) in Chinese. A useful tactic might be to contrast small and capital letters, then to look at a reading book to see where the capital letters are in relation to full stops, then to re-read the original story so that the writer can spot the problem for himself.

Photo 17   An attractive writing environment

Raising general awareness of sentences is important with all primary children. As Kress (1994) points out, the concept of 'sentence' is a difficult one – even among adults there is some flexibility, for example, in whether this sentence itself should be one, two, three or four sentences; not surprisingly it takes children time to develop control over punctuation. Eleven-year-olds are often vague about what is a sentence:

> Well, it's a group of words and at the end there's a full stop and you use it in a story a lot.

> It's all words put together with a capital letter at the front and a full stop at the end.

> You write a sentence down in your book, you write a line that makes sense in words.

One strategy is to use familiar material, select sentences singly or in pairs (without punctuation), and ask children if there are one, or two, sentences. Another is to develop sequencing activities with clauses, so that children match first and second halves of sentences, then sequence the sentences. A third strategy is to play 'Sentence Diets': progressively adding words to a short sentence to see how long it can get before it is better to split into two sentences, or reducing a long sentence by deleting words to see how small it can become and still remain a sentence.

Different perspectives on writing

Writing takes up time – about a third of class time in most primary class-rooms. Teachers commonly give a number of reasons why so much writing is important.

- Writing develops language skills in terms of fluency, accuracy and appropriateness, in the communication of meanings and messages.
- Writing reinforces and consolidates the learning of curriculum material and helps children learn: the act of writing helps to make explicit to the writer what he or she knows or is coming to know.
- Writing is the major means of assessing learning throughout the education system.

In spite of recent emphasis on the importance of oral language, most tests and many curriculum tasks are assessed on the basis of written performance.

Children often have a different picture of writing in school. The reasons for particular writing tasks and how they will be assessed are rarely explained, so children form their views on the basis of what they actually *do* and how their writing is received. Asked about writing in school, some 6-year-olds said:

We write 'cos the teacher tells us.

We write so we'll get better at writing.

To keep us busy and quiet, so the teacher can rest a bit.

Writing is working, it's when you do a piece of work and the teacher's writed something down, then you have to write it down and copy what she's done.

It means you're writing a word and don't copy it off other people or you'll get it rubbed out and you have to do it again.

The teacher writes on the blackboard and you write a thing and then he tells you the answer and then one day he won't tell you. You've just got to guess it in your head.

If you don't know how to do it, all you do is just go up to the teacher and she tells you how to do it.

The implication is that it is important to clarify the purpose of writing activities. Teacher-made worksheets sometimes include such instructions as: 'Copy and finish these sentences . . .' (science); 'Copy and complete . . .' (geography); 'Copy out in your best handwriting with the right spellings . . .' (English); 'Read the story and write out the first five verbs . . .' (English).

In such cases, it is worth asking whether the children actually *need* to write anything; simply marking the worksheet or writing only a few words (since copies are provided for each child) is sufficient to consolidate the teaching point. A lot of copying seems redundant or designed to keep children busy (but bored?). If such sheets are for handwriting practice this is rarely made clear to the children and almost never has a handwriting aim (such as letter formation, joining certain letter groups, or writing fluently and legibly within a time limit). The teacher should help the children to be aware of the purpose: by having clear tasks, discussing the purpose and outcome with children.

Process approaches

Broadly, a process approach to developing children's writing gives importance to what the individual writer wants to say and focuses on the process of planning, drafting and reviewing (Graves 1983; National Writing Project 1990). The emphasis is on *saying something to someone*, rather than on the product. Teachers adopting process approaches try to avoid treating children's written work as one-off, 'it's-got-to-be-right-first-time' pieces. They encourage children to talk about their writing in one-to-one or small group 'conferences' and to take responsibility for their writing by, for example, taking decisions about topic, form, content and revision (see Figure 11.2). It is widely claimed that such an approach leads to positive attitudes to writing – held by both teachers and pupils.

Process approaches have helped teachers to realize that many children can develop their knowledge and deepen personal experience in writing. They can be helped to clarify purposes and audiences, which is essential for writing development. They can gradually internalize criteria for revision of form and content, so that self-editing improves. They can identify with what they write and develop their own voices.

Studies of children's 'emergent' writing (Clay 1975; Temple *et al.* 1982; Hall 1987, 1989) have demonstrated that children bring concepts of literacy to school at the nursery stage, often using invented or adopted symbols to convey meaning. The example of May's writing in Figure 11.3 illustrates several points. Aged 4, and only able to write her name, May insisted that this was not a picture, but writing. Asked what it said, she sang: 'Oh, I do like to be beside the seaside, oh I do like to be beside the sea . . .'. She was reading the musical notation with direction and rising pitch (it goes up on the page). Further, the waves were created by a handwriting pattern which she had seen being practised by an older brother. This is a visual pun: a pattern of C's (seas) and M's, making her initials MC. This shows a degree of ingenuity and knowledge applied to the problem of how to convey meaning on paper. Children are rarely blank slates – they bring knowledge of fundamental aspects of writing (and other skills) with them when they arrive in school (the Chapters in Part 2 all emphasize this point).

Process approaches have shown the value of a range of early writing and planning techniques to sort out ideas and likely language, some of which have been illustrated in cameo 2. These could include the uses of:

A typical sequence might be:

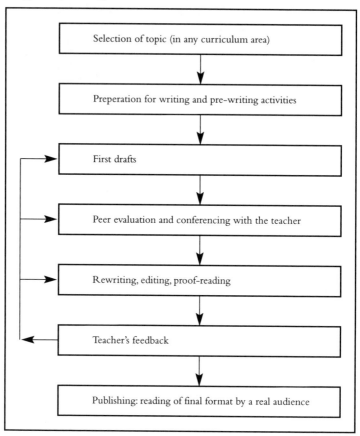

Figure 11.2   The writing process

- orally brainstorming ideas;
- making lists of key words and pre-teaching essential vocabulary;
- using dialogues, interviews, debates and role play as preludes to writing;
- using question words – who did what, how, when, where and why;
- using note-making techniques, such as planning on the left-hand page to sort out ideas and organization, then writing in full on the right-hand page.

As shown in Figures 11.4 and 11.5, a variety of visual planning techniques can be used. Some 5-year-olds wrote up the example shown in Figure 11.5 as:

The penny sank but the cork floated on the water.

The cork floated but the stone sank.

The coin and stone sank only the cork floated.

Figure 11.3 May's 'writing'

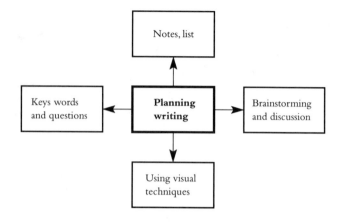

Planning writing

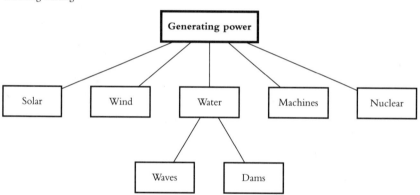

Figure 11.4   A diagram to plan writing about generating power

Object	Floated	Sank
Coin		✓
Cork	✓	
Stone		✓

Figure 11.5   A diagram to record an experiment and plan writing about floating and sinking

A useful exercise is to see how many different sentences can be made from such a chart, perhaps paying special attention to linking words (and, but, however, whereas, and so on).

The clarification of purposes and audiences can be helped by interactive writing (Hall and Robinson 1994). This process approach focuses on the participation of correspondents in the exchange of meaningful and purposeful texts over an extended period of time. The use of dialogue journals is one example which has been used for science: the teacher and pupil build up an exchange when they comment on the other's responses to an original piece of writing. Another useful example is seen in pen-friend letters between classes, exchanged by teachers working in schools reasonably close to each other. The tone of interactive writing can be seen in these brief samples of letters from 9-year-olds in Leicester schools:

Dear Mark:
I hope you enjoyed your Birthday and got lots of presents. I red your letter and I sean it when it said on Thurday we went up to Dunkerly Beacon which is 1750 feet above sea leavel I showed my freindes they could not belive there eyes.
Yours Sincerely,
Darren

Dear kevin,
I have just read your letter and your writing is very neat your letter was, was interesting and i'll tell you one thing you have better books than us. At the moment i'm reading a mystery story and its not bad.
Yours,
Sumit

Dear Jamie,
If I can get a photo of my self I will send it to you. And you went wrong in your letter could you tell me what you ment by I have a pode. I have a big garden too. And I have a bike with three geirs.
from Christopher

Dear Christopher,
In the storm on Friday it killed one of our baby budies. I ment I have a pond.
from Jamie

A dilemma for the teacher here is how, when, and how far to intervene to develop correctness in such writing without losing the spontaneity and personal investment in the exchange of meaning. Children may be learning each other's mistakes ('ment' in the Jamie–Christopher exchange, or 'leavel' in Darren's response). On the other hand, meaning also gets clarified when errors lead to a breakdown in communication if this is repaired, as seen in 'I ment I have a pond'.

Process approaches highlight several tensions which ultimately need to be held in balance. Children are seen as stakeholders in the writing process: concepts of authorship and ownership are developed. However, the role of the teacher cannot be solely to set up the writing environment and to encourage the process of children clarifying their ideas on paper. There is also a need for intervention, for teachers to adopt roles of remediation, instruction and correction.

Process approaches also raise issues of teaching writing across the curriculum. They have been successful in improving children's writing in English, but it could be very time consuming to use the approach systematically in all curriculum areas for all significant writing tasks. It could be argued that children will transfer their text planning and revision skills to other areas but this is unlikely to happen without action from the teacher. In fact, criticisms of process approaches are that they give heavy weighting to the writing of personal experiences and narrative at the expense of other types of text and that they are applied across the curriculum with different types of learning and knowledge. Approaches which do focus on types of text and knowledge structures are genre approaches and Mohan's framework of knowledge structures.

Genre approaches

The concept of genre has been elaborated by those who see the need for children to have clear guidance about the broad range of different types of text which commonly occur in schools (Kress 1994; Martin 1989; Cope and Kalantzis 1993). Children need to learn to write in different ways to meet the expectations of using writing for learning in the curriculum. This should not be left to chance or pupil choice; rather, children should be taught to recognize how meanings are organized in the overall structure of different types of text. Learning to write involves learning new genres. By learning to control genres, children develop writing for learning.

A genre is a kind of text structure defined in terms of its social purpose and relating to a social context. Using a genre for writing is about writing something to somebody and meeting the reader's expectations of form and social conventions. Ideas about genre in writing thus include notions of *purpose and audience*, but there is emphasis on the generalizability of learning about text structures.

In the second and third steps of the genre approach shown in Figure 11.6, the teacher could use charts or diagrams with labels to show pupils the text structure of the genre. For example, to write a 'report' with a Year 5 class, a teacher discussed several brief examples of reports about animals, showing how they were set out. Pupils were led to see that each report was factual and contained an initial general classifying statement followed by a series of sentences giving a description. Children were given copies of reports and circled the classification part, then identified different parts of the description. Some children drew a diagram to illustrate the parts of their report. The teacher then chose the topic of 'bikes' and through group

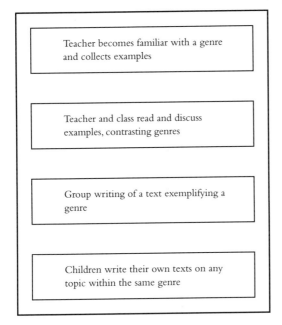

Figure 11.6 Steps in a genre approach

discussion built up a diagram with headings and supporting facts (see Figure 11.7). Children used this as a structured overview to produce their own writing. One child began:

A bike is a machine with two wheels that is pedal-operated. It has a frame with a seat on top and handlebars to steer it. You put your feet on the pedals and turn them. This moves the chain and makes the wheels turn . . .

The following list shows genres which commonly occur in primary school writing, approximately in order of development.

Label: a caption for an object or picture – 'This is our gerbil'.
Description: shows what something is like – 'This is my house. It has three bedrooms . . .'
Observation/comment: shows something observed; the comment gives a personal reaction – 'This is my mouse. It has a long tail. I like it.'
List: 'We saw lions, tigers and elephants'.
Recount: presents a series of events in the past, in time sequence – 'We planted seeds in different containers. We watered some of them.'
Narrative: resembles a recount but in addition has a complication (problem, dilemma) heightening human interest, leading to a resolution.

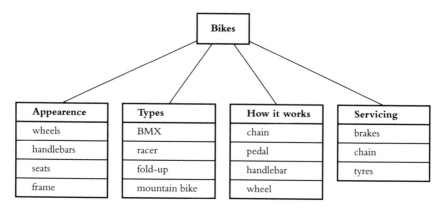

Figure 11.7 Example of headings and supporting facts, as part of a report genre

Procedure:	shows how something is done, gives a series of actions/instructions for the reader to follow.
Report:	shows what a class of things is like; has a general classification statement which relates the topic to a broader category of knowledge, followed by a description, i.e. a series of organized statements usually in the present tense.
Explanation:	gives a reason why a judgement has been made; a factual text which accounts for how something comes about or why things are as they are.
Exposition:	gives arguments showing why a thesis has been proposed; the thesis statement gives a position which is being argued, supported by arguments which recognize other positions.

These are the main factual genres: other familiar genres include letters, poems and play scripts.

A good way to become familiar with a range of genres is to take examples of children's writing, classify them generically and see if they might be improved by explicit instruction on the organization of the text. Another way is to rewrite texts from one genre to another, while preserving the basic content. Many texts are combinations or sequences of different genres.

Talking with children about genres gives them access to ways in which key types of writing in school are organized. There is no need for children to learn this by osmosis through teachers' indirect comments. They can learn to control relevant types of text through explicit teaching. Using labels, such as those used above, gives children a language to talk about texts.

Some teachers see a danger that teaching children about genres is to over-emphasize the product of writing and undervalue individual creativity.

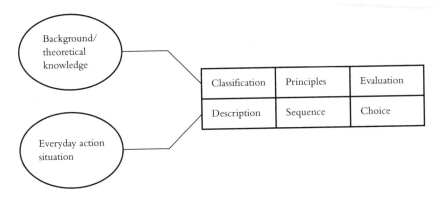

Figure 11.8   A framework of knowledge structures

However, a genre approach will take writing processes, purposes and audience into account, and genres are not seen as fixed types but as broad tendencies. There is much scope for choice and innovation within a genre, otherwise it would be a formula with little meaning. Meaning implies choice, and children will have access to a much wider range of choices in their writing when they have a degree of control over relevant genres.

Knowledge structures

The development of writing skills through processes and genres can be enhanced by drawing on a further approach which relates knowledge structures and thinking skills to language (Mohan 1986). This approach has been particularly useful for second language users of English to develop their thinking skills in all areas of the curriculum. It gives importance to visuals as planning devices, or bridges, between language and knowledge structures.

In the classroom, curriculum content is represented by learning activities and tasks. Many learning tasks are made up of content knowledge and skills and the language used to express these. Mohan (1986) offers a framework to integrate content objectives with language by identifying six principal knowledge structures, shown in Figure 11.8. Description is related to Classification; Sequence to Principles; Choice to Evaluation: the former in each case logically precedes the latter. A rough order of ease of learning is: Description, Sequence, Classification, Choice, Principles, and Evaluation, although this depends on how abstract the knowledge in question is. Each knowledge structure can be associated with characteristic thinking skills, and with visuals which typically illustrate those skills, and with likely language patterns. These are shown in Figure 11.9 and include some of the relevant language patterns (after Mohan 1986).

Description

Thinking skills	Visuals	Language patterns
observing	tables	present tense
describing	diagrams	comparatives
naming	picture	adjectives:
comparing	plans	size, colour,
contrasting	maps	shape, etc.

Sequence

Thinking skills	Visuals	Language patterns
time relations	tables with	here, there,
spatial sequence	numbered steps	first, second,
steps in a process	flow charts	next, before,
	cycles	precedes, follows
	time lines	

Choice

Thinking skills	Visuals	Language patterns
forming personal	decision trees	can, ought,
opinions	flow charts	should, would,
making decisions		better, preferable

Clarification

Thinking skills	Visuals	Language patterns
classification	webs	specific and
categorizing	trees	generic nouns
defining	tables	kind of, type of,
	graphs	
	databases	

Figure 11.9

Teachers can plan learning tasks using this framework by finding the main knowledge structures of topic information in a curriculum area, then targeting particular thinking skills, choosing relevant visuals to illustrate content, and highlighting relevant language patterns. Key visuals are more than just illustrations; they symbolize the knowledge structures. They make

Principles

Thinking skills	Visuals	Language patterns
explaining	tables	cause
predicting	diagrams	due to
interpreting data	graphs	result of
drawing conclusions	cycles	unless, if,
developing generalizations (cause, effect, rules, reasons)		therefore, because,
hypothesizing		consequence

Evaluation

Thinking skills	Visuals	Language patterns
evaluating	rating charts	I think, judge,
judging	rank orders	believe, prefer,
criticizing	grids	the reasons are,
justifying		as a result of,
giving preferences & opinions		ought, need,
recommending		should

Figure 11.9 (cont.)

communication clearer and lower the language barrier for second language users and all other pupils who may have difficulty. With due preparation they act as advance organizers for children's writing, so that they can plan and structure their writing. Children can be shown how to use the visuals associated with characteristic language, in tackling the thinking skills. The framework can be used in any area of the curriculum and it is highly generalizable. It can guide the transfer of writing and thinking skills from one curriculum area to others.

General strategies for developing writing

Setting up writing tasks

- Have a defined task and outcome in mind (beware of tasks which simply practise writing).

- Relate the task to a clear context.
- Check the nature of the envisaged outcome: should it be a word list, notes, a list of sentences, a complete text?
- Define the writing purpose with the children.
- Help children to define the audience and their knowledge and purposes for reading the writing.
- Select an appropriate genre and relevant knowledge structure: will children need explicit guidance about this?
- Choose a visual which will bridge the content knowledge and the planned writing.
- Consider a cycle or series of tasks in which writing is integrated with, and supported by, other skills.

During the writing process

- Help children to follow their planning.
- Refer children to writing purposes and audiences.
- Encourage writers to postpone major revision until ideas have been written down.
- Support children's search for the right words, without getting trapped into delays over spelling.
- Get children to use techniques to overcome hesitations, e.g. bracketing words of doubtful spelling, for checking later.
- When intervening try to give help, encouragement and support without interrupting.
- Use prompting questions sometimes (What happened then? What was the result? What is the reason? Can you give an example?).
- Observe children writing sometimes: are there difficulties which they are not telling you about, or strengths which you were not aware of?

Responding to writing

- Respond to the content and to the writer as an author; give a reader's understanding.
- Be positive and encouraging; see children's writing in terms of developments.
- Use variety: oral conferences, written comments, audio-taped comments, peer feedback, class feedback using an overhead projector and so forth.
- Assess accuracy of meaning; overall organization and text structure; appropriateness of language conventions; grammar, punctuation and spelling.
- Consider selective marking or comment; choose major areas for development or systematic errors.
- Check whether the school has a marking policy, e.g. use of a marking code if appropriate: p=punctuation, sp=spelling, etc.
- Check that feedback is clear, meaningful and useful for future development.

- Ask how pupils will use comments: do they have strategies for handling feedback?

Finally, revise this list: amend it and extend it according to the age group and levels of children you are teaching and in the light of what works for you.

References and further reading

Beard, R. (1984) *Children's Writing in the Primary School.* London: Hodder and Stoughton.

Brown, A. (1993) *Helping Children to Write.* London: Paul Chapman.

Clay, M.M. (1975) *What Did I Write?* London: Heinemann.

Cope, B. and Kalantzis, M. (eds) (1993) *The Powers of Literacy, a Genre Approach to Teaching Writing.* London: The Falmer Press.

Cowie, H. (ed.) (1984) *The Development of Children's Imaginative Writing.* London: Croom Helm.

Czerniewska, P. (1992) *Learning about Writing.* Oxford: Blackwell.

Graves, D.H. (1983) *Writing: Teachers and Children at Work.* London: Heinemann.

Hall, N. (1987) *The Emergence of Literacy.* London: Hodder and Stoughton.

Hall, N. (ed.) (1989) *Writing with Reason.* London: Hodder and Stoughton.

Hall, N. and Robinson, A. (eds) (1994) *Keeping in Touch, Using Interactive Writing with Young Children.* London: Hodder and Stoughton.

Harris, J. (1993) *Introducing Writing.* London: Penguin Books.

Kress, G. (1994) *Learning to Write,* 2nd edn. London: Routledge.

Martin, J.R. (1989) *Factual Writing: Exploring and Challenging Social Reality.* Oxford: Oxford University Press.

Mohan, B.A. (1986) *Language and Content, Reading.* MA: Addison-Wesley.

National Writing Project (1990) *Becoming a Writer.* Walton-on-Thames: Thomas Nelson.

National Writing Project (1990) *Responding to and Assessing Writing.* Walton-on-Thames: Thomas Nelson.

National Writing Project (1990) *A Rich Resource: Writing and Language Diversity.* Walton-on-Thames: Thomas Nelson.

National Writing Project (1990) *What are Writers Made of? Issues of Gender and Writing.* Walton-on-Thames: Thomas Nelson.

National Writing Project (1990) *Writing Partnerships: Home, School and Community.* Walton-on-Thames: Thomas Nelson.

Perera, K. (1984) *Children's Writing and Reading.* Oxford: Blackwell.

Temple, C.A., Nathan, R.G. and Burris, N.A. (1982) *The Beginnings of Writing.* Boston: Allyn and Bacon.

Part 3

RESPONSIBILITIES, ROLES AND RELATIONSHIPS

12

Keeping track
Assessing, monitoring and recording children's progress and achievement

Morag Hunter-Carsch

Cameo 1

Note made by a student teacher after observing and assisting with teaching a Year 5 class: 'How can I possibly manage to keep track of all that is going on in the classroom? It's tough enough being expected to plan for all the subjects in the curriculum and all the children including the ones with special needs but, on top of that, to have to keep records is what really concerns me. Where can I get help with sorting out how to do it all?'

Cameo 2

Note made by a student after attending a primary school staff meeting: 'The teachers were talking about the school's policy for testing children throughout the year. Whole-class screening of the children is to be carried out to find out who should be followed up with individual testing. They worked in year groups and they brought along records of test results and portfolios of children's work. There seems to be a computer-based record for everyone to use. What does it all mean? It looks very daunting – I wonder if I'll be expected to do all of this during my teaching practice?'

Cameo 3

Notes made by a student after an early experience in an infant school: 'There was the usual cluster of parents coming into the playground and entering the nursery at "home time". One mother with a toddler moved determinedly through the crowd and right up to the teacher and asked her, "Mrs W, can I have a word with you? It's really about the older one, Alan, – he's in Year 4 now – it's him I'm concerned about, but I just wanted to talk to you, particularly, and about the two little ones as well. You know how Alan was so slow with his reading, do you think it might be dyslexia? Do you think David and the little one might have it too?" I was very curious about how Mrs W would answer this. I don't know much about the details of how to recognize reading problems, let alone "dyslexia" – and just how to deal with a parent's questions. It was very impressive how Mrs W was so calm and organized and found just the right way of reassuring the parent – especially when she shared her records and her notes about David and she could remember the older child and talk about the details of his early literacy problems.'

Introduction

Keeping track of children's learning by observing, making assessments and recording their progress and needs constitutes a vital component of the primary teacher's work. In the current climate of concern about 'quality' and 'standards' in education, there are models of assessment continually being developed (see Gipps 1994). Beginning teachers need to get to grips with the developments in assessment as soon as possible both for account- ability purposes and, principally, in order to *use assessment to support teaching and learning*. This involves many skills and processes which are diagram- matically presented in Figure 12.1 which is adapted from the University of Leicester 'Curriculum in Action' Project.

It should be noted from the outset that there is no single ideal way for teachers or children to assess and keep track of activities and learning in the classroom. The important issue, Gipps advises, is 'fitness for purpose' (Maurice Galton discusses this in Chapter 1). This chapter aims to intro- duce you to concepts, terminology and procedures for assessing and re- cording for a range of purposes. All three of the cameos reflect interest and concern in sorting out priorities and getting to grips with assessment, record keeping and communicating with parents and colleagues about children's progress and problems. The chapter begins, therefore, with discussion prompted by these three situations.

Priorities and issues

The first cameo reflects a quite normal response to the daunting recogni- tion of the range of skills which teachers require to develop beyond simply 'managing' children. For the beginning teacher 'testing' and teaching might appear to be quite separate areas of responsibility and consequently 'testing' might seem to be an extra burden. With increasing experience it becomes easier to understand how assessment relates to teaching and learning and particularly how teachers' and children's records can provide information

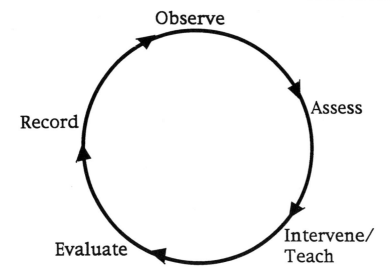

Six main questions to bear in mind:

1   What did the children actually do?
2   What were they actually learning?
3   How worthwhile was it?
4   What did I actually do?
5   What did I actually learn?
6   What do I intend to do now?

Figure 12.1   University of Leicester Curriculum in Action diagram and questions

which helps the teacher to plan in order to match the work as closely as possible to the children's needs: the essence of good teaching as shown by Janet Moyles in Chapter 6. However, it takes time to acquire expertise in assessment and record keeping, as indeed in all other aspects of teaching! It is helpful to be aware of a range of models and to have opportunities to explore different forms of assessing and recording children's progress and problems.

It would also be easier to develop greater understanding in this field if there was less conceptual confusion in some media reports on testing and standards, and relentless media interest in 'standards' and the issue of 'accountability'. It is not uncommon to hear or read angry comments about alleged falling standards in literacy and conclusions that 'half our children are failing'. Such reports may be based on popular misconceptions, for example the assumption that all children of a certain chronological age should be achieving at the same measured 'reading age'. A less dramatic but equally erroneous idea would be to report positively that 'half our children are succeeding beyond the average reading age for their chronological age'! What is required is greater clarity about the purposes and meaning of different forms of describing children's achievements. This is particularly important in the light of NC developments since the Report from the Task Group on Assessment and Testing (DES 1988). Teachers have been advised to employ a range of procedures for assessing and keeping track of progress, not least the developments of Records of Achievement (RoA) and the involvement of *children* in keeping track of their own achievement and planning for priorities in their own learning.[1]

As the second cameo reveals, you need not feel alone in dealing with these issues since the policies at national and local education authority level are increasingly supported by guidelines which are being implemented by collaborative teams of teachers in individual schools. Their work includes the development of cohesive policy statements and workable, informative practices for their schools, some of which I shall describe later, to ensure continuity and progression throughout the curriculum for all children including bi- and multi-lingual children and those with special educational needs.

The third cameo shows how teachers may be consulted by parents about matters which may require fairly specialized knowledge about diagnostic assessment and they will need to consider how best to respond to parents' concerns. This does not mean just a familiarity with detailed records of individual children's achievements but, as in this case, the teacher responded in regard to identifying children with specific learning difficulties, including dyslexia – the term used to highlight a condition in which children find it difficult to deal with letters and words in the effective and efficient way that most of us do.[2]

Questions about literacy and reading difficulties are amongst the most frequently shared areas of parental interest and concern. In recognition of the centrality of literacy for independent learning in and beyond the school curriculum, the illustrations in this chapter are mainly of literacy or reading records, though they equally apply to keeping track in other areas of the curriculum.

Questions and concepts

This section addresses some fundamental questions, provides reasons for making assessments and keeping track, and considers some basic concepts and procedures. Your task, through addressing your own competences as described by Neil Kitson in Chapter 4, will be to monitor, evaluate and plan requisite 'action' to lead you gradually to a greater understanding of these issues.

Why assess?

There are several purposes for assessing children's progress. They include:

- to investigate the progress of the individual child;
- to provide a profile of the child's achievements across the curriculum;
- to investigate the range of children's attainments in the class as a whole;
- to plan the teaching programme;
- to evaluate the teaching programme;
- to monitor standards.

For whom are we assessing?

The class teacher is the main user of information from educational assessments. In addition colleagues, nursery nurses and teacher assistants will be involved at various levels in both the collection, interpretation and use of information relating to assessment and record keeping. Results of formal assessments may be of interest not only within the school and to the school governors but also to parents and the wider community in the context of regional and national standards and international comparisons.

What is 'assessment'?

All teachers require skills for evaluating their own and the children's activities and outcomes. These skills include:

1 *Evaluation* is the measurement of learning in terms of competence, or the capacity of the child to achieve objectives. Evaluation implies some degree of judgement.
2 *Assessment* is a more limited form of evaluation. The assessment process is ongoing and should involve the learners. It forms a part of teaching and learning, informing future teaching and learning provision. It reflects the whole curriculum. There are different theoretical models of the process. The 'psychometric model' implies some form of measurement which is related to the performance of a particular group (norm-referenced assessment) or of a particular task (criterion-referenced assessment). The psychometric approach to assessment emphasizes *quantitative* descriptions or precise responses to selected criteria rather than *qualitative* descriptions of performance, the latter much more likely to be used with younger children in the context of observation (see Linda Hargreaves' examples in Chapter 3).
3 *Norm-referenced* assessment involves using tests of ability, achievement or attainment in which the individual child's achievements can be compared to a 'standardized sample' of children on whom the test was trialled. This

yields a description of the child's achievements in 'norm-referenced' terms (that is, compared to another group of a similar age). This makes possible the comparison of standards across different groups as long as the same measurement instruments are used and administered, scored and interpreted accurately.

4 *Criterion-referenced* assessment involves the use of specific criteria (for example the child can say the letters of the alphabet in order) against which the child's attainment can be matched. This is probably the most commonly used assessment in primary classrooms.

5 *Levels of assessment* include:

- screening or survey level which, at its broadest, helps teachers to find out about the range of a class of children's attainments in the particular aspect being assessed;
- individual or profile level which involves describing performance at a given date across a range of areas (e.g. curriculum subjects, skills or aptitudes) – this level of exploration may prompt a teacher to go on to study more keenly particular aspects of the children's learning abilities or difficulties at the next level;
- intensive or case-study level which involves collecting results of assessments over time – work at this level is likely to include both structured observations and diagnostic tests (detailed in Chapter 3).

6 *Types of assessment* may broadly be described as twofold:

- *formative* assessment which is the ongoing process of keeping track of how well the children are progressing over a period of time;
- *Summative* assessment which involves presenting a summary picture at the end of a given time.

7 *Assessment in the National Curriculum*: The programmes of study within the NC are intended to guide the planning, teaching and day-to-day assessment of 5 to 11-year-olds' activities. Standard assessment tasks and tests have been designed to assist teachers in making summative assessments and attainment reports at the end of Key Stages (though these have been hotly disputed since their advent in the early 1990s). Teachers use 'level descriptions' in making judgements on an individual child's achievement (SCAA 1994). A teacher's own assessments of children's performance are reported alongside the test results.[3] When the teacher's own assessment indicates that the child has largely achieved attainment targets at one level in an aspect, the teacher tests the children using tests selected from the catalogue of national test units to see if a child can achieve further.[4]

8 *Assessing bilingual children*: The NC requires that children should be assessed in the language of instruction and consideration given, in administering and interpreting their performance on assessment tasks, to the possible impact of their first language. A lively example involves the 'over-literal' interpretations of instructions in a mathematics task requiring the children to 'draw round half of the children' resulting in drawings

'through' half of each child rather than half of a group of children! The Leicestershire LEA in conjunction with the Bilingual Working Party (1989) has produced helpful descriptors of language levels to assist teachers in exploring possible gaps between children's social language, which might seem to be fluent, and their understanding of 'technical English' as applied to a range of school tasks.

9 *Assessing children under 5*: The majority of forms of assessment described in this chapter can be used with young children. However, it must be remembered that only 5-year-olds and above are included in the NC assessment procedures: younger children experience a much broader, less subject-dominated curriculum in a majority of under 5s contexts.

What is involved in record keeping?

Record keeping is a routine and essential part of teaching. Making records about professional work such as daily activity plans and children's responses to a range of tasks, forms the basis for decision making about what to monitor, which kinds of behaviours to observe more closely and, for example, what aspects of the interaction process of learning and teaching to select for further analysis.

Refining professional competence in keeping track should lead to self-evaluation, making informed choices about priorities for teaching and for further professional development and is included in the kind of self-reflection activities described by Neil Kitson in Chapter 4.

It is vital to keep records up-to-date – it is simply not possible to remember pertinent specific observations until, for example, the end of the day, week or term before making a note of them. It is also necessary to avoid trying to make notes of too many things. The challenge is to discern what records are essential and practicable and to maintain them, even if they are not ideal in every way. With practice it is possible to evolve an improved system for your own use. Teachers' records may differ in design according to their intended purposes (see Clift 1981; Fisher 1991) and can loosely be clustered into three main types – *'baseline' records, continuous records* and *summary records* – which correspond with the sequence of tasks likely to face the teacher throughout the school year (these will be explained later and examples given).

Portfolios and records of achievement

The School Portfolio consists of a collection of examples of work which demonstrate the standard of consistency between groups of teachers.

The Individual Portfolio consists of an annotated collection of work by an individual child, put together by the teacher in order to demonstrate the attainment for a particular child.

The Record of Achievement should:

• be a positive record of the achievements and experiences gained during the period of a child's education;

• embrace the wider interests of the student and not be confined to achievements and experiences within formal education;

• be drawn up through a process of discussion between a student, teacher and others over a period of time;

• be drawn up in a way which respects the student's right to privacy;

• be available to all children;

• be the property of the child to whom the record refers;

• facilitate the continuity of learning and transfer between stages of education and between education and adult life, from years 1–10 and beyond;

• be a catalyst for improving the teaching and learning within the school and fully integrated into the curriculum structure;

• encourage active learning styles through an emphasis upon the process of learning;

• encourage children to take greater responsibility for their learning by reviewing achievements and experience in negotiation with their teachers.

(from Eyres Monsell Primary School, Leicester)

Figure 12.2   Example of a 'Statement of Principles about RoA'

The Record of Achievement is child-centred (with samples of work selected by the child) and provides examples of achievement.

Schools generally provide handbooks for teachers regarding matters of administration and management of the curriculum and assessment which may include guidelines on principles of Records of Achievement. One such example shown in Figure 12.2 serves as a useful guide. Schools may provide their own style of records for different aspects of the curriculum to assist the child. Figures 12.3 to 12.6 provide a selection of record formats for children to use by colouring in as they acquire the relevant competences or by completing them.

As can be seen, the format of records can vary considerably from school to school and this flexibility is both interesting and desirable – if only to keep teacher motivation! Teachers frequently use class *lists* (alphabetical or other order of children's names) for the purposes of drawing up *matrices* to note, for example, tasks for children to complete or comments on their performance (see Figures 3.2 and 3.7 in Chapter 3).

Other lists, perhaps those for 'emergent reading', might be presented in the form of *tick lists,* sometimes with spaces for noting dates. The boxes for ticks or colouring are sometimes coded to allow for a range of additional messages to be quickly noted. The use of simple headed *columns* for entering comments is well illustrated in Manchester's Early Literacy Project (1988) shown in Figure 12.7.

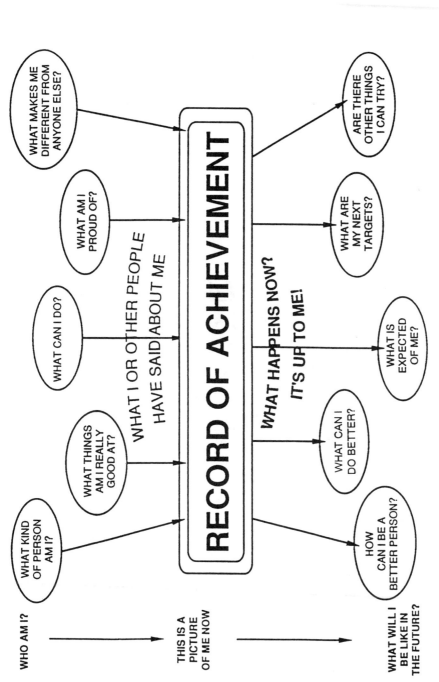

WHO AM I? → THIS IS A PICTURE OF ME NOW → WHAT WILL I BE LIKE IN THE FUTURE?

WHAT KIND OF PERSON AM I?

WHAT THINGS AM I REALLY GOOD AT?

WHAT CAN I DO?

WHAT AM I PROUD OF?

WHAT MAKES ME DIFFERENT FROM ANYONE ELSE?

WHAT I OR OTHER PEOPLE HAVE SAID ABOUT ME

RECORD OF ACHIEVEMENT

WHAT HAPPENS NOW?
IT'S UP TO ME!

HOW CAN I BE A BETTER PERSON?

WHAT CAN I DO BETTER?

WHAT IS EXPECTED OF ME?

WHAT ARE MY NEXT TARGETS?

ARE THERE OTHER THINGS I CAN TRY?

Figure 12.3

Early Years

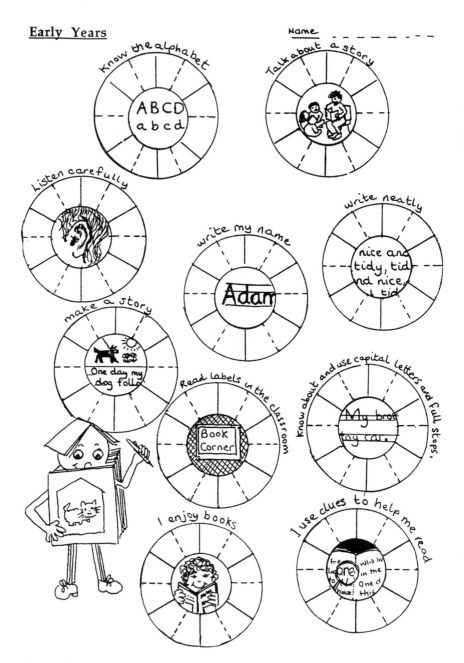

Figure 12.4

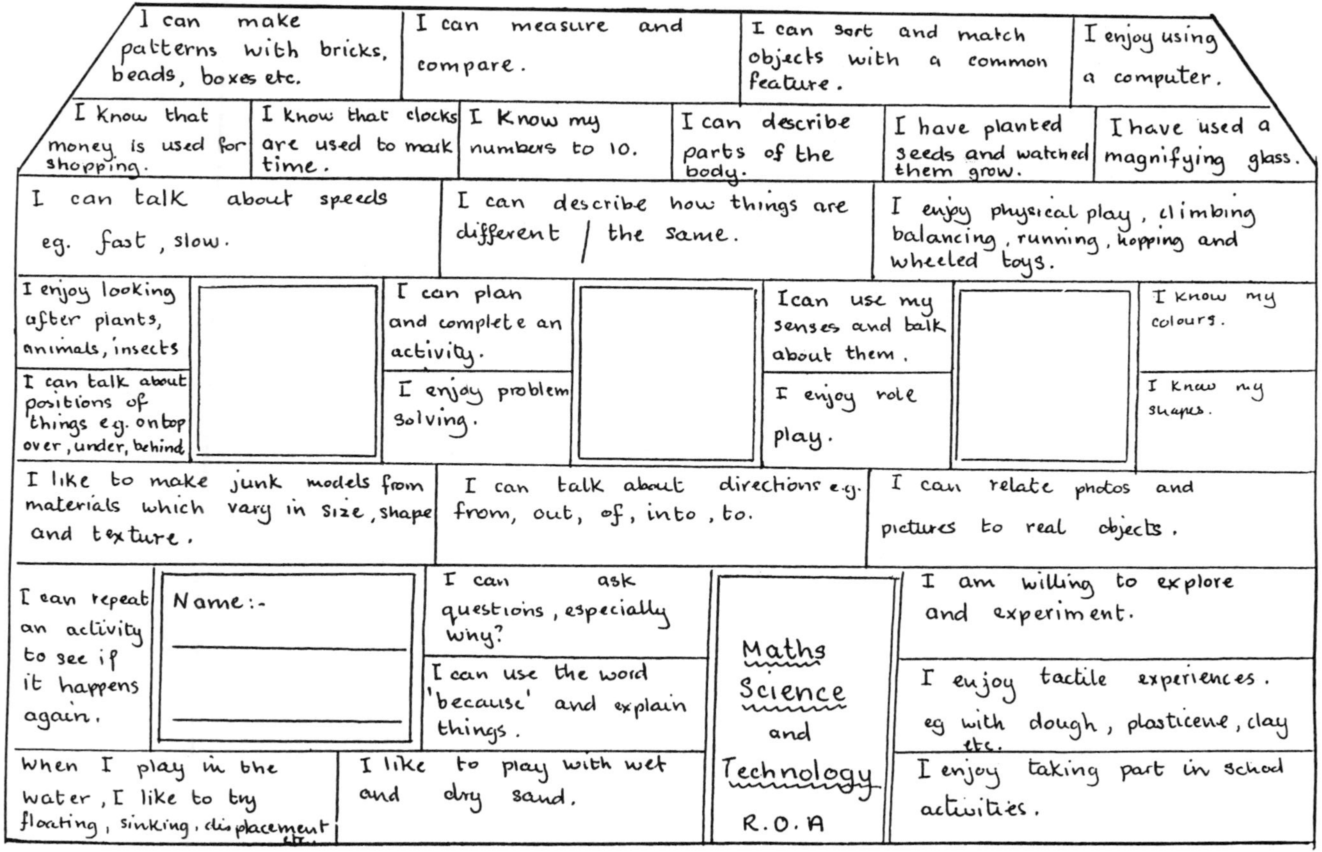

I can make patterns with bricks, beads, boxes etc.

I know that money is used for shopping.

I know that clocks are used to mark time.

I can measure and compare.

I know my numbers to 10.

I can sort and match objects with a common feature.

I enjoy using a computer.

I have planted seeds and watched them grow.

I have used a magnifying glass.

I can describe parts of the body.

I can talk about speeds eg. fast, slow.

I can describe how things are different / the same.

I enjoy physical play, climbing balancing, running, hopping and wheeled toys.

I enjoy looking after plants, animals, insects

I can plan and complete an activity.

I can use my senses and talk about them.

I know my colours.

I can talk about positions of things eg. on top, over, under, behind

I enjoy problem solving.

I enjoy role play.

I know my shapes.

I like to make junk models from materials which vary in size, shape and texture.

I can talk about directions eg. from, out, of, into, to.

I can relate photos and pictures to real objects.

I can repeat an activity to see if it happens again.

Name:-

I can ask questions, especially why?

I can use the word 'because' and explain things.

I am willing to explore and experiment.

I like to play with wet and dry sand.

When I play in the water, I like to try floating, sinking, displacement.

Maths Science and Technology R.O.A

I enjoy tactile experiences. eg with dough, plasticene, clay etc.

I enjoy taking part in school activities.

Figure 12.5

When you can use a piece of software well write its name on the correct screen above.

Please tick

I can use the concept keyboard ☐

I can load a disk ☐   I used the BBC ☐

I can save a disc ☐   I used the Nimbus ☐

I have used the printer ☐

Name .... **Class** .... **Year** ....

Figure 12.6   Example of a computer RoA

Date	Book	Comments	Initials
8 Oct	The Two Snowmen	Liked this book, needed a little help	Teacher *gcb.*
10 Oct	The Hen + the Rock →	this will need more help but the class enjoyed the story greatly.	Parent
		READ IT ALL BUT STRUGGLED WITH ALOT OF THE NEW WORDS.	*ll* Teacher
12 Oct.	Peace at Last. (it's a hot favourite) ←	A lovely book, that holds the child's interest from beginning to end.	*gcb.*
13 Oct	The little monster.	Rather tired tonight, James started to read the left hand side of the pages, but reserved to the right hand side after a drink.	*gcb.*
14 Oct	Hairy Bear (I think he's having a rest cure).	No problems tonight, James still finds this book amusing and told me he's going to have a midnight feast!	
	Glad he lives at your house! ←	James interested in the story especially their adventure in the tree house. ↓ James read this to me really well.	
15 Oct	The Pirates		
	☺		
16 Oct	Hungry mouse.		
19 Oct	To Town	Must be having a rest. Book·partner easy	*gcb.*
20 Oct	The Rat. What a surprise.	Only like you or I reading "Woman's Own"! Read upto P.10: enjoying the story so far Read some more to Mrs. Logan.	
21 "	Little Monkey.	at low ebb tonight. Full of a cold. Hence not much reading done	
23 Oct	Boys + Girls	He's asked for it again. Read at his mamma's	*gcb*

Figure 12.7 Parent comment card

Photo 18   Assessing and recording learning

How and when to assess and record

How, when and exactly what to record depends on the purpose of the assessment or record. Together with the detailed documentation to assist teachers with formal assessment of the NC, the following aspects aim to provide a framework and to develop points made above.

A framework for keeping track

You first need to be clear about the requirements in law within the NC. In order to establish your own knowledge base you will need to:

1 Consult the NC framework and study the requirements for children's learning and assessment across the full curriculum.
2 Consult the LEA guidelines and teacher colleagues about ways in which these guidelines extend understanding of the national requirements and relate particularly to your locality.
3 Consult the School Policy Statement and teacher colleagues about the practical planning and implementation of the school's policies.
4 Decide on the particular purpose(s) of your assessment or records.
5 Select or design the assessment procedure or record you require. Decide on the purpose(s) of the particular record.
6 Try it out, evaluate it and adapt as appropriate.

You will need gradually to establish your own ways of using (and where relevant, devising) records for the range of purposes mentioned previously. The most immediate ones will be:

1 *Day-to-day records* – projective plans for organizing, managing and teaching class, groups and individuals which:
  • mainly relate to teaching activities (self/teaching assistants/visitors/ parents and other helpers);
  • mainly relate to individual children's progress;
  • can be records made by children about their work;
  • can include samples of children's work.

Other records which you will use in time include:

2 *Summary records* – these can be weekly/monthly/termly plans and reviews for all subjects and/or topics to include:
  • teacher's plan;
  • class achievement/attainment test results;
  • transition records (across phases, for example Early Years or Infants to Juniors or Upper Primary) for individual children;
  • transfer records (between schools when child moves).
3 *Diagnostic records*, including case studies (for example of 'gifted' children, bilingual children, travelling children or children with special educational needs) and involve:
  • screening/identifying special needs (see DfE 1994);
  • noting plans for individual educational programmes or relevant support strategies based on assessment.
4 *Welfare records* which indicate liaison with outside agencies.
5 *Reports to parents* which relate the child's achievements to previously stated (and noted) plans and expectations based on previous assessments (or home-school liaison in the case of children just starting school). It is preferable that parents are regarded as partners with teachers at all levels of their children's education, and that their knowledge is taken into account, as well as the child's views, particularly at the case-study level of assessment. This is particularly so where 'on-entry' assessments are made of children just beginning the process of schooling (see Wolfendale 1993).

Time	Plan Curriculum subjects/ Activities (class/group/ind) Organization/resources needed	Record Were plans carried out? What changes were needed? Comments? Reminders?

Figure 12.8   A sample day-to-day record

Each of these five types of records relates to different forms of practice. The first two are more fully explored below and reference sources are provided for further information about all five kinds of records in the chapter notes.

Day-to-day records – the teacher's log

In addition to recording attendance, you will generally keep notes of daily plans on which to make comments on significant events. One of the purposes of informal daily records can be to remind you to adjust the timetable or the content of particular work sessions in the light of 'happenings'. A simple three column layout for a 'day record' might look like Figure 12.8. Such daily notes may form part of a 'teacher's log' or 'journal' which could also include spaces for dated entries about significant events in children's or your own learning.

Informal continuous assessment

Advice on routine, informal assessment is provided in the Teacher's Guidebooks for most published 'schemes' across the range of subject areas. Increasingly there are examples of record formats for use *by children* in groups, pairs or individually. Very useful examples of such records are to be found within the Oxford Reading Tree Scheme as part of the 'Factfinder Resources' (see References).

With early years children, informal recording is the most usual means by which to identify children's activities. This may be as simple as merely noting what the child actually *does* within the choices available (see Figure 3.3, Chapter 3) but will also be related to *how* children approached activities, who else was involved, how long they persisted, language competence and the presence of adults (see Moyles 1989). These will nearly always be related to specific observations from which assessment will be made (see Drummond 1993).

Observation records may be made for assessment of particular activities or tasks. These may be for routine purposes of checking understanding at the beginning or end of a unit of activities. Such records may be made by teachers, assistants or children. In recording direct observations of children, objectivity in data collection and interpretation will need to be studied (see Chapter 3). Take-home tasks may also include records for children or parents, for example where comments are sought from parents on their observation of children's reading at home.

Making speedy notes while talking with an individual child in the course of moving around the class as children work, the TIC Record format, shown in Figure 12.8, has proved to be helpful as it relates to the immediate interaction and provides an instant check on the child's capabilities. It consists simply of two intersecting lines in which to organize notes. Such notes take only a little time to make while talking with the child and up to four children might be 'visited' during a single day. Thus, by using a class list, a rota can be established to remind the teacher to 'check' and have an encouraging word with every child in the class over a period of a week or two prior to starting the rota again. The notes can be added to logs, 'mark books' or portfolios. Such notes are particularly helpful in discussions with mentors or parents as you will have a ready vignette to bring to mind.

'Mark Books' (and 'Remark Books') or cumulative lists of comments about children's progress may be kept by teachers in a different location from their day-to-day logs or journals. Such 'mark books' record class and individual outcomes of periodic assessments throughout the school year. The results should yield information about the range or spread of attainment levels and developmental levels within the class as a whole. Mark books may also include information about individual children's profiles across the curriculum. A useful framework for individual assessment in reading is that provided by the Individual Assessment Record of the Reading 2000 Storytime 2 materials (1993), reproduced in Figure 12.9.[5]

Summary records

At the end of each period of transition, such as moving from nursery to reception, infants to juniors and junior to secondary school, summary records will be required. These may be drawn upon for reports to be communicated to parents and for passing on to the next teacher. There may be some aspects of *confidentiality* to be considered and undoubtedly there will be areas relating to curriculum continuity and progression which require to be 'connected' for efficient planning for the next stage.[6]

For summary records, as for informal ongoing records, it is important that the information they contain can be readily related to plans for further learning. They should point towards likely requirements for support for learning and provision of further access to the curriculum through independent learning and collaborative learning. Also, where possible, records should be designed to bring about a sense of personal valuing of learning

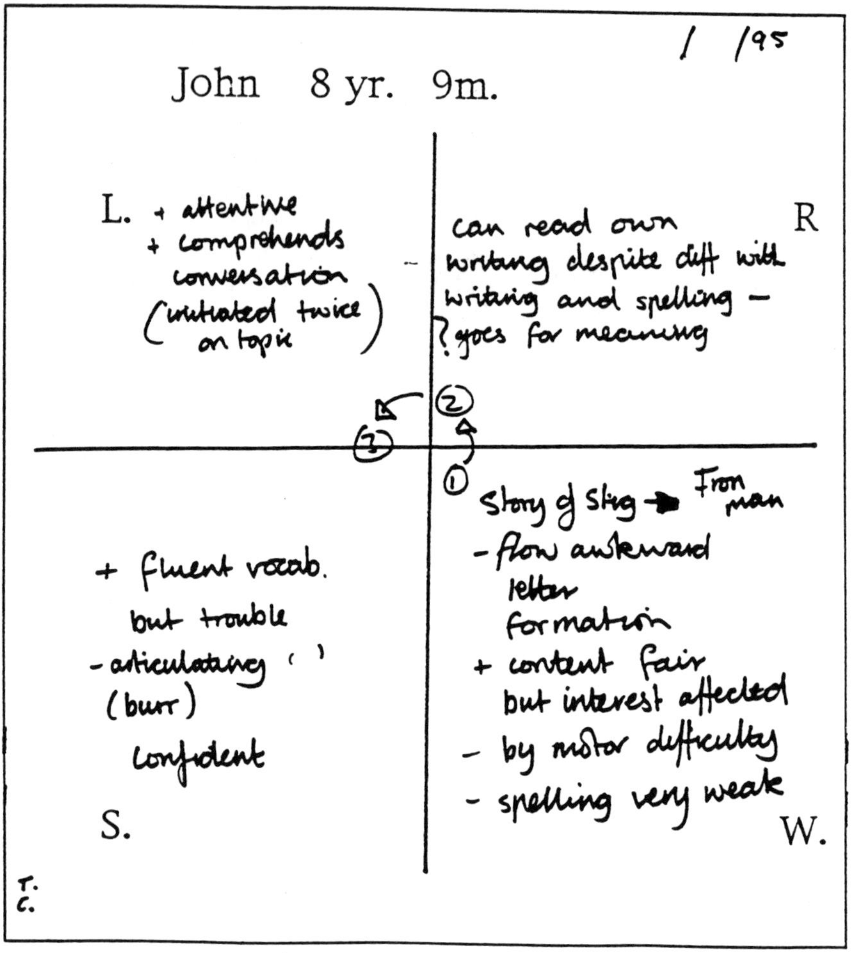

Figure 12.9 TIC Record

and recognition of achievements in the personal assessment statements by the individual child. A record system which involves the children in setting their own goals through dialogue with peers and teachers and recording their attainment of these goals, is likely to be both enjoyable and effective in guiding children towards greater confidence in continuing to set goals and responsibly keeping track of their activities and achievements.

Conclusion

Knowledge and skill in assessment and record-keeping procedures are very much a part of 'real teaching'. It might seem daunting at first but remember,

Individual Assessment Record : School Netherlee

Name Hannah

Age (D of B) 6yrs 2mths

Class P1

Date June '96

Strengths

Hannah came to school already very interested in and enthusiastic about books. Within 2 months she could read very well. Her oral reading is fluent, expressive and meaningful. Reading silently she is capable of reading and understanding 'novels' as well as picture stories. She is skilled in understanding characters' behaviour & feelings. When using follow up material from her class reading book she can readily find information needed to give an appropriate answer.

Comments

Hannah is a very able pupil in every area of the curriculum. Her reading skills are well in advance of her peer group and I have come across no reading material which she has been unable to read although she may not be able to understand some areas outwith her experience.

Developmental Needs

Hannah needs to be given reading materials which will extend and consolidate her skills and encourage her enthusiasm for reading to develop even further.

Support Strategy

Each week Hannah spent two twenty minute periods with a learning support teacher, working with other able children, in order that she could develop her full potential.

Outcomes

Hannah was able to print out her own stories on the computer.

Future Targets (Next Steps)

Increased experience of a variety of texts to improve and develop her comprehension and reference skills further.

Teacher Isabel J. Eden   Date June '96.

Parent _____   Date _____

Reading 2000 Storytime. Teacher's Guide 2

Figure 12.10

you have already demonstrated some of the necessary competences. For example, you have managed to organize your own note-making for planning, learning, reviewing and coping effectively with many practical events in your own life including successful completion of several examination courses.

This chapter has emphasized that, through your use of appropriate assessment procedures and attractive and efficient modes of record keeping shared with children, you will be contributing in a directly and strongly motivating way to individual children's increasing self-confidence, competence and control as learners.

Notes

1 See also the NC; RoA National Steering Committee (RANSC) Report (1989); and the trend towards greater use of 'formative profiling' and goal setting through discussions between children and teachers.

2 With reference to specific learning difficulties (SpLD), and perhaps spurred on by the media through, for example, the National Literacy Campaign and the Dyslexia Campaign, several professional associations as well as LEAs and schools are involved in developing resources to assist teachers and children in this aspect of their work. Sources for further information include: the DfE (1994) Code of Practice in Identifying and Assessing Children with Special Educational Needs; National Literacy Campaign including the '99 by '99 Campaign; British Dyslexia Association; UK Reading Association; The Schools Library Association Library Power Campaign (1995); Language and Reading Centre, Reading University.

3 In Scotland, the National Guidelines: English Language 5–14 (SOED 1991) provide descriptions of attainment targets which are set out in five levels of increasing demand (A–E). In *Assessment 5–14* Scottish teachers are required to 'report on children's learning and attainment across the whole curriculum, using their professional judgement and the evidence available to them from their own continuous assessment throughout the year' (SOED 1991: 1). They are provided with helpful guidelines including also *Reporting 5–14: Promoting Partnership* (SOED 1992).

4 Further information is contained in an HMI 5–14 publication *A Practical Guide for Teachers in Primary and Secondary Schools* (SOED 1994). The Scottish Examination Board 5–14 Assessment Unit provides a catalogue of national test units (August 1994) from which teachers may select reading, writing and mathematics units.

5 Further information about reading tests and literacy assessment may be found in Wray and Medwell (1991) and Pumfrey (1985 and 1991). For further diagnostic information on literacy development see Kemp (1989) and Clay (1993). For information regarding assessment in other areas of the primary curriculum and of children's development, abilities and difficulties in learning, see Blenkin and Kelly (1992) (who include discussions on bilingualism and assessment) and Harding and Beech (1991). Further information on the practicalities of ongoing record keeping can be found in *Primary Language Record* (Barrs et al. 1990).

6 If you are particularly concerned with young children, Bartholomew and Bruce (1993) offer very useful guidance on making assessments and keeping appropriate records.

References and further reading

Bartholomew, L. and Bruce, T. (1993) *Getting to Know You: A Guide to Record-Keeping in Early Childhood Education and Care.* Sevenoaks: Hodder and Stoughton.

Barrs, M., Ellis, S., Hester, H. and Thomas, A. (1988) *The Primary Language Record Handbook.* London: ILEA/CLPE.

Barrs, M., Ellis, S., Hester, H. and Thomas, A. (1990) *Patterns of Learning.* London: ILEA/CLPE.

Barrs, M. and Johnson, G. (1993) *Recording Keeping in the Primary School.* London: Hodder and Stoughton.

Blenkin, G.M. and Kelly, A.V. (1992) *Assessment in Early Childhood Education.* London: Paul Chapman.

Clay, M.M. (1993) *An Observation Survey of Early Literacy Achievement.* Auckland, NZ: Heinemann.

Clay, M.M. (1993) *Reading Recovery: A Guidebook for Teachers In Training.* Auckland, NZ: Heinemann.

Clift, P. (1981) *Record Keeping in the Primary School.* London: Schools Council/Macmillan.

Department of Education and Science (1988) *National Curriculum Task Group on Assessment and Testing: A Report. (The TGAT Report).* London: DES/WO.

Department for Education (1992) *Code of Practice on the Identification and Assessment of Special Educational Need.* London: DfE Central Office of Information.

Department for Education (1994) *Assessing 7–11 year olds in 1995,* Circular 21/94. London: HMSO.

Drummond, M-J. (1993) *Assessing Children's Learning.* London: David Fulton.

Fisher, R. (1991) *Recording Achievement in Primary Schools.* Oxford: Blackwell.

Gipps, C. (1994) *Beyond Testing: Towards a Theory of Educational Assessment.* Lewes: Falmer Press.

Harding, L. and Beech, J.R. (1991) *Educational Assessment of the Primary School Child.* Windsor: NFER/Nelson.

Kemp, M. (1989) *Watching Children Read and Write: Observational Records for Children with Special Needs.* Australia: Thomas Nelson.

Leicestershire Local Educational Authority in conjunction with the Bilingual Working Party (1991) *Assessing Bilingual Pupils at Key Stage 1 and Key Stage 2. Advice for Primary Schools.* Leicester: Leicestershire County Council.

Manchester City Council Education Department (1988) *Manchester Early Literacy Project: A Framework for Assessment.* Manchester: Manchester City Council.

Mitchell, C. and Koshy, V. (1993) *Effective Teacher Assessment.* London: Hodder and Stoughton.

Moyles, J.R. (1989) *Just Playing? The Role and Status of Play in Early Childhood Education.* Milton Keynes: Open University Press.

National Curriculum Targets Class Record KS1 (1990) Blackburn: Educational Services Ltd.

Oxford Reading Tree Fact Finders Teacher's Guide 1 (1994) Oxford: Oxford University Press.

Pumfrey, P. (1985) *Reading Tests and Assessment Techniques,* 2nd edn. Sevenoaks: Hodder and Stoughton in association with the UK Reading Association.

Pumfrey, P. (1991) *Improving Reading in the Junior School: Challenges and Responses.* London: Cassells.

Records of Achievement National Steering Committee (RANSC) (1989) *Records of*

Achievement: Report of the Records of Achievement National Steering Committee.
London: DES/WO.
Reading 2000 Storytime Teacher's Guide (1993) Harlow: Oliver and Boyd.
Schools Curriculum and Assessment Authority (1994) *The Review of the National
Curriculum: A Report on the 1994 Consultation.* London: SCAA.
Scottish Office Education Department (1991) *Assessment 5–14.* Edinburgh: HMSO.
Scottish Office Education Department (1992) *Reporting 5–14: Promoting Partnership.*
Edinburgh: HMSO.
Scottish Office Education Department (1994) *A Practical Guide for Teachers in Primary
and Secondary Schools.* Edinburgh: HMSO.
Scottish Office Education Department (1995) *Taking a Close Look at English Lan-
guage.* Curriculum Assessment in Scotland 5–14. Edinburgh: HMSO.
Wolfendale, S. (1993) *All About Me.* Nottingham: NES.
Wray, D. and Medwell, J. (1991) *Literacy and Language in the Primary Years.* Lon-
don: Routledge.

Acknowledgements

Thanks are due to the following people for their generous assistance and permission
to include examples of records: Mrs A. Baker and Knighton Fields Primary School,
Leicester for Figure 12.5; Miss M. Hardy and Mrs S. Seth for information about
the Leicester Bilingual Project; Mr A. James, Headteacher, Levens Primary School
for Figure 12.3; Manchester Education Authority for Figure 12.7; Mrs H. McLullich,
the staff of Netherlee Primary School, Glasgow and Oliver and Boyd for Figure
12.9; Mr P. Ranson, Headteacher, Mrs J. Putick and the staff of Eyres Monsell
Primary School, Leicester for Figures 12.2, 12.4 and 12.5; and, finally, Mr R.
Reobuck, Mrs C. Hutchinson and Mr E. Spencer, HMI, for information from
SOED.

13

It's not fair!
Equal opportunities in practice

Wendy Suschitzky

Cameo 1

Most of the children in my teaching practice class live on the council estate and several are of Asian origin. Also, sometimes a boy with a hearing impairment comes in to work with the other children. I'm all for equal opportunities but where do I start in the classroom?

Cameo 2

Beginner teacher: How do you deal with equal opportunities in the classroom?

Teacher: I treat them all the same. I do not see that a child's colour or sex are important. Look over there, both boys and girls are playing with the train set.

The beginner teacher observes the group and finds that it is the boys who are building the track with assistance from the girls. Once play with the trains starts, the boys dominate and the girls quickly become excluded.

Cameo 3

After a class visit to a local Hindu Temple, several children taunt a Hindu member of the class saying 'Your priest wears pyjamas'.

Introduction

The issue of inequality in our society and the educationalists' response requires careful and considered attention. The demands on teachers today are greater than ever before and there is a danger that, in their efforts to prioritize, issues of inequality do not feature strongly. However, the implementation of equal opportunities for all children must not be marginalized. Discussions on how to achieve this in practice can challenge deep-seated values which may even result in rejection of the issues or lack of action for fear of making mistakes. Giving every child entitlement to quality education is *just good practice*.

> Schools would be wrong to accept the view that inequalities in the outcomes of schooling merely reflect inequalities and differences in wider society, and that there is nothing that education can do to counter them.
>
> (Runnymede Trust 1993: 12)

This chapter aims to help you to understand the individual teacher's role in addressing inequalities in education by examining the effect on children's learning. Practical guidelines will be provided for making a classroom the context in which all children have equal access to learning and where positive attitudes towards others are formed.

Learning contexts and the teacher's role

The response given in the second cameo is frequently given by teachers to questions about equal opportunities in the classroom. However, equality of educational opportunity is not achieved if we treat all children the same. The outcome of the above scenario is the continuation of stereotypical behaviour which may deny girls the opportunity to develop technological skills. In order to provide equality of outcome different provision may be necessary (Hogben and Wasley 1989). Technology tasks can sometimes be set for a 'girls only' group. If boys have greater experience of these skills from home then they can easily become frustrated with the girls lack of experience and so be too assertive. A better response to the student's question would be 'I treat them all equally *while recognizing each child's identity*'. Wishing to treat all children the same can hide an underlying reluctance to acknowledge that some children are, for example, black or disabled.

It is now very common in schools to use artefacts, food sampling and visits to introduce children to different ways of life. These are vitally important aspects of the curriculum but, as the example demonstrates, background knowledge of other religions is insufficient to change attitudes and may still result in holding negative views. There is a danger that the exposure actually feeds the intolerance as in the third cameo above. The aim of learning about other ways of living is to understand the factors that have led to the development of that culture and so help children to be able to challenge stereotypical and negative views. It should be acknowledged that culture is not static but is constantly evolving and that the similarities between groups are more important than the differences. As Swann (DES 1985: 323) states in 'Education For All':

> Multicultural education can only develop positively from a serious analysis of the cultural and racial assumptions in the 'normal' British education system. The rejection of an ethnocentric approach requires a commitment to equality which can only come from within each individual.

Each of us must be clear when setting the learning objectives for multicultural activities just as we do for other activities (see Chapter 12).

Framework

There is a framework regarding equal opportunities within which teachers must work. The Education Reform Act (1988) calls for a broad and balanced curriculum which 'promotes the spiritual, moral, cultural, mental and physical development of pupils at the school and of society'. It is clearly stated that pupils must be treated as individuals and that individual needs should be met. Schools must provide equal access to the curriculum and other aspects of school life. The Act also states that schools should challenge myths and stereotypes. Criteria for evaluating a school's arrangement for equal opportunities are given in the Framework for the Inspection of Schools (OFSTED, 1994). So legislation requires that children have entitlement to the curriculum, learn about difference and similarity, and increase their respect and understanding of other cultures. How is this to be interpreted? Is it apparent in the organization and content of the curriculum?

Most LEAs have policies concerning equal opportunities practices in schools. Individual schools also develop policies which they feel are relevant to their particular context, which should express the fundamental values to which a school aspires and be as explicit as possible. However, these can be paper exercises which are long on rhetoric and short on specific action. The task of the classroom teacher is to implement the policy in day-to-day school life. As with any policy, different interpretations will be made dependent upon an individual's perspective. Open discussion by teachers, governors and parents in a climate of trust is vital for the success of any whole school policy as is the continued reflection of the individual practitioner as clearly outlined by Neil Kitson in Chapter 4.

Where do I start?

Primary teaching is concerned with human relationships and is, as Schmidt (1961: 58) points out:

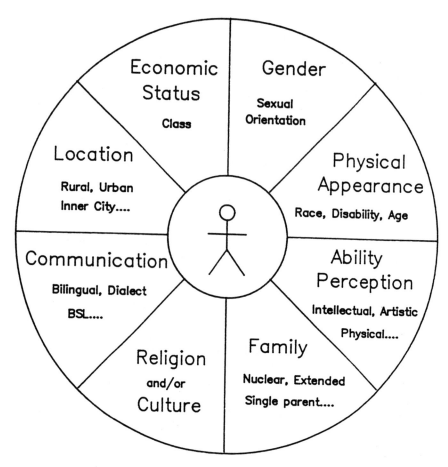

Figure 13.1

. . . a complex activity . . . It is directed by complex organisms – human beings. The recipients of the teaching activity are complex individuals, students, whose characteristics are undergoing continuous and complex change.

As teachers we must start by acknowledging who we are and how our personal value system has evolved. There is a commonly held assumption that schools provide a neutral environment for children's learning but the teacher's verbal and body language, the classroom procedures, the resources provided are not culture free. As Figure 13.1 shows, our self-identity consists of many factors. The relationship between each is significant. For example, a black woman from an ethnic minority background has a different experience of being a woman to that experienced by an indigenous white woman: although there is much commonality, perspectives are different. To be a man or woman is as much concerned with dress, gesture, occupation and social position as it is with biological factors (Oakley 1985). Recognition of diversity and the unequal value that society places on aspects of this is vital to teachers. 'Diversity is itself embodied in subordinate social groups who face a range of inequalities and discriminations' (Hazareesingh *et al.* 1989). This discrimination can be caused by any of the elements in the identity diagram. The important issue is that the consequences of discrimination for certain elements such as racism and sexism are of much greater significance. The task for teachers is to help all children:

• to value themselves;
• to find similarities between their lives and those of other children;
• to be receptive to others and learn from each other;
• not to learn feelings of superiority over any other child for reasons of race, gender or ability.

How do young children absorb negative views about others?

Attitudes are developed by the processes of seeing, hearing and interpreting surroundings (Lane 1984). It is recognized that the early years are the most formative time of life (Janet Moyles explores this further in Chapter 6) but the fact that children as young as three can already have developed negative attitudes is often treated with scepticism. Researchers give evidence that young children can recognize racial difference and are already placing unequal value on groups in society (see Jeffcoate 1979; Milner 1983).

The main influences on children's views come from the home, peer group, media, locality and school. Children today are bombarded by images from television, computer games, comics, magazines, catalogues and roadside hoardings which present a confusing mixture of messages. It is from these that they learn that in our society we award unequal status to certain groups. The absence of women, black and disabled people in prominent positions is apparent. Comics and catalogues reinforce stereotypical behaviour by portraying boys' interests as active and exploratory and girls' interests as domestic, bland and creative. Black people are frequently represented as being a problem or inferior. For example, a Caribbean island can be described as an 'underdeveloped banana republic' until a pop star visits when it becomes a 'tropical paradise'. The images can not only devalue a discriminated child's sense of self but can increase feelings of superiority in other children. The pressures to be the 'same' as the dominant group are considerable. Black children have been known to scrub themselves in the mistaken belief that they can become white.

However, there have been some recent attempts to redress the balance with black programme presenters, news readers, and actors in advertisements challenging stereotypical behaviour. However, this is only one small part of the influences on young children's attempts to make sense of their world.

Where do I start in the classroom?

In order to address the issues in relation to classroom practice, ask yourself the following questions. As you set criteria for evaluating your practice, ensure that you include equality issues.

Am I making a negative assessment of the home experiences of working-class or ethnic minority children?

Recognition must be given that parents are a child's first educators and that an important factor influencing learning is what the learner already knows (Roger Merry explores this in Chapter 5). Teachers must, therefore, recognize each child's prior experience and attempt to understand whatever children hold to be meaningful and significant about their lives (Hazareesingh *et al.* 1989). You can:

• in conjunction with parents, build profiles of the children's home experiences to include family membership, health, customs, housing conditions, rural life-style;
• find ways to stress the similarities and positive aspects of home life;
• encourage children to talk and write about home experiences;
• when making reference to the family, show that you are sensitive to the varied make-up of families today – for example, the production of Father's or Mother's Day cards could cause distress to children from single parent (or Jehovah's Witness) households;
• when inviting parents to assist with classroom activities, discover their particular expertise;
• avoid stereotypical assumptions such as inviting a mother to help with cooking and a father for woodwork.

Do I recognize the language of the home and the child's additional skill of speaking and listening in a second language?

Conflicting messages can be given if the child's first language is devalued at school. At home this language is spoken by those whom the child loves and respects such as grandma or the priest. Siraj-Blatchford (1994: 47) offers a definition of a bilingual child as 'one who uses more than one language regularly and effectively'. The different levels of attainment in each language will be dependent on many factors. Research has shown that a well-developed first language aids the development of a second (Cummins 1984). The Swann Report (DES 1985: 399) offers one model of bilingual education as 'the structuring of the school's work to allow for the use of a pupil's mother tongue as a medium of instruction alongside English'.

This is applied in early years classrooms where the first language is the channel through which early conceptual development takes place. The use of a first language should be encouraged in all phases of the primary school and not just the nursery and reception class where it is considered acceptable until the children have acquired English. This can be achieved by working in partnership with teachers and other adults who share the linguistic background of the children.

Strategies must be developed to enhance the bilingual child's sense of self-esteem and also give status to ethnic community languages so that all children view them positively. You can:

- ask if the school has a policy on first language development;
- make sure that you are aware of the linguistic background;
- avoid negative references to children who have little confidence in English such as 'he has no language';
- read stories from books with dual language texts;
- expose children to writing in varied scripts;
- give equal status in presentation (watch for typed English and hand-written Gujarati);
- encourage children to speak in their first language in paired or group work;
- give bilingual children additional support with English by working alongside children whose first language is English;
- provide good models of communication and its effective use;
- provide tasks that enable learning to take place in practical ways rather than through reading.

Can all children use appropriate methods of communication such as computers, Braille and signing in order to gain access to the curriculum?

Where children with special educational needs are integrated into a class, activities such as art, drama or puppets will enable everyone to express themselves through speech or non-verbal communication. Activities can be devised to allow children to experience Braille and learn some simple signs in British Sign Language in order to understand the significance of their use within the disabled community.

Relationships

Do I have different expectations of children owing to factors of gender, class and race?

Children absorb messages about the kinds of relationships established between teacher and children. One aim is to create an environment where all children feel accepted and stretched to their full potential but teachers are often unaware that their behaviour is discriminatory. For example, if a teacher always stumbles over Asian names showing irritation, then children will receive a message that Asian children are a nuisance. A study investigating teachers' talk in the classroom (Biggs and Edwards 1991) found that interactions with white children were more frequent and extensive than with ethnic minority children. In addition, girls received fewer directions and reprimands than boys. Coates (1986) reports that boys demand more teacher attention than girls, thus giving its own messages about gender 'importance'.

The under-achievement of working-class or ethnic minority children is frequently blamed on their own inadequacies or that of their family. However, we must examine the system to see if our expectations of children's success matches their true abilities, as Janet Moyles takes up in Chapter 2. Second language learners are often not sufficiently challenged cognitively until they have mastered English (Siraj-Blatchford 1994). So:

* when assessing children be aware that assumptions may be based on race, gender or class;
* take account of the process of learning when assessing children and not only of the end product;
* assess bilingual children by their understanding of concepts rather than on their level of written English;
* make a positive stand to raise the self-esteem of working-class children;
* avoid rewarding or reprimanding behaviour that fits with sex role expectations, such as scolding girls more readily than boys for rowdiness or fighting;
* avoid remarks such as 'Young ladies don't do that'; 'Big boys don't cry'; 'Can I have a strong boy to lift this table';
* encourage all children to express a range of emotions, e.g. boys can be sensitive and caring;
* set the same expectation of independence in learning for girls as that set for boys;
* when assigning classroom duties ensure that boys carry out their share of tidying;
* set high expectations of success for girls in maths and science;
* ensure that interactions with children with special educational needs are not patronizing;
* obtain information about the backgrounds of all children, but particularly those from ethnic minority families, and find out how to pronounce names that are unfamiliar to you.

How do I answer children's questions concerning race and disability?

Often teachers experience confusion and embarrassment and do not answer with the same frankness and truthfulness that is now mainly given to children's questions about sex. The reason may be due to our own internalized attitude which we need to recognize and learn to overcome. Try to:

- encourage children to talk about their bodies, discussing basic aspects of hair colour, eye colour, skin colour, body parts and so on as factual information;
- ensure that children have access to positive pictures depicting people from many races and with varied physical appearance;
- make sure that paint and crayons are available in appropriate skin colours.

Can I handle with sensitivity incidents such as racist name calling?

Too frequently there is over-reaction and a great fuss made of the perpetrator while the victim is forgotten. Children from ethnic minorities need to know that racism is not their fault so you should:

- provide support for the victim;
- encourage children to express their feelings;
- adopt a calm but firm approach referring to school policies;
- insist on the latter being carried out effectively.

How do the adults in the school relate to each other?

The adult-to-adult relationships formed within a school present role models to the children. It may be necessary to:

- examine the way that tasks are shared by gender;
- give status to ethnic minority personnel;
- when speaking to parents who do not share your language, aim for a balance between speaking too fast and idiomatically and being patronizingly simple and loud.

Curriculum

Do I plan for children's learning with equal opportunities in mind?

Issues of equality must be integral to all children's learning experiences and not be considered as a few isolated inputs. So the planning of concepts, skills and knowledge for children's learning must take into account the fostering of attitudes and inequalities of delivery. We must ensure that children grow up with 'fundamental concepts of justice, fairness, equality, co-operation and sharing' that are not distorted (Siraj-Blatchford 1992: 109) and in order to do this we should:

- give recognition to all children's prior experiences;
- use group work that will help children to develop co-operation and understanding of others within the class (strategies for this are included by Sylvia McNamara in Chapter 10);

- plan opportunities for girls and ethnic minority children to take a leading role;
- plan tasks that allow for differentiation (as explored in Chapter 2);
- encourage the acquisition of the skills of analysis, criticism and evaluation (in children as well as yourself);
- arrange for girls-only technology groups, if necessary;
- encourage the use of first language in pair work;
- set the context of mathematical and scientific work in non-stereotypical settings (Tina Jarvis gives some useful examples in Chapter 7);
- recognize that stereotyping by sex disadvantages both girls and boys;
- ensure that there is opportunity for all children to experience a range of roles such as both nurturing and active ones within a range of curriculum opportunities.

Does the content of the curriculum reflect an ethnocentric or gender restricted perspective?

The content should reflect our socially and culturally diverse society and its interdependence with the wider world. It should acknowledge the contribution of women and academics from non-Western cultures to our knowledge base. Jeffcoate (1979) suggests that a curriculum that reflects this is more stimulating, interesting and challenging for all children. This is also true for the teacher. Emphasis should be placed on the similarities and differences between the ways that societies address their basic needs. Examination should be made of the perspectives from which history and geography are written. A global approach is particularly important in science which previously has presented a narrow outlook influenced by the discoveries of Western males. Of course, that is not to deny that provision of knowledge of British culture is also important in order to understand the context of the British way of life. It is vital, however, to:

- find out if any member of staff within the school holds a responsibility for equal opportunities in the curriculum and talk to that person;
- make certain you present accurate information that a) challenges stereotypical views, b) helps children to understand the reasons for change in our society and c) does not devalue non-European contributions;
- use the power of stories to shape children's perceptions of the world by encouraging traditional tales that reflect working people and ethnic minority groups (Jane Hislam explores this aspect more fully in Chapter 9);
- ensure that, in history sessions, the lives and contributions of ordinary people from a range of different backgrounds are presented;
- introduce varied counting systems and pattern work such as Islamic patterns for developing geometrical concepts;
- use traditional games from a range of cultures in PE and other areas of curriculum;
- give accurate reasons why people have come to settle in the UK;

- ensure that expressive arts reflects the richness of non-Western art, music, dance, drama and architecture (a point very clearly expressed by Martin Wenham in chapter 8).

Do I present resources which demonstrate the invisibility of ethnic minority, disabled people and of working-class culture? Do materials portray stereotypical life-styles?

The way learning experiences are presented is crucial in addressing inequality: the use of positive images and non-stereotypical contexts can influence children's sense of identity and their view of the world. Frequently materials are presented where Western culture is seen as the standard by which other cultures are measured. Every communication non-verbal, verbal and written expresses an individual's particular view of the world. Klein (1985) argues that, when examining the bias of an author of children's books, one needs to ask whose bias is being reflected? If the bias reveals a view of one group as superior to another then this is unacceptable. Many schools have addressed this issue in recent years and it would be worthwhile to:

- find out if any member of staff holds responsibility for checking resources for bias and whether this has been undertaken (if not, at least you can do it yourself for your particular classroom using the following points);
- obtain information about specialist suppliers and publishers from the school or from your local college library;
- find out how to access the LEA's multi-cultural resources;
- examine materials for representation of certain groups in a tokenistic way;
- ensure that all people are presented in a natural, everyday range of settings;
- choose books that address issues such as disability or age in a sensitive way;
- choose materials that reflect the life-style of modern, British, minority group members;
- examine resources for negative portrayal of ethnic minorities, disabled people, the aged and single parents;
- ensure that materials reflect varied family life and not just that of a nuclear family;
- ensure that true facial characteristics and clothing are presented (watch for the white face which has been coloured brown);
- choose books with lively female characters and people in non-traditional occupations;
- examine materials for use of racist and sexist language;
- provide materials where common experiences are emphasized for diverse groups;
- ensure that multi-cultural equipment is used in the classroom, such as the objects provided for counting or weighing or home corner contents;

- encourage older children to recognize bias in books and the media by examining newspaper articles, television programmes and toy catalogues.

If you have difficulty obtaining information and resources keep asking. The more requests that resource staff and libraries receive the more materials will be produced. The response that 'we haven't got the knowledge' only perpetuates the inequalities.

If the school's population is predominantly white, do I present the curriculum and resources in a way that reflects our multi-racial society?

It is vitally important that white children learn to value others and not to absorb ideas about superiority through ignorance. Children do not fully develop emotionally and intellectually if they are allowed to hold negative views of others (Lane 1984). However, the use of multi-cultural resources can raise the response from parents 'but there is no problem here'. Open discussions must be held with parents to explain the reasons for their use and the effects of discrimination and stereotyping. It may be useful to find out if the school in which you are currently working has approached these issues with its parents and governors so that you know where you stand.

Do I accept the special circumstances of traveller children?

Understanding is required of traveller life-style, and acknowledgement should be given of the extreme hostility which these children may encounter. The use of positive images reflecting the traveller way of life, such as mobile homes and fairgrounds, is needed to counter negative attitudes.

Obtain information about each individual's life-style to ascertain needs. Children may come from housed families, mobile groups with infrequent attendance at any particular school or show-ground families, who are settled for the winter months. Remember to:

- keep detailed records to ensure continuity;
- consider distance learning materials which may be required to help the family to support the child.

Do I view the local community in a negative way or see it as a valuable resource for the school?

It is important to understand the influence that the local neighbourhood has on the lives of children. But we must also recognize the multi-faceted nature of any locality. If the school recognizes this and values the richness of the community then it can be a useful resource. It would be well worth the time involved to:

- explore the school's neighbourhood – Antonouris and Wilson (1989) suggest producing a 'locality trail' to include industries, commercial, cultural, educational, religious, and public services;

- invite local people to share their expertise with you and the children on relevant topics;
- consult community members for authenticity of resources;
- invite grandparents to talk with the children to confront assumptions about the elderly;
- plan topic work to include outside visits to the locality.

Conclusion

As a person just setting out on a career in teaching, you have a crucial role to play in addressing inequality. This means being proactive. It is all too easy to respond only when there is a perceived need concerning a particular child or group. This approach reflects a view that these children are a problem and so only short-term actions are required. We must expand our horizons and plan long-term strategies. Classrooms should be places where every child feels safe and important. We must expect high achievement from all children and examine the processes required in achieving this. In order to value others, children must first value themselves. They need to perceive a sense of justice in the education system and should be given the tools to challenge inequality. As teachers, we do have the power to redress the imbalance and challenge the acquisition of negative attitudes.

A few thoughts

1 Where do you currently stand on issues of equal opportunity?
2 Have you ever been in circumstances where you have felt aggrieved at receiving what you considered to be unequal treatment?
3 How did you handle this situation?
4 Scan the next television news you have a chance to watch and reflect on some of the issues raised in this chapter in regard to images of different groups in society such as ethnic minorities, the disabled, the elderly. Are they fairly represented?
5 When you next plan a session with the children, how will you account for equitable differentiation?

References and further reading

Antonouris, G. and Wilson, J. (1989) *Equal Opportunities in School*. London: Cassells.
Biggs, A. and Edwards, A. (1991) 'I treat them all the same': teacher-pupil talk in multi-ethnic classrooms. *Language and Education*, 5 (8): 161–76.
Coates, J. (1986) *Women, Men and Language*. London: Longman.
Cummins, J. (1984) *Bilingualism and Special Education Issues in Assessment and Pedagogy*. Clevedon: Multi Lingual Matters Ltd.
Department for Education and Science (1985) *Education For All* (The Swann Report). London: HMSO.

230   *Wendy Suschitzky*

Department of Education and Science (1988) *The Education Reform Act.* London: HMSO.

Hazareesingh, S., Simms, K. and Anderson, P. (1989) *Educating the Whole Child.* Save The Children.

Hogben, J. and Wasley, D. (1989) *Learning in Early Childhood.* Australia: Education Department of South Australia.

Jeffcoate, R. (1979) *Positive Image. Towards a Multiracial Curriculum.* London: Writers and Readers Publishing Co-operative.

Klein, G. (1985) *Reading Into Racism.* London: Routledge.

Lane, J. (1984) Childcare shapes the future – the need for an anti-racist strategy. *Commission for Racial Equality Education Journal,* 7 (2): 2–4.

Milner, D. (1983) *Children and Race. Ten Years on.* London: Ward Lock Educational.

Oakley, A. (1985) *Sex, Gender and Society.* Aldershot: Gower Publishing Company Ltd.

Office of Standards in Education (1994) *Framework for the Inspection of Schools.* London: OFSTED.

Runnymede Trust (1993) *Equality Assurance in Schools.* London: Trentham Books.

Schmidt, J. (1961) Factor analysis of teaching complexity. *Journal of Experimental Education,* 30 (1): 58.

Siraj-Blatchford, I. (1992) Why understanding cultural differences is not enough, in G. Pugh (ed.) *Contemporary Issues in the Early Years.* London: Paul Chapman.

Siraj-Blatchford, I. (ed.) (1993) *'Race', Gender and the Education of Teachers.* Buckingham: Open University Press.

Siraj-Blatchford, I. (1994) *The Early Years, Laying the Foundations for Racial Equality.* Stoke-on-Trent: Trentham Books.

14

It takes two to tango!
Working with experienced others in the school

**Wendy Suschitzky and
Barbara Garner**

Cameo 1

The beginning teacher is on a visit to a teaching practice school:

Mentor: Have you got any questions?
Beginner teacher: I don't really know what I need to know.

Cameo 2

Beginner teacher observing mentor teaching: Child A asks permission to go to the toilet and is allowed. A few minutes later, child B requests the same and is refused with the mentor referring to the class rules that all children should go to the toilet at playtime.

The beginner teacher's interpretation is that the mentor is inconsistent and that making class rules is a waste of time. The beginner teacher does not have the mentor's knowledge that child A has frequently wet herself in the past. When making the rules together, the class had also agreed that anyone who is really desperate could go to the toilet.

Introduction

Traditional models of teacher education are being challenged by the establishment of new routes into teaching and changes to existing courses where a greater emphasis is being placed on the training provided by schools. This is, in itself, part of a larger, overall onslaught on primary education, explored by Maurice Galton in Chapter 1. As a result new relationships and responsibilities are being created. Recent education reports highlight the quality of teachers as the prime factor in school effectiveness, so those engaged in teacher education must ensure that the training of teachers is of the highest calibre. The success of this is dependent upon the establishment of a real partnership between those who are engaged in teacher education and those who are undertaking training, where each side respects and understands the other.

The terms 'mentor', 'mentoring', 'mentee' and 'protégé' have entered educational jargon. The word 'mentor' originates from Greek mythology, where Ulysses appointed Mentor, his trusted friend, to care and guide his son, Telemachus, during his absence. During an initial teacher education course, the student teacher will be placed with an experienced teacher (mentor) in whose classroom teaching experience will take place. A newly qualified teacher is now required to have an assigned mentor in their first post, who has responsibility for induction into the art of teaching.

This chapter will help you to benefit from various school-based experiences by examining both aspects of the partnership with experienced teachers, who are at least in part responsible for your learning.

Let the dance begin!

Mentoring is sometimes likened to apprenticeship, where a master craftsperson passes skills to young recruits to the trade. However, in teacher education, a beginner teacher should also gain a high level of understanding of the *purpose and place* of those skills (Monaghan and Lunt 1992). Learning how to teach must be valued as an intellectual discipline (Aldrich 1990). The tasks of learning to teach and of mentoring are, therefore, complex; neither is acquired without some effort.

Both mentor and beginner teacher need to develop skills and strategies. For example, in cameo 1, an inexperienced teacher will have insufficient knowledge to ask appropriate questions to such an open invitation. The mentor must take the lead by providing basic information so that questions will arise. As cameo 2 demonstrates, each classroom situation and the interactions found in it are unique and sometimes apparently contradictory. In order to learn how to teach, one must understand the underlying reasons behind professional judgements. Superficial observation of performance does not provide this. Only by mentor and beginner teacher exploring together the meaning of a teaching episode can mentoring be effective. As Linda Hargreaves suggests in Chapter 3, there are many ways in which this observation may occur.

In every school setting you will work alongside many people, so although the relationship with a mentor will be the most important one to establish, ways of working with other adults in the classroom will need to be examined.

Photo 19   Working with a mentor can help a beginner teacher to evaluate her own performance

Mentoring

While there is uncertainty in the educational establishment about the increase in school-based training, there is no opposition to the principle of the mentor role (Jacques 1992). In fact, teachers have always been involved in the training of new entrants to the profession during that aspect of initial teacher education courses commonly called 'teaching practice', 'school experience' or 'partnership'. However, as Jacobi (1991) states, at a superficial level everyone knows what mentoring is, but on closer examination there is a wide variation in practices. The greater the understanding of the concept of mentoring and its implications for schools, the greater the effectiveness of the process. Being a good classroom teacher does not necessarily mean that one will be a good mentor (Jacques 1992; Harber 1993). The skills and knowledge required for teacher education are in many ways different to those considered valuable for the education of children. Mentoring makes new professional demands on classroom teachers, not least that they must begin to articulate practices and processes which have become established patterns of behaviour over their years of teaching. It is clear that schools must recognize their new role and give time and support (Wilkin 1992). However, it is doubtful whether this can be fully achieved in the primary school until teachers have class non-contact time awarded to them, as is common practice in secondary education.

What is the difference between the role of a university tutor and that of a mentor?

There is a danger of the two roles becoming indistinguishable. Hirst (1990) argues that the mentor and university tutor bring different criteria to the assessment of teaching, based on individual backgrounds of school practice or theoretical and research work. McIntyre and Hagger (1993) suggest that a mentor's unique knowledge of the school setting, coupled with frequent contact with the beginner teacher provides a greater degree of continuity and a more valid diagnosis of strengths and weaknesses. A university tutor can focus on specific areas for evaluation, whereas a mentor has an overview of the practice. These perspectives must be seen as complementary and both must acknowledge the other's role in the teacher education partnership.

Nias (1989) states that teaching demands a massive investment of 'self', so teacher education is not just concerned with teaching skills but with the development of the beginner teacher's personal and professional welfare. In order for effective professional development to take place, acknowledgement must be given of the learners as adults and they should be treated accordingly. The establishment of a constructive relationship between the mentor and beginner teacher provides a framework for the mentoring process but what type of relationship should be formed? Should the relationship be one of 'critical friend' or 'critical colleague'? If the mentor and beginner teacher are from different cultural or social backgrounds, or there is a gender or age difference, then recognition must be given of value judgements which may be made, based on these factors. Objectivity is essential to avoid stereotypical assumptions by either partner (see also Wendy Suschitzky's previous chapter).

The first few meetings between beginner teacher and mentor are therefore crucial. An agenda might include:

- reaching a shared understanding about the purpose of the teaching experience;
- sharing of expectations of each other's role;
- understanding of each other's priorities such as the classroom teacher's commitment to her class or the student teacher's workload from college;
- sharing views on the process of adult learning and how this will be carried out – will a sink or swim approach be used or practice followed by evaluation;
- giving recognition to the beginner teacher's prior experience and skills;
- recognizing that beginner teachers will have individual values and theories about teaching, albeit tentative ones;
- making an assessment of needs (of both people);
- setting realistic targets;
- agreeing the format of discussion times;
- recognizing the need to induct beginner teachers into the hidden culture of school, such as where to sit in the staffroom, which mug to use and how to address the headteacher!

Structures and strategies

Until the training of mentors is fully established, and schools are given the time and resources to release teachers from their main function of educating children, mentors and schools will vary considerably in their ability to fulfil an effective mentoring role. We could say that:

THE IDEAL MENTOR IS . . .
An excellent, well-organized, experienced teacher, who is a perceptive observer and a good communicator, in a school that appreciates the education and training role and has a sound policy for its interpretation.

No mentor could be all of those things all of the time: most will have strengths and weaknesses in varying degrees in varying situations. You are most likely to measure your mentor's skills against your own needs whatever you perceive these to be. What you define as excellent/poor, or well organized/poorly organized will relate to *your* level of understanding of good primary practice and may not be the interpretation of others. Since you will wish to emulate what you perceive as successful practice and reject the opposite, it is only by continuous questioning of your assumptions that you will further your development. Goldsberry (1988) defined three models of supervision:

• nominal – shallow form of supervision;
• prescriptive – supervision is there to correct;
• reflective – skilled support, stimulate enquiry into the 'ends and means of teaching'.

It is imperative that beginner teachers know how to get the best out of the situation in which they are placed. In order to achieve the best possible supported teaching experience, you need to clarify your own needs by giving *structure* to your thinking processes and to have *strategies* for meeting those needs. Remember that each of the highlighted mentor qualities above is a quality *you* wish to develop further yourself. Taking each of the main statements about the ideal mentor, we must first ask the following questions.

What is a 'perceptive observer'?

A perceptive observer notices your strengths, weaknesses and needs, not from continual comparison with their own methods, but from the interaction between you and the children. They note in which circumstances you and the children relate well and the causes of this. They recognize the symptoms that arise from difficulties in establishing complex relationships. They are aware where there is a lack of understanding on either side so that needs can be clarified. This maintains a balance between your needs, those of the children and the relationship as a whole. Valuable observations are made, not only during lessons, but from any interactions between you and the children, from how you and they deal with any number of situations and learning strategies.

Structure for considering the 'perceptive observer': Unless the act of observing is approached systematically, both you and your mentor are likely to be confronted with more information than is manageable. It is quite common to feel totally overwhelmed by the number of things that require attention and for mentors to assimilate so much that there is neither time for discussion nor useful depth of observation.

How can a systematic approach be developed between you and your mentor? You have to know what it is you need help with and to make this the basis for observations. Together you need to choose a specific focus by using *Individual Action Plans* or statements of competency – those things it is agreed you will be able to do at the end of a given period of training (see Neil Kitson explanation in Chapter 4).

When setting a focus, you need to see it not only in the light of your own performance but in the light of its effectiveness in creating learning. Feiman-Nemser *et al.* (1993) report that in mentor/beginner teacher interviews the focus was on the performance of the lesson and little attention was given to the underpinning theories. There was a lack of emphasis on aims of lessons and on children's actual learning. You need to try to ensure that your foci are not solely concerned with *your* development but also with the *children's learning*.

Strategies for dealing with the mentor as 'perceptive observer' (or otherwise!): Consider the beginning teacher who stated: 'My mentor never seems to spend time watching me. What can I do?' Discuss the chosen focus with the mentor and decide on the particular focus for a day. This means that even if the mentor, for all manner of reasons, is unable to be in the classroom for any length of time, observations remain focused during even the briefest of opportunities. An experienced teacher can quickly see what is actually happening.

What is a 'good communicator' in relation to the teacher educator role?

A 'good communicator' is primarily looking to develop your learning, and secondly, to share their greater experience and expertise with you. By questioning, they seek your understanding of a given situation. They share their positive observations of what was successful and ask why you think that was. They help you look at what was not successful in the same way, drawing upon your understanding, rather than unloading theirs on to you. They encourage you to develop strategies of your own, sharing possible strategies of theirs. A good communicator only talks in response to your needs and if you are not recognizing them, no amount of good advice is going to be acted on by you. They will leave you with questions unanswered rather than answers for which there have been no questions formulated.

Structure for considering the 'good communicator': The best possible structure for effective feedback is to agree a time and place, ideally once a day, or at least once a week. A formal session takes the training role seriously: incidental feedback often only fulfils the supportive role that keeps things running smoothly. This time the beginning teacher suggests: 'The feedback I receive is very unhelpful. What can I do?' Communication is a two-way process. Good teachers cannot separate their learning from their teaching. Learning involves listening and asking the right questions, in order to know what needs to be taught. Successful teaching takes place when the answers to the questions provide information which is eagerly assimilated and accepted by the recipient. Good teaching can be said to have taken place if that information proves invaluable. That is how you should feel after a good feedback session.

Calderhead (1987) states that teachers can demonstrate their craft admirably in the classroom but often have difficulty describing it verbally. In order to get the best from feedback:

1 *Know exactly what it is you want to know.* This should be directly related to the focus you have chosen. If you expect the entire lesson or day to be dissected then this is unhelpful and often results in clichés and unqualified statements. You will want to know what went well and why; what can be improved upon and any advice, strategies or information in respect of criticism.

2 *Ask the right questions.* It is important to recognize that misunderstandings will occur if you have not established that you and the mentor are referring to the same focus for your discussion. McAlpine *et al.* (1988) recommend that your questions concentrate on the positive events in the lesson, are framed to explore specific happenings, are open-ended and that you allow plenty of time for the mentor to respond.

3 *Make your questions very specific* as time for feedback will probably be limited. 'How did it go?' will probably result in 'Fine. You're doing very well', or 'Not too badly. I think you are going to have to be firmer, don't you?' The former is encouraging but does not further your learning and the latter leaves you wondering how.

If you are to benefit from your mentor's observations, this framework should help:

• With regard to —, what did I get right?
• What aspects of — could I improve upon?
• Can you give me any (advice/strategies/information) in respect of — ?

The discussion based on these three questions, however brief, is far more likely to make you feel positive, the task at hand manageable and the mentor more able to answer your needs. More importantly, theories underpinning practice will be reflected upon. For example, in answer to your request for strategies, your mentor may advise that to ensure children do not finish too quickly and become potential nuisances, you should examine whether the material being used is appropriately differentiated and that you have extension tasks to hand.

Here are a few other questions raised by beginning teachers in relation to communicational aspects:

> I am constantly being criticized and given advice I haven't asked for! What shall I do?

Strategy: Even though the mentor means well, this can have an undermining or overwhelming effect. If you first show gratitude for the help then you can use the three questions suggested above, focusing on points raised that concern you and so make sense of the overload.

> My mentor gives me lots of written feedback but never seems prepared to discuss things with me face-to-face.

Strategy: Put your three questions in written form for the mentor to handle when time allows.

What is meant by a 'teacher who appreciates the education and training role'?

Mentors who appreciate their role in this way will give as much help and guidance as possible, passing on how they work, record, observe, plan and organize, providing forms, lists and information about children (a good mentor will be using all those strategies mentioned by Morag Hunter-Carsch in Chapter 12). They will only expect you to use their methods if these are appropriate and will encourage development along your own lines. They will allow mistakes to be made but will assist in evaluation. They will let you know that they are there to help and will arrange the practice so that you are not thrown in at the deep end unless you wish this. A partnership will be formed giving as much assistance as possible. Such a mentor will have the children at heart and place importance on their learning as well as yours. As previously stated, the root of effective mentoring is the establishment of the relationship between beginner teacher and mentor. This takes time and thought and other demands and pressures may prevent its easy fulfilment. You can do much to establish a good working relationship regardless of the difficulties, if you first acknowledge this. Then you can identify your needs in respect of the mentor's role.

Structure: You must have a clear perspective on what your mentor's role is if you are able to relate effectively to it and benefit fully from it. The relationship whereby this can happen, is built up through good communication, so the key words are:

- *Communicate*   • *Ask*   • *Question*   • *Share*   • *Praise*

The mentor's role is to teach you by providing a learning environment, to support you, to protect you in respect of your inexperience, to challenge you and to accept you as a developing professional. Each of these aspects is discussed in turn below.

Teach

Listen and be open to what your mentor is saying or doing. A learner is exploring beliefs and trying out possibilities. Learning has stopped if you think you know the answers.

> My mentor seems constantly to lecture me and tell me what to do. I don't feel as if I ever use my own ideas.

Strategy: You may ask if this is an effective way of creating learning for you (or children). You will have to try and focus your mentor by asking specific questions. You may disagree with what you are told but your views may come from inexperience. How does theory work in practice? Until you have tried your mentor's way and then your own, you have no evidence on which to base your judgements. Are you a realist moving towards the idealistic, or an idealist moving towards reality?

Support

In order to support you, your mentor must appreciate your needs, which you must communicate. Fear of appearing ignorant, vulnerable or incompetent might stop you doing so. Remember that your mentor may not be unhelpful but may be suffering from anxiety too. One of the complexities of the job is to know when to intervene, challenge, accept your levels of competency or leave you to find out for yourself. Watkins (1993) suggests that this is because experienced teachers do not have an explicit set of understandings to work from.

> My mentor doesn't ever seem to really listen to me or understand what my needs are.

Strategy: There could be a variety of reasons for this, such as other pressures. If you ask your mentor 'Who should I ask about –', the required support may be proffered or another member of staff with expertise identified. If neither happens then go and find someone yourself to offer support.

Protect

This means that your mentor has to make judgements as to what you should be protected from at what stage in your learning. The mentor will also have the children's and school's welfare at heart in making some protective decisions. You may feel you are being underestimated. There is a very fine line between allowing errors that are valuable tools and stopping potentially damaging situations. We all learn by making mistakes but we don't want this to be continually happening otherwise it is undermining of confidence.

> My mentor tried to protect me from everything . . . or nothing!

Strategy: The more able you are to voice your inexperience/experience, uncertainties/certainties and doubts/confidence, the more able the mentor will be in taking appropriate action. For example, 'I am feeling much more confident with the class now. Shall I have Paul (behavioural difficulties) in my lesson tomorrow?' Or, 'As I'm having the whole class tomorrow, I feel inexperienced in handling Paul. Could he be excluded until I find my feet?'

Challenge

Your mentor has to recognize your potential and your ability to take risks but so do you! How you react to pressure gives you the opportunity to know yourself better, where your limits lie and whether you view difficulties as problems or challenges. Remember, a problem cannot be overcome until you see it as a challenge.

My mentor just leaves me to sink or swim.

Strategy: If your mentor thinks that you have to provide all the ideas or that your training institution will have prepared you for all eventualities, then they may see your practice as a test and not a learning experience. If you are sinking, is it because you have not followed the structures recommended above? If you are swimming and so have been given little feedback during the last few weeks of practice, have you sought out your mentor to ensure further communication? Have you considered what challenges the school itself can offer you such as volunteering to do an assembly or take on an after-school activity?

Acceptance

In order for your mentor to accept you, you must be someone who is prepared to respect the conformities of the school, and to seek to understand the individual expectations of your mentor. You will not easily be accepted if you are seen to be rejecting the status quo: it is a case of being professional. If you accept the reality of your situation then energy will not be wasted fighting it but, instead, used to enhance it or reach a happy compromise through understanding.

If the relationship established with your mentor is based on the clearly defined role given above, then it will provide the best possible training. However, you should recognize that 'the way we relate to others is affected by the way we relate to ourselves, and particularly how we perceive ourselves'. Also 'the way we perceive others has a strong effect on the way we relate to them' (Hall and Hall 1988). A good working relationship is a two-way process, for half of which the beginner teacher is responsible.

I don't think my mentor really likes me – it's very difficult having to work together.

Strategy: First, ask yourself and then your mentor whether you are behaving in an acceptable way. Then ask yourself whether you actually like your mentor. You could be projecting your negative feelings on to the mentor who is then sensitive to your resistance, which is an extremely common defence mechanism (Hall and Hall 1988). You need to concentrate on the professional role of the mentor, as outlined above, and not their weaknesses as perceived by you. Any anger you feel will come from negative rather than positive action on your part. Tensions arising between you and your mentor may build into mutual dislike for each other through a series of judgements and misunderstandings. It then becomes impossible for either of you to communicate effectively with the other as you both feel threatened. You need to take responsibility for your half of the relationship if you wish to resolve the uncomfortable situation. You could start by asking the mentor if you are to blame and can improve the situation. Try to appreciate what your mentor does for you even in a small way and give positive feedback on their help. You will not overcome difficulties by pride or anger or by seeing yourself as guiltless and the mentor as guilty.

As schools develop policies for teacher education to take place, many of the difficulties described above will cease. However, we must remember that teachers are individuals. How a beginner teacher relates to a mentor will reflect the quality of the relationships formed with children in the classroom. Any number of strategies may fail you if you are not working within a clear framework. It is from this framework that you can safely learn and move forward in your professional development.

Working relationships with other adults

In primary classrooms, you will find that teachers work alongside many adults with whom relationships need to be established. Before a main teaching experience you should request a list of people who will be present in the classroom and the times and frequency of visits. A typical list may include ancillaries, language support teachers (monolingual and bilingual), home school liaison officers, special needs teachers, students (who may be teenagers on a community course from the local secondary school), parents, volunteers, governors and personnel from outside agencies. Interactions with such a wide range of people require a high level of interpersonal skills from planning partnership teaching with language support staff to requesting practical help from busy ancillaries.

Strategies

- Gather as much information as possible concerning the role of classroom supporters and their expectations of your role.
- Find out the procedures for briefing support staff.
- Provide explanations of what children should be learning from an activity and not just what the children should do.
- Ensure that children understand the adult's role and behave accordingly (Moyles 1992).

- Prepare lessons which include plans for the work of other adults and review these in lesson evaluations.
- Communication is important so that staff who work intermittently in the classroom can have relevant information concerning the teaching situation.
- Establish common policies of discipline, organization and assessment.
- Acknowledge that you and support staff are working together to solve common problems.
- Value the different perspective that other adults bring to the classroom especially culture, language and gender.
- Avoid stereotypical or negative assumptions when working in cross-gender contexts or with staff from ethnic minorities.
- Discover the talents and specialized knowledge of all support staff to improve classroom management and extend children's learning.
- Give specific tasks to parents and volunteers in order to make them feel useful.
- Maintain confidentiality at all times.

Working with the youngest children

Collaborative teaching in nurseries and under 5s classrooms requires careful consideration. Many nursery nurses believe that they are doing the same job as nursery teachers (Moyles and Suschitzky 1994) which can arouse feelings of frustration as pay and status are less than that of teachers. In recent years the roles of the two have become blurred in the name of equality, with teachers sharing the 'chores' and nursery nurses teaching number and reading skills. During the planning of a teaching experience, communication of expectations of the role of each nursery staff member is vital in order to establish good working relationships. A young beginner teacher can easily feel threatened by an experienced nursery nurse. Information concerning the beginner teacher's course content and assessment procedures should be shared with nursery nurses and other permanent classroom personnel.

Conclusion

Learning to teach is a demanding process but, with skilled support, you can succeed. If both mentor and beginner teacher appreciate the complexity of the task then the mentor can take satisfaction from witnessing the professional development of the beginner teacher. The new entrant to the profession can feel that they have gained access to the knowledge experienced teachers use in their teaching and that they have received the best possible education and training from an experienced and thoughtful mentor to complement and support their college-based activities.

A few points to consider

1 What are the three main models of supervision identified by Goldberry?
2 Take a few moments to think about 'mentors' in your prior experience; then ask yourself: Which of these models have I experienced? How do I know? How helpful or otherwise was each type of supervision?
3 Make some notes about how you will:

(a) clarify your own understanding of the models;
(b) identify what it is *you* want from a mentor;
(c) identify the strategies you will need for getting the best from the mentoring situations in which you find yourself.

References and further reading

Aldrich, R. (1990) The evolution of teacher education, in N. Graves (ed.) *Initial Teacher Education*. London: Kogan Page.
Calderhead, J. (1987) *Exploring Teachers' Thinking*. London: Cassells.
Feiman-Nemser, S., Parker, M. and Zeichner, K. (1993) Are mentor teachers teacher educators?, in D. McIntyre (ed.) *Mentoring*. London: Kogan Page.
Goldsberry, L. (1988) Three functional methods of supervision. *Action in Teacher Education*, 10 (Spring): 1–10.
Hall, E. and Hall, C. (1988) *Human Relations in Education*. London: Routledge.
Harber, C. (1993) Overseas students and democratic learning. *British Journal of In-Service Education*, 19 (2): 72–6.
Hirst, P. (1990) Internship: the view from outside, in P. Benton (ed.) *The Oxford Internship Scheme*. London: Calouste Gulbenkian Foundation.
Jacobi, M. (1991) Mentoring and undergraduate academic success: a literature review. *Review of Educational Research*, 61 (4): 505–32.
Jacques, K. (1992) Mentoring in initial teacher education. *Cambridge Journal of Education*, 22 (3): 337–50.
McAlpine, A., Brown, S., Hagger, H. and McIntyre, D. (1988) *Student-Teachers Learning From Experience Teachers*. Edinburgh: The Scottish Council for Research in Education.
McIntyre, D. and Hagger, H. (1993) Teachers' expertise and models of mentoring, in D. McIntyre (ed.) *Mentoring*. London: Kogan Page.
Monaghan, J. and Lunt, N. (1992) Mentoring: person, process, practice and problems. *British Journal of Educational Studies*, 4 (3): 248–63.
Moyles, J. (1992) *Organizing for Learning in the Primary Classroom*. Buckingham: Open University Press.
Moyles, J. and Suschitzky, W. (1994) The comparative roles of nursery teachers and nursery nurses. *Educational Research*, 36 (3): 247–58.
Nias, J. (1989) *Primary Teachers Talking*. London: Routledge.
Watkins, C. (1993) *Mentoring: Resources for School-based Development*. Harlow: Longman.
Wilkin, M. (1992) *Mentoring in Schools*. London: Kogan Page.

15

Don't make a drama out of a crisis!
Primary teachers and the law

David Turner and Mark Lofthouse

Setting the scene

This chapter is breaking with the established pattern for previous chapters in that all litigation against schools and teachers is brought because something goes wrong! Rather than frighten you immediately with harsh tales of disaster, the cameos are interwoven throughout the chapter in contexts where they can be explained and expanded. As you read you must remember that, thankfully, such incidents are still relatively rare and many teachers go through a career spanning nearly forty years without any such incidents occurring. The 'secret' (if there is one) is in considering yourself to be what the law describes as '*in loco parentis*' – adopting the role and responsibilities of a 'good parent' – and thinking through the care and attention to detail you will need in order to organize and manage children on a day-to-day basis in schools. As we shall see, these two aspects have led to some interesting and sometimes surprising outcomes of litigation.

Introduction

It is claimed that we live in an age of litigation. Newspapers and the media bombard the public with court hearings and details of disputes which often serve to define shifts in social attitudes. It is doubtful whether there is anything substantially new in what is surely an age old process. For example, in Victorian Britain, Dickens and Gilbert and Sullivan all concentrated upon the majesty of justice, and the mockery of the law that served it. What has changed is that constant media attention feeds public consciousness as to

Photo 20 A teacher's legal responsibility for children is even greater during field trips

the impact of the law, thereby fuelling a readiness for each and everyone to reach for the law as a redress for every slight and injury: this has already happened in the US.

Teachers cannot escape from a world grown more contentious and fractious. They carry the challenge of children's developing lives and concerns within the potentially hazardous world of the classroom and the school. Teachers are bound by codes of conduct and professional ethics which stem from an examination of cases where teachers have been held responsible for such things as children using sharp-ended scissors, for example, or handling dangerous substances, leaving school premises (with or without permission) and incurring injuries in PE activities. Through attention to case law, much of it made available through teaching unions, teachers are alerted to the nature and extent of legal hazards associated with teaching. They can also learn much from these about how to handle day-to-day situations efficiently and effectively.

Before turning to these sometimes harsh examples, it is important to acknowledge how threatening and anxiety-provoking such accidents and incidents are for all teachers. Most primary teachers are caring and responsible people, who enter the profession with high ideals and a real sense of vocation. As many of the case examples show, misfortunes often arise from what teachers have *not* done; sins of omission rather than of commission! In terms of inexperienced teachers, there is security in knowing what professional responsibility means and how this is expressed in practice.

Therefore, care and common sense have to be made visible in codes of conduct covering:

- supervision of children arriving and leaving school premises, during playtimes and in classrooms during inclement weather;
- supervision of children leaving school premises and seeking/obtaining parental permission/explanation for absence;
- supervision of children in classrooms and around the school, including sporting and playground activities;
- behaviour codes setting out expectations of behaviour between pupils and behaviour between teachers and pupils;
- professional codes setting out means and methods of communications between teachers and parents, teachers and governors;
- codes of practice as to actions and procedures to be followed if a child becomes ill or suffers an accident.

This particular list is potentially endless and, as such, is potentially intimidating! As a beginning teacher you will have enough to do coping with the immediate and the everyday. Heads, deputies and mentors (as we have seen in Wendy Suschitzky and Barbara Garner's preceding chapter) play a vital role in inducting new staff into codes and procedures which compose the elements of 'extended professionalism'. Such professionalism is now the hallmark of good teaching at every level. Understanding and embracing codes of good professional conduct are the surest way of avoiding the kind of pitfalls which are now explored through a cameo and other examples.

Cameo

A small 4-year-old boy is in a nursery class with other children being prepared to go out for a walk with the teacher. She leaves the pupils for a brief period of time to get her coat. While out of the classroom she comes across another child who has cut himself so she attends to this child. The teacher is away from the classroom for about ten minutes during which time the small boy in question gets out of the classroom. He makes his way out of the building into the school playground and through an unlocked school gate, down a lane into a busy road. Here he causes the driver of a heavy lorry to swerve so that it strikes a telegraph pole as a result of which the driver is killed.

This startling story is taken from a real life legal case history and illustrates how an apparently minor incident can trigger a chain of events that can have calamitous consequences. That accidents will happen is a fact of life but, when they do happen, someone, somewhere, will be concerned and conscience-stricken. Although no crime has been committed it may well be that someone will be *legally liable* for what has happened. *What do you think may have happened in this case?* (We promise to return to the outcomes towards the end!)

Education is no different from any other service in our society and is regulated by many branches of both the criminal and civil law as laid down by acts of parliament and, indeed, by custom, practice and precedent which it is important for you to know.

Firstly, duties are imposed on parents by the 1944 Education Act which requires them to ensure that their children are properly educated (though not necessarily at school). Local authorities must provide schools, teachers and equipment. The role of LEAs has recently been modified with various legislation passed in the 1980s, relating to school government, and by the 1993 Education Act which established the Funding Agency for schools to share responsibility with LEAs subject to certain conditions. In addition to existing independent schools, city technology colleges and grant maintained schools (also independent of LEAs) have also been established. As was emphasized by Janet Moyles in the Introduction, through the NC, children have specific entitlements under the Education Reform Act 1988.

Secondly, the recruitment and selection of school staff, together with their terms and conditions of service, are regulated by various employment law statutes supplemented by the Teachers' Pay and Conditions of Service Act 1987 (details of which are set out in the Teachers Pay and Conditions of Service booklet sent annually to schools).

Thirdly, the Sex and Race Discrimination Acts should protect the intending teacher from unfair treatment as far as employment matters are concerned, while ensuring that all pupils are afforded equal opportunities and fair treatment (discussed by Wendy Suschitzky in Chapter 13).

Family law also influences the education service and, in particular, The Children Act 1989 which takes teachers, among other aspects, into areas of child abuse and neglect. Since a teacher's work offers day-to-day contact with children they have a positive role in child protection (see David 1992). At the same time because of their day-to-day contact teachers are vulnerable to accusations of child abuse. Every care should be taken to avoid situations which have the potential for this or from which accusations from pupils or parents may arise.

As schools are moved more into what might be called a 'consumer market', commercial laws regulate certain activities by schools as do the Data Protection Act and Copyright Design and Patents Act. Moreover, Health and Safety legislation is playing an increasingly important role in regulating the conduct of schools.

The teachers' duty of care

All of these Acts and laws form what may be described as *the legal aspects of schooling*. While the various acts may seem extensive and intrusive, in reality, law relating to education is light and sketchy in comparison with, for example, maritime law. While a modicum of laws relating to education may seem of benefit to teachers, the outcome tends to promote grey areas. Because the law is 'thin', great importance is placed in teaching on custom and precedent. Most of the latter is focused on *teachers' duty of care* which has its origins in the nineteenth century, when the national system of education became established.

Duty of care has been substantially amplified since 1865 when a dispute arose which came before the courts, about the extent to which a schoolmaster [sic] has authority over his scholars. In *Fitzgerald* v. *Northcote* (1865) it was stated that the master of a school has the same authority over his scholars as the parents would and may impose reasonable restraints and that, when a parent places his child with a schoolmaster, he delegates to him all his own authority so far as it is necessary for the welfare of the child. This duty of the schoolmaster was subsequently given greater clarity and definition in the famous case *Williams* v. *Eady* (1893). The teacher had left a bottle containing phosphorus in a conservatory to which the boys had access. Young Kenneth Williams took the bottle and played with it. The bottle burst, the phosphorus exploded and the young boy was injured. It was concluded that the schoolmaster had been neglecting his duty and Lord Esher, in an often quoted remark stated:

> The schoolmaster was bound to take such care of his boys as a careful father would take of his boys and there could be no better definition of the duty of the schoolmaster . . . he was bound to take notice of the ordinary nature of young boys, their tendency to mischievous acts and their propensity to meddle with anything that came in their way. When having phosphorus in the house he was bound not to leave it in any place where they might get at it.
>
> (Adams 1992: 103)

It is this notion of *loco parentis* which should inform a teacher's conduct regarding how to act as a caring, prudent parent would act, and it is the standard which has been applied in disputes ever since. This is no mean feat for either teachers or parents given the complex and sometimes confounding ways in which children react to, and interact with, the world as discussed by both Janet Moyles and Roger Merry in Chapters 2 and 5 respectively.

What counts as 'reasonable' is, of course, not an unchanging standard in a changing world. Since such issues are seldom clear-cut, a substantial body of often colourful case law continues to amplify the notion of 'reasonableness'. To give a flavour of the hazards that await the unwary there have been cases involving acid, coke lorries, caustic soda, contractor's equipment, cookery lessons, children falling through glass roofs, dangerous doors, crackers, cricket rollers, gymnastics apparatus, golf balls, lollipop men, oil cans, paper pellets and paper-clips, pen-tops, playground games, rugby tackles by teachers, saws, slippery floors, school buses, sheath knives, scissors, shot-putting, slipping on ice, tea-making for teachers, trampoline elastic, and toy soldiers!

However, the *loco parentis* principle has itself been subject to considerable development since its establishment. Teachers are *qualified professionals* and the law expects such people to show the average amount of competence associated with the proper discharge of the duties of that profession. Therefore teachers, because of their training, should be in a position to visualize more clearly the results of their acts and, more importantly, their omissions.

It should be remembered that teachers are not working in home domestic situations but in the context of a school – usually a larger and more complex environment. In *Lyes* v. *Middlesex County Council* (1962) a boy was injured when he put his hand through an ordinary eighth-of-an-inch thick glass panel in a swing door. The boy had attempted to push open the door which led to a changing room but another child had stopped the door with his foot. In awarding damages against the authority the judge, commenting on the *loco parentis* principle, asserted:

> I hold that the standard is that of a reasonably prudent parent judged not in the context of his own home but in that of a school, in other words a person exhibiting the responsible mental qualities of a prudent parent in the circumstances of school life.
>
> (Adams 1992: 103)

The higher standard expected from teachers as professionals was articulated again in *Beaumont* v. *Surrey County Council* (1968). Whereas parents have generally few pupils, some schools can contain hundreds and the standard expected from those acting as reasonably careful parents has to be modified to fit the circumstances. In this case a nine feet length of trampette elastic had been placed in a wastepaper bin where pupils congregated in the playground. During a break time the children were in the playground but because of a breakdown in the system of supervision the duty teachers had not yet arrived, the elastic was removed from the waste-bin by some of the pupils. It was used in 'horseplay' with the result that a bystander pupil suffered serious injury. Given the known propensities of children to engage in such rough play the authority was held liable, the judge stating:

> It is a headmaster's duty [sic], bearing in mind the propensities of boys and indeed girls . . . to take all reasonable and proper steps to prevent any of the pupils under his care from suffering injury from inanimate objects from the actions of their fellow pupils, or from a combination of the two. That is a high standard.
>
> (Nice 1986: 206)

Although the concept of *loco parentis* requires the teacher and other school staff to act in a way that a reasonably careful parent would, the legal framework through which a 'plaintiff' – that is one who has suffered somehow – could bring an action to seek redress and money compensation for a breach of duty lies nowadays with the law of tort, and in particular the tort of negligence.

Tort and criminal law are quite different in that the former relates to actions between legal entities whilst the latter is concerned with the enforcement of legal rules (laws) laid down, for example, through acts of parliament. However, it is worth noting that criminal prosecutions can and do arise in some instances. So far as teachers are concerned, whilst a body of case law had begun to emerge from the beginning of the twentieth century at around the time that LEAs had become established, the legal framework and the concept of negligence – that is by careless action or careless lack of it someone causes harm to another – was given substantial clarity and definition through *Donoghue* v. *Stevenson* (1932).

This case, on the face of things, has apparently little to do with education. However, its implications for teachers in respect of their liability in law for negligence were far reaching. A bottle of ginger beer had been purchased and given to a friend in a cafe to make ice cream soda. The friend drank some of the ginger beer but then discovered that the opaque bottle contained what appeared to be the remains of a dead snail! She developed severe gastroenteritis and, not unnaturally, suffered nervous shock. When the case eventually reached the House of Lords the tort of negligence was confirmed as a separate tort and their lordships stated:

> You must take reasonable care to avoid acts or omissions which you can reasonably foresee would be likely to injure your neighbour. Who, then, in law is my neighbour? The answer seems to be – persons who are so closely and directly affected by my act that I ought reasonably to have them in contemplation as being so affected when I am directing my mind to the act or omissions which are called in question . . .
> (Adams 1992: 107)

To successfully bring an action for negligence then against either a teacher, or other member of staff or employing authority, it must firstly be *proved* that a duty of care was owed by that person, the defendant. This was established so far as schools were concerned by the *loco parentis* decision of *Williams* v. *Eady*, subsequent court judgements and by the neighbourhood principle set out in *Donoghue* v. *Stevenson*. However, the issue is not always straightforward. When, for example, does the duty of care begin? There have been several legal case histories, for example, relating to the times surrounding the beginning and end of the school day – an issue over which many of you will be concerned, particularly those teaching the youngest children.

Many children do, in fact, arrive in school before the start of the school day but this does not mean that, as a consequence, schools have a duty of care or should provide supervision simply because the parents have chosen to send them early. In *Mays* v. *Essex County Council* the judge said:

> . . . a parent has no special right to impose responsibility for his children on to the teachers outside the official hours of school. On the other hand, most schools open their playground gates before school begins – what does this mean? Is it an invitation to leave children there and an implied acceptance of responsibility once they enter on the premises of the school or is it an act of grace offering the

comparative safety of the playground when compared with the street outside but signifying no acceptance of responsibility for the behaviour within?

(Nice 1986: 214)

Despite the absence of a strict legal obligation, it has become custom and practice for many schools to accept responsibility for pupils for up to ten minutes before the start of the session. Again, applying the *loco parentis* principle, it might also be argued that locking pupils out of the playground would be in many areas to deny them a place of safety. Whatever the arrangements, parents certainly need to be advised of them by the school. So far as the end of the school day is concerned case law suggests that teachers must be meticulous in not allowing children to leave early unless due notice has been given. In *Barnes* v. *Hampshire County Council* (1969), for example, damages were awarded against the authority when a 5-year-old girl was let out early, knocked down by a car and injured on a main road.

Having demonstrated that a duty of care was owed, the second stage in law must be to show that there has been a breach of that duty of care. Simply because an accident happens and, as a result, someone is injured does not automatically mean that a teacher has been careless.

The key to understanding this issue lies in the notion of 'foreseeability' as articulated in *Donoghue* v. *Stevenson* described above. Two legal case histories serve to demonstrate the point. In *Wright* v. *Cheshire County Council* (1952) a boy in a party of ten others taking part in gymnastic exercises was injured whilst vaulting over a buck. All the boys had experience of the exercise and were taking it in turns. It was the duty of the boy who was last over to wait at the receiving end of the buck to assist the next boy to come over. During the exercise the school bell announcing the start of playtime rang and the boy at the receiving end of the buck ran off without waiting to receive the next boy who, as a result, fell and was injured. Since it was established that the exercise was being conducted according to recognized custom and practice, the claim for negligence was dismissed since it could not have reasonably been foreseen that the boy at the receiving end would run off and, therefore, there was no legal liability upon the teacher for the injury to the child.

In reading through the detail of these legal case histories a number of 'ifs and buts' will undoubtedly arise in your mind. It is sometimes impossible to predict what the reaction of the court will be and what is reasonably foreseeable in one year might not have been so clear-cut in previous years. Two cases involving the use of scissors neatly illustrate this point. In *Butt* v. *Cambridgeshire and Isle of Ely County Council* (1969) a class of Year 5 children had been given pointed scissors with which to cut out illustrations. Although the teacher had warned the pupils that they should put the scissors down when not needed, an accident occurred in which a girl in turning round to speak to a fellow pupil who had attracted her attention sustained serious injury when she was struck in the eye by the scissors that her fellow pupil was holding. In court it was stated that the pointed scissors were desirable educationally, the teacher was supervising her class properly and that therefore the accident could not have been foreseen. Although judgement initially went with the plaintiff, it was overturned on appeal. In *Black* v. *Kent County Council* (1983), however, some fourteen years later the defendants were held to be guilty of an error of judgement since it was held that it was reasonably foreseeable that sharp-ended scissors involved greater risks than blunt-ended models, more so since a booklet *Safety in Schools* published by the then DES and used in evidence had recommended the use of scissors with rounded ends!

It will be recognized that it is not only in the use of equipment or the method of instruction that the notion of foreseeability is considered when deciding whether there has been a breach in a teachers duty of care – the *age of the pupils* is also an important factor.

The third condition required for an action for negligence to succeed is that damage has been sustained as a result. Minor injuries from which children make full recovery are unlikely to be admissible. Moreover, it has to be said that the vast majority of parents are reasonable people – and that it is not unreasonable to expect their offspring to get into scrapes of one kind or another as they grow up. Indeed, the courts have long taken the view that, while teachers should act in the way that a reasonably careful parent would act, that does not mean an over-anxious or over-cautious parent! *Mays* v. *Essex County Council* is a good illustration. Here a serious accident was sustained by a child sliding on ice in the playground before the start of the school day. In rejecting the claim that was put forward the judge remarked,

> If I thought that any school authority was seriously prepared to de- clare sliding on ice is a dangerous game and should be stopped, I would feel obliged to make some sort of declaration that children in this country are free to slide on ice in a sensible and orderly manner whenever a suitable opportunity arises. They and their elders have been doing it for centuries.
>
> (Nice 1986: 197)

So . . . what should you do if something goes wrong?

The above judgement, radiating robust common sense, should give en- couragement to beginning teachers everywhere. Accidents happen in the best regulated families and are treated for what they are – unintentional and unexpected mishaps. However, the first year in teaching has aptly been described as a roller-coaster ride of highs and lows, the lows being not infrequently associated with anxieties provoked when you first confront difficulties and mishaps. As the latter are inevitable, be prepared!

Point 1

Remember Corporal Jones in 'Dad's Army' – *don't panic!* You will know by now that a large part of the teacher's role is in projecting an image (see Chapter 2). When accidents happen, part of your role is to stay calm and look calm – even if you don't feel it!

Point 2

Retaining calmness and self-control will enable you to *respond* promptly and professionally. In terms of professionalism, good fortune favours the well-prepared mind. Make sure you *know* the codes of conduct and procedures operating in your school. Be careful to *apply* them.

Point 3

When an incident is dealt with and a suitable moment arrives (playtime, lunch-time), *write down* what has happened, remembering to deal with facts rather than emotions (think objectively in the ways considered by Linda Hargreaves in Chapter 3). If you read the small print on a motor car in-surance policy, 'What to do in the event of an accident', this will give you a good grasp of the salient facts you should capture, namely: time, place, people and relevant contextual details.

Point 4

Communicate what has happened to your mentor or another member of staff – two heads are better than one! Nine times out of ten you will find that what you feared to be a major crisis is, in fact, just another everyday incident of school life. Unfortunately, more experienced colleagues may not immediately appreciate how much emotional stress you have experi-enced in coping with something they find commonplace. Therefore, be kind to yourself, remembering that calmness during an incident may be followed by varying degrees of shock which can strike you many hours after the incident has occurred.

Point 5

If you are *extremely* unlucky, and an incident in which you are involved is the subject of legal proceedings, *do not play at being your own lawyer.* If legal proceedings are threatened, your response is that of a Mastermind contestant who is confronted by too difficult a question – *'pass'*. Your employers (LEA or school governing body) are the bodies liable and they have access to lawyers who can act for them and for you. If you want the peace of mind that comes from knowing you are permanently protected, think carefully about joining a professional association which provides legal services and cover as part of membership benefits.

Point 6

Don't make a drama out of a crisis. When you first begin teaching, every day can seem like walking through a minefield. Be assured, it does get better! Even though the mines are still there, you get more adept at avoiding them. Your colleagues are your greatest asset in enabling you to gain a sense of what is professionally appropriate. Therefore, be sensitive to their needs as well as your own. By listening and observing you can quickly learn what is a crisis (or has the potential to become one) and what are merely incidents in life's rich tapestry. While you will encounter plenty of the latter, you will be most unfortunate to be involved in a case like the one described at the opening of this chapter.

So . . . what about the small boy?

And what of the case of the small boy who ran into the road causing the death of a driver of a heavy lorry described at the opening of this chapter? The widow of the driver who was killed brought an action for negligence. But the judge exonerated the teacher saying:

> . . . her duty was that of a careful parent. I cannot think that it could be considered negligent in a mother to leave a child dressed ready to go out with her for a few moments and then, if she found another of her children hurt and in need of immediate attention, she could be blamed for giving it . . . it seems to me that she acted just as one would expect her to do.
>
> (Adams 1992: 111)

However, in a neat yet perhaps unexpected twist, their Lordships went on to add:

> . . . the actions of a child of this age are unpredictable and I think it ought to have been anticipated by the appellant County Council or their reasonable officers that in such a case a child might well try to get on to the streets and if it did a traffic accident was far from improbable. It would have been very easy to prevent this and either lock the gates or, if that was thought undesirable, to make them sufficiently difficult to open to ensure they could not be opened by a child so young he could not be trusted alone on the street.
>
> (Nice 1986: 195)

Conclusion

This all serves to highlight how easy it is to be wise after the event – the moral of this chapter is to draw attention to the importance of being wise *before* the event! The major responsibilities of being *in loco parentis* need to be thought through on an individual and a collective basis. Where thought has been applied, negligence is difficult to prove. However, as we have seen, the road to hell is paved with good intentions! The sometimes bizarre incidents recorded in this chapter demonstrate how quickly minor problems can develop into major crises. Such crises bring in their wake much individual unhappiness, and for schools, a great deal of unwanted publicity. For all these prudential reasons, it is sensible to remember the proverb, 'the law was made for the obedience of fools and the guidance of wise men and women'. Wise teachers review the law so as to put in place systems, codes and practices which go beyond the law. Good practice, consistently defined and applied, is the best way of ensuring that laws are redundant because the standards upheld within a school go beyond what is legally demanded.

Before you leave this chapter:

1 Think through what '*in loco parentis*' means to *you*? (If you are already a parent this will help – if not, talk to colleagues who are!)
2 Jot down a note of anything which, in reading the above, gives you particular concerns – and *go and talk to a professional colleague about them* rather than leave your concerns unvoiced.

References and further reading

Adams, A. (1992) *Your School and the Law*. London: Heinemann.

Barrell, G.R. and Partington, J.A. (1985) *Teachers and the Law*, 6th edn. London: Methuen.

Coleman, J.E., Liel, P. and Saunders, J.B. (1984) *The Law of Education*, vol. 3, 9th edn. London: Butterworth and Company.

David, T. (1992) *Child Protection and Early Years Teachers*. Buckingham: Open University Press.

Harpwood, V. and Alldridge, P. (1989) *GCSE Law*. Blackstone Press Limited.

Harris, N. (1990) *The Law Relating to Schools*. London: Fourmat Publishing.

Lowe, C. (1988) *The Teacher, the Pupil and the Law*. London: Secondary Heads Association.

Nice, D. (ed.) (1986) *Education and the Law*. London: Councils and Education Press.

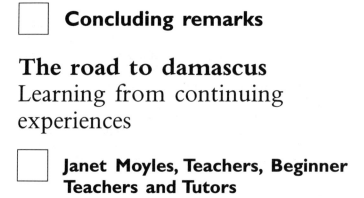

Concluding remarks

The road to damascus
Learning from continuing experiences

Janet Moyles, Teachers, Beginner Teachers and Tutors

One group of PGCE students asked to pass on their own messages to readers of this book, chose to make their offering in a 'Recipe for the perfect teacher' which is faithfully reproduced in Figure 16.1. To my mind, this shows just the kind of warmth, humour and beliefs about primary teaching which characterize the new teachers of today and is worth preserving in our teachers of tomorrow through a balanced and supportive teacher education programme. Moves towards even more school-based training are met with some scepticism in both training institutions and schools, for the priority task of primary school teachers is to teach *children*. The skills of classroom teacher and course tutor have many similarities but working with other adults is very different to working with children – as many class teachers learn when they take on a mentoring role. Teacher educators have themselves all been class teachers: not many class teachers have also been teacher educators or have the time available to acquire the relevant new skills. Many course tutors have spent considerable amounts of time in school and regularly work with practising teachers through continuing professional development and research activities. Having the combined perspectives of tutors, teachers and students themselves benefits everyone involved in the processes of teacher education, especially the children.

Having worked in schools with teachers, many students come back to the university desperate to know more about the theory behind classroom strategies or behaviour techniques or dealing with parents. Even when teachers have this knowledge (and many do), it is not always easy for them to articulate their effective practice as it is often 'second nature' (a point Maurice Galton raised in Chapter 1). Opportunities for training will need

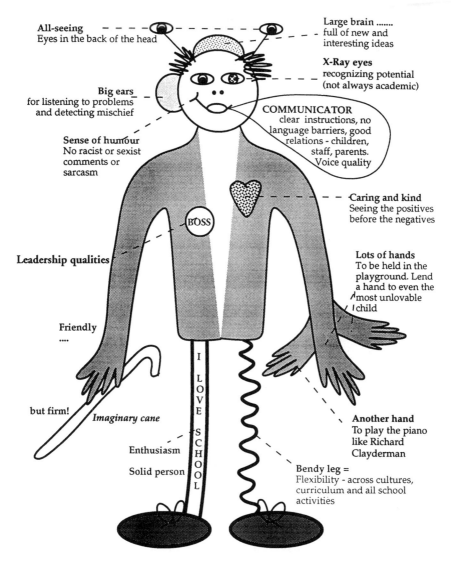

Just add 30+ children. Place in a hot classroom and bake for 25 years or more.

Figure 16.1 Recipe for the 'perfect' teacher

to be given to classroom teachers for this to happen which, at the end of the day, mean more money (rather than less) being put into teacher education. In the meantime, education tutors frequently have this information to hand and the experience of dealing with adult groups to link the theory and practice effectively and efficiently.

The final statements in the book are left to those teachers just entering their first posts in primary schools all over the country and to those who are part of the teacher education system. Students just leaving a PGCE course and some who had left in the previous year, were asked to reflect (through the individual action planning processes mentioned in Chapter 4) on what advice they would wish to pass on to others in a similar situation. Teacher education tutors were also asked for their comments, and reflections were also gathered from experienced teachers. The sample from all four groups constitutes much food-for-thought for beginner teachers and, probably, teachers at every stage in their careers.

We hope that, having read this book, you will be able to adopt (and adapt) some of this advice as you set out on the complex but rewarding professional journey that is primary teaching. Whereas some of the 'tips for teachers' might be familiar to you, there are others which, though unusual, are worth remembering. Many of these reiterate, albeit in a different way, the wealth of messages and insights which have comprised the chapters of this book.

Think twice! (teacher)

Know your own self-worth: value the skills you have and enjoy the children with their skills and understanding. (tutor)

Be up-front about our weaknesses with mentor teachers and tutors: share with them your own ideas and priorities. They will be grateful to you for the guidance of what they can help you with. (student teacher)

Avoid the perils of becoming a chocoholic – the pressure of the job leads to comfort eating on a massive scale. A 'Mars-a-day' is guaranteed to slow down your work, rest and play! Save the choc for the day you've been on playground duty! (tutor)

I think everyone has a good cry during their first year of teaching – but it doesn't mean you're useless! (NQT)

Learn the children's names as quickly as you can and use them as much as possible. You must *act* like a teacher – look as if you expect children to listen to you and they probably will! (tutor)

Don't be too proud or stubborn to learn from tutors and teachers: they have lots of experience and are there to help you to become a good teacher. (student teacher)

I've learned that all good teaching is based on relationships. Remember that children, like adults, tend to mirror the behaviour shown to them (especially if it's negative!). Always be patient, calm and courteous to the children whenever you can and don't 'lose your cool' (except as a deliberate strategy)! (teacher)

Treat children and others in school just as you would wish to be treated yourself. That way, you usually all find life as you like it. (tutor)

Try to ask yourself every day – 'What did *I learn* in school/on the course today?' (student teacher)

Make one weekend day your own and cultivate friends who are not teachers – you will find that they offer a hearty laugh at some of the antics which go on in schools and thus offer you a sense of proportion. (tutor)

On my final teaching practice, I found that using practical activities with the children was less stressful than endless paper exercises. I found out more about what and how children were learning. When children did produced paper work, I wrote a comment on what they had shown they could do, or needed help to do, etc. and read this to the children. Even 5-year-olds appreciated this and it gave them motivation to try their best. (student teacher)

Good teachers have to be good learners. They have to learn *exactly* what it is the children (and they themselves) don't understand and then move heaven and earth to teach is so that they both *do* understand. (teacher)

Don't upset the caretaker and other support staff! (student teacher)

Try out new things on a Friday afternoon: that way you (and the other staff) can forget any disasters by Monday! (tutor)

Do your evaluating and assessing straight away after a lesson. When things are fresh, it helps you to think and helps you to work out progression for the children. (student teacher)

Having done written assignments on your teacher education course, you must use them as a tool for your work in school – if you have found out the theory and reflected on how you or others put that into practice (or not!), stop and then think about *how* this will affect your practice. Don't just rush on regardless! (NQT)

Getting the class 'with you' so that the child misbehaving becomes embarrassed without you having to shout! First give the child 'the withering look', then make them stand up (just for a little while), then ask them to settle down. It has usually worked for me. (student teacher)

Do remember that 'difficult' behaviour is usually the sign of an unhappy child – it is a challenge to you but it is not, at the end of the day, your *personal* problem. (course tutor)

Don't forget to speak clearly and *listen* hard to what the children are telling you. (student teacher)

Don't make promises you can't keep. If you say 'The next child who talks I'll get your parents in' and someone talks, get the parents! (Worst still, you might be tempted to suggest you'll throw them out of the window!) The corollary of this is *keep your promises.* (course tutor)

Especially with young children, don't be too shy to read stories in 'funny' voices. When I did, the children were 'knocked out' by my Oscar-winning performance and I think I commanded much more respect afterwards. (student teacher)

Yes – you'll be tired, worn out, all-in, kn——ed (and every other exhaustion word you can think of!). *But* it's worth it at the end of the day when even one child shows you s/he has actually *learned* something new. (teacher)

It would be unforgivable to leave a book about primary education and 3–11-year-old children without giving some of them the final word. After all, it is because of children that most people enter the teaching profession in the first place.

Photo 21 Please will you come and be our teacher?

Index

ORGANIZING FOR LEARNING IN THE PRIMARY CLASSROOM
A BALANCED APPROACH TO CLASSROOM MANAGEMENT

Janet R. Moyles

What is it that underlies classroom organization, routines, rules, structures and daily occurrences? What are the prime objectives and what influences the decisions of teachers and children? What is it useful for teachers to consider when contemplating the issues of classroom management and organization? What do different practices have to offer?

Organizing for Learning in the Primary Classroom explores the whole range of influences and values which underpin *why* teachers do *what* they do in the classroom context and what these mean to children and others. Janet Moyles examines teaching and learning styles, children's independence and autonomy, coping with children's differences, the physical classroom context and resources, time management and ways of involving others in the day-to-day organization. Practical suggestions are given for considering both the functional and aesthetic aspects of the classroom context. Opportunities are provided for teachers to reflect on their own organization and also consider innovative and flexible ways forward to deal with new and ever increasing demands on their time and sanity!

> This book is to be highly recommended for all primary school teachers . . .
> *(Management in Education)*

> . . . indispensable to courses in initial teacher education and to providers of inset.
> *(Child Education)*

> Janet Moyles brings her long experience of the primary school to *Organizing for Learning in the Primary Classroom* . . . I particularly like the attention she gives to the physical envoironment, giving lots of advice about arrangements of furniture and the role of the teacher's desk . . .
> *(Times Educational Supplement)*

Contents
Introduction: Polarizations and balance – Teachers and teaching: beliefs and values – The learning environment: organizing the classroom context – The children and their learning needs: balancing individual and whole class approaches – Grouping children for teaching and learning: providing equal opportunities and promoting appropriate behaviour – Time for teaching and learning – Deploying adult help effectively in the classroom: delegation and responsibility – Evaluating classroom organization and managment – Conclusion: the primary classroom, a place and a time – References – Index.

208pp   0 335 15659 2 (Paperback)   0 335 15660 6 (Hardback)

SPECIAL EDUCATIONAL NEEDS IN THE PRIMARY SCHOOL
A PRACTICAL GUIDE

Jean Gross

Local management of schools and cutbacks in central support services mean that the responsibility for meeting special educational needs is resting ever more squarely on the shoulders of ordinary classroom teachers. Yet few feel wholly confident in their ability to adapt work within the national curriculum to meet the whole range of needs, or coordinate successful action plans for children who – for whatever reason – are not learning as well as they might.

This book will increase that confidence. Aimed at busy class teachers, special needs coordinators, heads and teachers in training, it shows how the teacher can build differentiation into planning lessons and schemes of work. It describes workable strategies for managing the most common behaviour difficulties and meeting special needs in language and mathematics.

At a whole school level, it offers practical guidance on developing special needs policies, assessment, record keeping, and the managment of time, roles and re-sources. The focus is on the ways in which schools can do a good job in meeting special needs themselves, within everyday constraints of time, money and energy, and in doing so hold back the tide of increasing marginalization of vulnerable children within the education system.

Contents
Current perspectives on special educational needs – Developing a whole school policy – Special needs and the national curriculum – Assessment and special educational needs – Action planning and record keeping – Managing time – Managing roles and resources – Managing behaviour – Communication and classroom relationships – Special needs in speaking and listening – Special needs in reading – Special needs in writing – Special needs in maths – Beyond the school – References – Index.

240pp   0 335 19035 9 (Paperback)

EFFECTIVE EARLY YEARS EDUCATION
TEACHING YOUNG CHILDREN

Anne Edwards and Peter Knight

In this concise and accessible guide, the authors are sympathetic to the particular demands of teaching three to eight year olds and offer practical solutions to the complex issues that are currently faced by early years educators. In recognizing the demands on practitioners, they provide new and challenging frameworks for an understanding of the practice of teaching young children and draw upon international research to offer a sound model of early years subject-structured teaching which has the quality of children's learning at its centre. Their aim is to support teaching expertise through stimulating teachers' thinking about children's development, motivation, ways of learning and the subjects they teach. These topics are clearly set in the complex institutional settings in which practitioners work and ways of taking and evaluating action are offered.

Contents
Introduction: education from three to eight – Becoming a pupil – Children's learning – A curriculum for the early years – Subjects and the early years curriculum – The organization of the learning environment – Parents and professionals – Developing the curriculum – Developing the organization – Endpiece – References – Index.

176pp   0 335 19188 6 (Paperback)   0 335 19189 4 (Hardback)